GERMANIE

GAULE CISALPINE

ALPES

MER MÉDITERRANÉE

MER ADRIATIQUE

ITALIE

Nimègue · Bonne · Mayence · Belfort · Bâle · Milan · Turin · Aquilée · Jorat · Genève

Rhin Fl. · Danube Fl. · Lac de Constance · Lac Léman · Rhône Fl. · Elbe Fl. · Oder · Moldau R. · Eger R. · Beraun R. · Main R. · Neckar R. · Lahn R. · Fulde R. · Werra R. · Sieg R. · Ruhr R. · Lippe R. · Tessin R. · Adige R. · Pô Fl. · Stura R. · Arno · Tibre R. · Ombrone R. · Inn R. · Lech · Iser R. · Ens R. · Mur R. · Drave R. · Save R. · Raab R. · Piave R. · Tagliamento R. · Tar R. · Moselle R. · Meuse · Doubs · Danube Fl.

monts Faucilles · Jura

200,000 — Milles

400 · 50 · 0

D1388117

9030 00005 5880 3

ancière 10

CAESAR'S
FOOTPRINTS

BIJAN OMRANI is a historian and classicist and the author of *Afghanistan: A Companion and Guide* and *Asia Overland: Tales of Travel on the Trans-Siberian and Silk Road*. He formerly taught Classics at Eton and Westminster. He is known as a writer of English and Latin verse. Extracts of his Horatian Ode on the 2012 London Olympics were published in the *Evening Standard*. He has also written for the *Spectator* and *Literary Review*. Bijan Omrani is a Fellow of the Royal Geographical Society and the Royal Asiatic Society. He can be followed on Twitter @bijanomrani.

CAESAR'S
FOOTPRINTS

JOURNEYS TO ROMAN GAUL

Bijan Omrani

First published in the UK in 2017 by Head of Zeus Ltd

1 3 5 7 9 10 8 6 4 2

A CIP catalogue record for this book is available
from the British Library.

ISBN (HB) 9781784970659
(E) 9781784970642

Printed and bound by CPI Group (UK) Ltd, Croydon, CR0 4YY

Head of Zeus Ltd
5–8 Hardwick Street
London EC1R 4RG

www.headofzeus.com

To Sam, Cassian and Beatrix

The Amphitheatre at Nîmes. Like that of Arles, it was built around AD *70, and was converted into a fortification by the time of the Visigoths. It functioned as a town in its own right, until being restored to its more recognizably Roman form (and function), for bullfights and other public spectacles, in the mid-nineteenth century.*

Contents

List of Maps · xi

A Note on Terminology · xiii

Introduction · 3

I · Gaul Before Caesar · 9

II · Caesar's Command · 45

III · The Taming of Gaul · 81

IV · Tales of the Imagination · 119

V · When in France · 145

VI · High Life and City Chic · 175

VII · Country Life · 199

VIII · The Dignity of Labour · 225

IX · In Their Own Words · 245

X · Blood of the Martyrs · 277

Epilogue: From an Empire to a Dream · 321

Bibliographical Notes · 347

Bibliography · 357

Picture Credits · 371

Acknowledgements · 373

Index · 375

List of Maps

1 • The tribes of Gaul at the time of Caesar • 2

2 • The course of the Rhône from Geneva to the Pas de L'Écluse • 68–9

3 • The Battle of Bibracte • 75

4 • The Battle of Gergovia • 96–7

5 • The Battle of Alésia • 112–13

6 • Julius Caesar's invasions of Britannia • 132–3

Maps 2–5, together with the map that appears in the endpapers, were prepared by Colonel Stoffel in the 1860s during the archaeological investigations ordered by Napoleon III into the Gallic conquests of Caesar. They were first included in Napoleon III's *Histoire de Jules César*, published in 1866.

A Note on Terminology

The use of the words 'Celtic', 'Gaul' and 'Gallic' caused considerable difficulty to classical authors, who could not agree on their exact meanings. There was a debate as to whether all Gauls were Celts, or whether they were mutually exclusive, and whether the term Gallic should be used to denote just those peoples living in the southern and western areas of modern-day France (as opposed to those who lived in the Belgic or Aquitanian regions). This difficulty exists as much for contemporary authors. For simplicity, I use the word 'Gauls' to describe those people who lived in the area designated by Julius Caesar as Gaul.

Another challenge is the use of ancient and modern place names. Here, I make no great claims to consistency. In general, I have tended to use ancient place names when talking about the places in the Roman context. However, this is not always the case. For example, I have stuck with Autun rather than persistently using the lengthy ancient name of Augustodunum. Both ancient and modern names of places are given in the index for clarity.

CAESAR'S
FOOTPRINTS

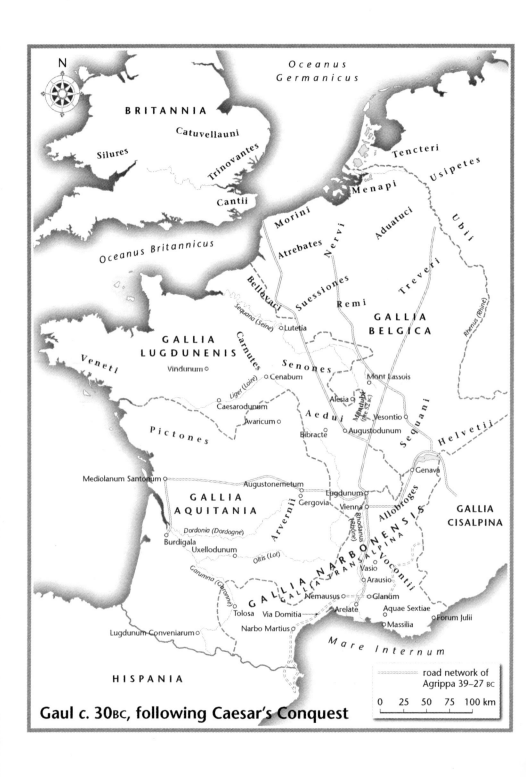

N

*Oceanus
Germanicus*

BRITANNIA

Catuvellauni

Silures

Trinovantes

Cantii

Tencteri

Usipetes

Morini

Menapi

Oceanus Britannicus

Atrebates

Nervi

Aduatuci

Ubii

Bellovaci

Suessiones

Remi

Treveri

Sequana (Seine)

Lutetia

GALLIA
BELGICA

Veneti

GALLIA
LUGDUNENSIS

Carnutes

Senones

Vindunum

Liger (Loire)

Cenabum

Mont Lassois

Rhenus (Rhine)

Caesarodunum

Alesia

Mandubii
(fle 52 BC)

Vesontio

Sequani

Helvetii

Pictones

Avaricum

Aedui

Bibracte

Augustodunum

Mediolanum Santonum

Augustonemetum

Genava

GALLIA
AQUITANIA

Arvernii

Lugdunum

Gergovia

Vienna

Allobroges

GALLIA
CISALPINA

Dordonia (Dordogne)

Burdigala

Uxellodunum

Oltis (Lot)

Rhodanus
(Rhône)

Vocontii

Garumna (Garonne)

GALLIA NARBONENSIS

GALLIA TRANSALPINA

Vasio

Arausio

Lugdunum Conveniarum

Tolosa

Via Domitia

Nemausus

Glanum

Arelate

Aquae Sextiae

Forum Julii

Narbo Martius

Massilia

Mare Internum

HISPANIA

road network of
Agrippa 39–27 BC

0   25   50   75   100 km

Gaul c. 30BC, following Caesar's Conquest

Introduction

THE IDEA FOR WRITING THIS BOOK came to me a few years ago, while I was teaching a Latin lesson. It was a Wednesday morning deep in the winter term, period two. I was conducting a Latin language session with a bright but not especially motivated lower sixth. The unfortunate fodder for this exercise was the fifth book of Julius Caesar's *Commentaries on the Gallic War*, describing his conquest of Gaul between 58 and 50 BC.

There was something almost ritualized about the pupils' misery during these sessions. The use of Caesar as fodder for teenage children to take their first steps in translating 'real' Latin, after leaving behind the safety of language textbooks, is an ancient tradition. Say 'Caesar' to anyone who has been subjected to an education containing a classical component, and there are two likely reactions. One the one hand, a cheerful reminiscence of how good Caesar was for them: how wonderfully hard his writing worked their brain, as if his dialogues were specifically designed – like some formidable fibre-laced breakfast cereal – to improve their cerebral motions. On the other, a cross-eyed stab of agony, like thinking back to a mental version of the Somme, where all was muddy quagmire and barbed-wire entanglements formed of indirect statements enmeshed with ablative absolutes and gerundives of obligation. My lower sixth form class was very much in the latter camp.

I hated it that, for generations of schoolchildren, this was the miserable end to which Caesar's account of the Gallic Wars was put. During that lesson, as someone, floundering in a particularly long and vicious stretch of *oratio obliqua*,* paused and expressed his total disgust for Caesar, *The Gallic Wars* and the whole exercise, I felt compelled to pause and make a defence, if not of using Caesar for grammar bashing, then at least of Caesar's writing. It was, I pleaded, rather more than a random tale of legions being marched and legates being dispatched. The text stood as an extraordinary account of the very foundation of modern Europe: for it was by taking the heart-lands of Gaul under their control that the Romans introduced the culture of the Latin Mediterranean to the European north. Without this conquest – which was not a historical inevitability, and which was undertaken on the spur of the moment because of Caesar's own political circumstances and all-consuming ambition – the Roman empire would likely never have had the reach or staying power that it attained. The modern languages of Europe would probably have been more Celtic than Latinate in nature. The literary classics of Virgil, Cicero and Ovid, and the masterpieces of ancient Greek literature that influenced them, might not have had such a profound impact on the Western tradition. The same is the case for classical ideas of philosophy, law, rhetoric, music and architecture. Christianity like-wise would perhaps never have penetrated Europe as deeply as would prove to be the case. Without Caesar's conquest of Gaul, the map of modern Europe would look entirely different. There would have been no European neurosis springing from the memory of the barbarian invasions across the Rhine in the fifth century AD; no Charlemagne; no modern state of France; no Renaissance in the fifteenth and

---

* Indirect speech. For example, '*Magister est stupidus*' (The teacher is stupid) is direct speech. '*Putat magistrum stupidum esse*' (He thinks that the teacher is stupid) is indirect speech.

sixteenth centuries – and very little likelihood that we would have been sitting in that classroom reading a classic work of Latin literature on a cold Wednesday morning.

I expressed myself largely and eloquently. My class essentially told me to sod off. Not one to give up on a fight with my students, I determined then that I would do something to save Caesar from the slough of grammar and syntactical misery to which he – perhaps as fitting punishment from the Furies for the Olympian scale of his ambition – had been condemned.

Modern interest in Caesar tends to concentrate on what he did in Rome rather than on what he did in Gaul. It is the political intrigue that marked his rise to prominence and his victory in the civil war, and the period that led up to his assassination, that captures the twenty-first-century imagination. His time in Gaul, and his bloody activities there, are by contrast relegated to the classroom, and the wretchedness of grammatical exercises for reluctant schoolchildren. My aim in writing this book is to redress the balance: to place centre stage what Caesar – and the Romans who followed him – achieved in Gaul, and to explore their lasting and highly visible cultural legacy.

The purpose of this book is not to give a military account of Caesar's time in Gaul; nor, indeed, is it exclusively devoted to Caesar. There are many excellent works that already fill this niche. It is intended rather to examine the circumstances that led to the Roman conquest of Gaul, and to consider the reasons why, after the initial bloodletting of the Gallic Wars, it would prove to be such a long-term success: how the Roman transformation of Gaul laid the foundations of modern Europe. It therefore looks at the history of the engagement of Rome and Gaul and the cultural and economic impact of that connection. Physical evidence of this can still be seen on the ground, and parts of the book are devoted to the surviving vestiges of Roman Gaul – amphitheatres, aqueducts, triumphal arches, temples and mausoleums. I will also trace the impact of Roman Gaul on cultural ideas, literary remains and religious traditions.

The question as to how Rome managed to knit Gaul to itself so effectively that it remained a part of the empire for half a millennium has an enduring relevance. In an age in which the aspiration for European unity looks increasingly chimerical despite the blessings of technology and the modern era, it is instructive to look back to when this ideal, under Rome, was first born, how it was brought about and what – in the example of Gaul – was its cost. It is tied up in questions not just of material change, but also culture, and in particular how Rome dealt with outsiders and migration. The Roman movement into Gaul was arguably born as a response to the first European migration crisis for which we possess an eye-witness account (however slanted it may be). To describe Caesar and the conquest of Gaul is also to describe how Rome treated the 'barbarian other'. And this demands that we look at Caesar not just as a grammatical exercise, but as the brooding presence – the 'vast ghost' in the words of Lawrence Durrell – that still hangs over a Europe which struggles to be at one.

Detail of the Vix Krater, c. sixth century BC.

CHAPTER I

Gaul Before Caesar

Factum eius hostis periculum patrum nostrorum memoria
'We have made trial of this foe in the time of our fathers'
JULIUS CAESAR, *De Bello Gallico*, 1.40

MARSEILLES

·

GREEK MIGRANTS

·

SAINT-RÉMY-DE-PROVENCE

·

GALLIC MIGRANTS

·

GALLIA CISALPINA

·

ENTREMONT

·

TEUTONIC MIGRANTS

·

ORANGE

·

THE CRAU

·

MONTAGNE SAINTE-VICTOIRE

·

POURRIÈRES

·

AIX-EN-PROVENCE

OUR STORY BEGINS IN THE OLD port of Marseilles, where the masts of a vast fleet of sailing boats are reflected, ribbon-like, in the opalescent water. These are the same waters that lap at the harbour walls of cities across the length and breadth of the Middle Sea: Ajaccio, Genoa, Algiers, Athens, Alexandria. Water, boats and masts seem to vaporize in the heat, suspended in a haze of ochre and peach dust above the grand frontages measuring the length of the quay. At the traffic lights, a figure in a brown chador washes windscreens for a handful of cents. In a shuttered doorway, sitting on a sleeping bag, an Arab man skins plastic from copper cables with a crooked knife, his young son curled up beside him on a bed of cardboard and dirty cushions.

Their origins may lie elsewhere, but Marseilles is *their* city. Just as, east of the city, the limestone cliffs of the Massif des Calanques shelter a diverse array of herbs and flowers, so Marseilles has always provided a refuge for new arrivals from foreign shores. A curtain of low mountains – the Garlaban and Massif de l'Étoile – is draped beyond the city's suburban shoulder like a protective cowl, shielding it from the suspicions of the north. Marseilles was founded not by Romans but by Greeks: it is, therefore, older than Caesar, though not older than Rome. But it was a place of wealth and taste long before Rome made its mark on the wider world. It had no great aspirations to empire or dominion like Rome, no serious martial tradition, but was happy, like Venice after it, to cling to a redoubt in a hostile hinterland – so long as it could make money as a middleman from trading upon the sea.

But, in truth, this city is a cousin to Rome. They are alike in the stories of their birth. They were early friends. They shared their fears, neuroses and hypocrisies. It was through Marseilles that the culture of the Mediterranean made its original entry into Gaul and so into northern Europe. Marseilles prepared the way for the coming of Caesar and the Romans, and presaged the mindset that drew Caesar into conquest. To understand the lure and the myth of the ground that Caesar would tread in Gaul, we must first understand Marseilles.

They came in search of a better life. Their original home, the Ionian Greek city of Phocaea, lay far to the east, clinging to the rocky scourings off the coast of Asia Minor, modern-day Turkey, north of Izmir. The land was crowded, stony and infertile. The Phocaeans thus became accustomed – according to the Gallo-Roman historian Pompeius Trogus, writing in the first century BC – to wandering and making a living from the sea. They were the first of all the Greeks, so Herodotus says, to make long journeys on the Mediterranean for the sake of trade. They conducted business past the Hellespont in the north, Egypt in the south, and Spain in the west. But the demographic pressures on their native city led many of them not just to travel, but to abandon Phocaea altogether and settle elsewhere. Some of their colonies, such as Lampascus in the Dardanelles, were close to home; others – Aléria in Corsica or Empúries in Catalonia – were far away. The first wave of Phocaean migration, at the end of the seventh century BC and early in the sixth, was voluntary; the second, in the middle of the sixth, came about as a result of war. Cyrus, king of Persia, determined to seize the Greek hinterland in Asia Minor and captured Phocaea in 546 BC; its entire population fled.

Marseilles was born of the first wave of Greek migration, and augmented by the second. Gaul would not have been completely unfamiliar to the Phocaeans, but it was certainly replete with mystery and danger. The tenth labour of Heracles* – to kill Geryon, the three-bodied giant, and steal his cattle – led him to traverse the coast of the

---

* Heracles is the Greek name for the hero Hercules.

Mediterranean through Spain and southern Gaul. The land even bore the scars of his journey: chased by the Ligurian tribes, Heracles was aided by his father Zeus, who flung rocks from the sky at his pursuers to cover his escape. According to local legend, the rocks that Zeus threw can still be seen in the dry, stony landscape around the town of Saint-Martin-de-Crau near the mouth of the Rhône. Closer to the Phocaeans' own experience, the Phoenicians of the Levant, the Etruscans from northern Italy and other Ionian Greeks had – over a number of centuries – carried on a fitful trade with the coast-dwellers of southern Gaul, but there was no sign that they had put down a permanent presence.

The Phocaeans were to change this. At the beginning of the sixth century BC, according to Trogus, Phocaean ships sailed into the mouth of the Rhône and found it to be an inviting place. Quite apart from its favourable location, at the hub of a trading route that could stretch from the furthest reaches of the Mediterranean, via the river Rhône, into the unexplored interior of Gaul, there were safe natural harbours and fine stretches of pleasant land protected by an encircling wall of hills.

Attracted by promising reports from these early visitors to southern Gaul, a fleet of migrants assembled in Phocaea. Its captains were Protis and Simos. They crossed the sea safely and arrived at the mouth of the Rhône, but they still had to win the right to settle the territory. The inhabitants of the area were the Segobrigii, whose king was Nannus. The legend of the coming of the Phocaeans is recounted not only by Trogus but also by Aristotle. They arrived on the very day that Nannus had appointed for his daughter, Gyptis, to be betrothed. When they approached Nannus to ask him for land on which to settle, the Greek captains found themselves invited to the nuptial festivities.

It was the custom at these events for the bride herself to choose whom she would marry. The suitors would gather, and the bride would parade around them clutching a goblet of water, or wine, says Aristotle, before finally giving it to the man she wished to be her husband. That night, after the local chiefs had assembled with the newcomers in their midst, they were astonished when Gyptis handed the goblet to Protis. Nannus, believing that a god had guided her choice, did not stand in her way, and granted the Greek migrants the site of Marseilles, then called Massalia.

Trogus's account of the legend is broadly similar to that of his Greek predecessor, but Aristotle gives the protagonists different names. In Aristotle's version, Protis was the son born of the marriage of the Greek newcomer and the daughter of the native king; the Greek captain's original name was Euxenus, meaning 'good stranger'; while the king's daughter was Petta (although she changed her name to Aristoxena – 'best stranger' – on marrying Euxenus). The descendants of Protis still constituted a noble family in Massalia when Aristotle was writing in the fourth century BC. Whatever the truth of the legend of the marriage, the kernel of the story suggests that a union between

Remains of the ancient Greek and Roman port of Massalia, now silted up a few streets inland from Marseilles' old port.

the migrants and the native inhabitants took place at the moment of Massalia's foundation.

The city was a great success. Standing in the ancient harbour of Massalia, now silted up a few streets inland from the old port, it is difficult to envisage the prosperity of the early days of the Greek colony. One cannot see the theatre or the temples the Phocaeans built nearby for their migrant gods, Artemis and Apollo. The harbour walls, water tanks and tower bases built of well-squared Roman blocks overtop the Greek originals of the earliest generations; it is only beneath the elegantly grooved Cassis* stone slabs on the Roman roadway leading from the quayside that traces of the sixth-century Greek road, which lies below the Grand-Rue of the modern city, can be discerned.

To see the early success of the colony, one must look beyond the city to wider Gaul and to the impact that the Greek presence had on the tribes deep in the Gallic heartland. In the sixth century BC, the interior of Gaul was under the sway of a proto-Celtic society – the Hallstatt culture, as it is conventionally termed by archaeologists. It was a society of the warrior chieftain. It possessed a special skill in metalwork, particularly iron, and the manufacture of weapons. The highest members of its aristocracy, perhaps ultimately migrants from the eastern steppes, were buried in timber chambers beneath tumuli, laid out on four-wheeled chariots decked in bronze. They displayed their power through ownership of an abundance of rare and exotic goods, which they could freely distribute to enhance their prestige and also attract new followers. It was the presence of the Greeks that gave them access to these desirable items, and even prompted them to develop this hierarchical society. Greek traders, with their links to the ateliers in the east, brought luxuries to Massalia and from there they were transported along the Rhône and Saône to the deep heartlands of Gaul. Perhaps in return for tin, or iron, or slaves, the noble classes were able to secure fine examples of Greek workmanship as tokens of their own authority.

* Limestone has been quarried at Cassis, a town east of Marseilles, since early antiquity.

By examining some of the archaeological finds of this age, it is possible to imagine how Gallic tribesmen might have reacted when they first set eyes on the luxury imports of the Greeks. For a vignette, let us set the date at 520 BC, at a Gallic settlement on the flat-topped hill of Mont Lassois by the upper reaches of the Seine in northeastern Burgundy. A number of boxes have been brought up the hill into the camp of wooden huts and palisades. The boxes contain together just one item, but being a heavy import, it is flat-packed for self-assembly. Fortunately, there are instructions – scratched-on Greek letters, indicating which part should be joined to which. As the tribesmen labour to join the pieces together – handles, stand, cover – the item takes shape. It is not easy work. The item is metal, refulgent hammered bronze, weighing over 200 kilograms, with individual components of as much as 60 kilograms. When finished, it stands at least as high as the tribesmen, at 1.6 metres (5 foot 4 inches). This is no simple bookshelf or bedstead, but a colossal 1,200-litre wine cauldron, or *krater*. It is the largest such item known from the ancient world, and is intricately and skilfully worked. Gorgons, menacing, with snakes in their hair and tongues sticking out through grimacing smiles, glare from the handles, as do rampant lions, their muscles taut and claws digging into the metalwork, while their tails echo in their curve the elegant whorls and scrolls chased into the rim and the volutes of the handles. In a band below the rim that runs the whole circumference of the *krater*, Greek soldiers, hoplites, march in an endless parade. They are naked save for great fan-crested helmets (whose plumage reaches down to their waist), greaves and round, dish-like shields strapped to their left arms. Some ride on chariots whose horses, ambling and stately, peer inquisitively at the new owners of the *krater*.

The tribesmen, who then had no native tradition of sculpture, would have felt similarly curious. They would have recognized and appreciated the chariots, but the panoply of Greek art and decorations – and the complex religious and social ideas that they expressed – would have been quite incomprehensible to them at this point in time. In a classical Greek context, such a *krater* would have been used for mixing wine and water at a symposium, or drinking party, where the atmosphere would have been that of easy aristocratic conviviality. In the Gallic context, however – to judge from investigations of other such *kraters* dating from sixth-century BC Gaul – it seems more likely they were used for mead, not wine. Their role in Gallic feasting was not simply as a drinking vessel, but to impress on the guests the power of the owner: they expressed hierarchy, not conviviality. They might even have had a religious function. In the very earliest stratum of Greek culture, the cauldron was associated with death and rebirth, a symbol of the abundant power of nature for regeneration. Such profundities were less likely to occupy the mind of a Greek party-goer of the sixth century BC, but these ideas were also indigenous to Celtic culture, and visible in surviving Celtic mythology.* Perhaps it was for the power of its religious symbolism that the cauldron was put to its final use, to accompany a lady of high status to the grave.

When the *krater*, now named the Vix Krater after the village nearest to the grave, was discovered in 1953, it provided compelling evidence of the impact of the Greek newcomers on the interior of Gaul in those early times. They had not at that stage brought about a fundamental change in culture, but they had introduced a material presence that would gradually affect Gaul in myriad ways. Following the import of *kraters* and ceramic items, Greek methods were introduced into construction, agriculture and the arts. Solid buildings were built, with mud bricks on top of stone bases. Even on Mont Lassois, huge structures of wood but in imitation of Greek halls, or *megara*, were erected. In the areas near Massalia, the olive and vine began to be cultivated. Local productions of ceramics in imitation of the Greek imports began. Silver coins, like those of the Greeks, were struck. The Greek alphabet was tentatively used for inscriptions in the local

---

* The Irish father-god Dagda possessed a cauldron with powers of rejuvenation. Similarly, the cauldron of the mythical character Da Derga could not only provide an unending supply of food, but also had the power to bring back life to the dead.

languages. Motifs from Greek art were taken up by indigenous artists: the figures and patterns from the imported wares formed the basis for the familiar style of what became known as Celtic art.

At the end of the sixth century BC there was an apparent breakdown in trade along the Rhône, as Etruscan rivals began to compete for business in the interior of Gaul using overland routes from northern Italy. Sites like Mont Lassois were abandoned, and Massalia turned its attention more to the southern coast of Gaul. The colony spawned a cluster of daughter colonies during the fifth century BC – Nice, Antibes, Agde, Monaco – increasing the Greek cultural presence in the south and marking a divergence from the northern interior. 'Such a radiance was shed over both men and things', writes Pompeius Trogus, 'that it was not Greece which seemed to have immigrated into Gaul, but Gaul that seemed to have been transplanted into Greece'.

The Vix Krater, an ancient Greek import into Gaul, discovered in 1953.

The Gauls had given the Phocaeans refuge and permitted them to found Massalia, but they were nonetheless uneasy. Trogus relates that a subject complained to the king of the Segobrigii by telling him the following fable: 'A bitch once asked a shepherd, when she was pregnant, for a place to give birth to her puppies. When he agreed, she asked again to be allowed to bring them up in the same place. Later, when her puppies were grown up, and she could depend upon their support, she seized the place as her own.' In such a way, the subject continued, 'the people of Marseilles, who are now regarded as your tenants, will one day become masters of your territory'.

The king began to fear. The immigrants were now too powerful to expel by open warfare, so he decided on a plot to remove them. Some of his strongest warriors would enter Massalia openly, as friends to the newcomers, to join in a festival. Others would lie concealed in carts, covered with baskets and branches. The king himself would hide with an army in the hills outside the city, waiting for the moment when – as the Massalians slept off the day's carousing – his agents within the city would throw open the gates. But, after the plot was set, one of the king's relatives told her Massalian lover what was afoot, and he rushed to alert the city authorities. The alarm was sounded. The Massalians, putting their celebrations on hold, scoured the city, rooting out and killing the intruders, before marching out of the city and destroying the army that was ready to trap them; even the king of the Segobrigii was killed. Thus did a reprise of the Trojan horse fail to overcome the Greeks.

This was not the only battle the Massalians had to fight. There were skirmishes in the sixth century BC with the north African city-state of Carthage, then the dominant naval power in the western Mediterranean, and their north Italian allies the Etruscans. Massalia and Carthage clashed over the capture of fishing vessels and perhaps the liberty of trade within Gaul itself. But it was on the landward side that the danger to the Greek colony was perhaps the greatest. Sometime before the end of the fifth century, Massalia was besieged by a large army of Gauls under a prince named Catumandus. It appears that, in response to Massalia's ever-growing prosperity, the neighbouring tribes had come together under Catumandus's banner/leadership. The legend of how Massalia came to be saved on this occasion, again recorded by Trogus, is telling. One night during the siege, when Catumandus was asleep outside the city walls, he saw a vision of a fearsome-looking woman. She told him she was a goddess, and ordered him to make peace with Massalia. Terrified, he begged the Massalians to allow him to enter the city by himself to worship their gods. As he came into one of the unfamiliar temples he saw, in a portico, a statue of Athena. Recognizing her as the goddess who had appeared in his sleep, he told the Massalians of his dream, and said that, since they were under the protection of the gods, he would leave them in peace. Before departing, he left what must have seemed to the onlookers a barbarous offering on her shrine: a Gallic neck torque, laid in submission to the most Greek of goddesses.

It is difficult to believe that the Gauls were easy neighbours for the Greek incomers. Some scholars, it is true, do not hold to this opinion. They observe that the stories portraying the Gauls as barbarous warriors who terrified their opponents are seen only in texts after the third century BC, particularly following wide-ranging Gallic attacks on Delphi and Asia Minor (Trogus was writing in the first century AD). They also point out that the Gauls bought goods from the Greeks, and began over time to imitate Greek ways. However, the Gauls used many of those Greek ways and ideas in a fashion that the latter must have found unnervingly beyond their cultural comprehension. The Gauls scarcely ever received good press among Greek authors based in mainland Greece. Authors such as Aristotle asserted that the Gauls were warlike, obsessed with drinking, cruel to their children for the sake of toughening them for battle, and bold to the point of irrationality. It might be easy to dismiss such writings as the projection of cultural clichés on a distant other. But setting eyes on some of the remains, one wonders if these Greek writings had more than a modicum of truth in them.

In the centre of St-Rémy-de-Provence, a dozen miles south of Avignon, stands a complex of Roman baths. Its walls are mostly intact, though the ancient buildings have been integrated into a warren of tall and handsome Renaissance townhouses. The little square outside is filled with tubs of white flowers. It was near here, in the Asylum of St Paul about a mile outside the town, in the midst of wide olive groves, that Vincent van Gogh spent the last months of his life. But in the inner recesses of the baths, which now house a selection of the archaeological finds from the nearby Gallic settlement of Glanum – a town based around a healing spring that fell strongly under the Greek influence of Massalia – is an item that speaks of more than a severed ear. Next to a storeroom, laid out on packing crates, is a stone door lintel from Glanum. From a cursory glance, one might think it an unremarkable Greek or Roman relic. The surface is well-squared, although battered by time, and topped with finely carved egg and dart mouldings. More arresting, however, are the six visible head-shaped niches gouged into the polite Greek stonework. These niches were, indeed, for heads. A Greek scholar, Posidonius, who travelled in Gaul at the end of the second century BC, records his difficulty in getting used to the sight of severed human heads on public display. On occasion they were strung like beads on a bracelet to adorn the neck of a horse, or preserved in linseed oil and kept in store chests to be proudly brought out on special occasions. Sometimes they even served practical uses. Livy writes that in 215 BC, the general Lucius Postumus, who was campaigning in Gallia Cisalpina, was captured and killed by members of the Gallic Boii tribe who then proceeded to clean out his skull, cover the scalp with beaten gold, and use it as a drinking vessel. No Gaul would want to part with the heads that they had won or inherited. They were marks of success in war, and a sign of the endemic competitiveness between Gallic warriors for the greatest glory in battle. Examples of lintels and pillars for displaying heads have been found at Roquepertuse and Entremont, sometimes with the skulls of the victims themselves pierced with iron spikes to secure them to the display space. The custom of exhibiting the severed heads of enemies would have been deep rooted when the Greeks arrived, and remained the norm even in the area close to 'civilized' Massalia throughout the Greek period. For all the willingness of the Gauls to adopt Greek artistic and architectural styles, Greek consciousness of the Gallic proclivity for head-hunting must have induced a fear of their underlying bellicosity, a primal terror of the brutalities they were capable of inflicting.

The 'Terror Gallicus' was the abiding impression that the Gauls left behind after their first encounter with the Romans. And it was an encounter that very nearly led to Rome's early extinction.

The Celtic Gauls, according to some accounts, were first present in the north of Italy as early as the sixth century BC. A grave stele found at Bologna, dating to the fifth century BC and depicting an Etruscan on horseback in combat with a characteristically naked Celt, suggests that Gallic warrior bands had taken up residence south of the Alps by this time. However, the first major incursion of Gauls into Italy appears to have taken place in the fourth century BC.

The ancient historians offer various explanations for their arrival. One reason given is the desire of deprived northerners for the luxuries of the south. According to Pliny the Elder, a Gallic craftsman from Switzerland who lived in Rome for a time sent back to his homeland dried figs and grapes, as well as samples of olive oil and wine. 'We may offer some excuse, then, for them, when we know that they came in quest of these various productions, though even at the price of war,' remarks Pliny indulgently. Livy reports a legend that one citizen of an Italian town sent presents of wine to Gallic warriors to lure them south of the Alps; once they arrived, he hoped to employ them to rid himself of an otherwise untouchable local dignitary who had been sleeping with his wife.

Perhaps the vintages of the south were indeed one of the leading attractions for the Gauls. However, the ancient historians acknowledge that there was more to their movements than this alone. Both Polybius and Livy (writing respectively in the second and first centuries BC) state that, as was the case with the Greek migration from Phocaea, Gallic migrations into northern Italy were triggered primarily by overpopulation in the Gallic heartlands. Livy explicitly recognizes the analogy between the southward movement of the

Stone heads from the Gallic oppidum *of Entremont, second century* BC.

Gauls and the northward movement of the Phocaeans. Placing the movements at the same time in the sixth century BC, he says that the wandering Gauls took the migration of the Phocaeans to Massalia as a good omen, and that each helped the other in their journey. To explain the circumstances of the Gallic migration, Livy tells the tale of one of the most powerful kings in Gaul, who had been so successful and had obtained so many followers that his kingdom had become overpopulated and difficult to manage. As he himself was growing old, he ordered his two nephews to set out in search of new kingdoms. He told them to take as many followers as they needed to overcome any opposition they might encounter on their journey. The nephews looked to heaven for signs indicating which way they should take: the less fortunate of the two found himself heading for the uplands of southern Germany; the other was assigned 'the much pleasanter road' to Italy.

This legend may reflect part of a wider truth. Archaeological evidence suggests that there was a rapid depopulation in Champagne and around the upper stretches of the Marne at the beginning of the fourth century BC. This was the starting point for an established route that led south, via the Rhine, to the Great St Bernard Pass and across the Alps. However, Livy's legend may also reflect an economic impetus behind the Gauls' southward migration. As has been said, Gallic chiefs relied on abundant wealth for their prestige. Aside from sporadic trade, the other source of such wealth was raiding. A successful chief who had gained a large entourage of warriors after a spell of local raiding would be compelled to raid further afield to support them. As the quantity of plunder increased and the warrior entourage swelled in number, the chief was caught in a vicious cycle of success. He had to lead his ever-increasing band of followers further and further afield to win sufficient plunder to maintain his authority and prestige. Eventually, the raids necessary to sustain him covered such a distance that they took on the character of a sudden long-distance exodus. Whether or not it was such an imperative that led the

Gauls into Italy, the Gallic culture of raiding goes some way to explain the character of the first encounter between the Gallic migrants and Rome.

Classical authors spoke admiringly of the movement of the Phocaeans and the foundation of Massalia. It represented, among other things, an extension of the Hellenic world, and hence civilization. Aristotle himself wrote a work in praise of the constitution of Massalia. But the movement of the Gauls south into Italy was not so well regarded. By about 400 BC, the Gallic migrants had established a number of settlements in the valley of the River Po. The Greek historian Polybius, writing about 250 years after this time, reflects an impression of the new arrivals that would have been commonly held by his Roman readership, even if he errs in the detail or repeats *idées reçues*. They lived, he says, in unwalled villages, and had no knowledge of the refinements of civilization. They were unacquainted with art or science. They slept on straw and leaves, ate meat, and had no occupations other than war and agriculture. Polybius's account hints at a raiding culture. Their only possessions were cattle and gold, since these were easily portable. It was of the greatest importance to have a following, and whoever had the largest following was the most powerful and the most feared.

The Romans, at this time, knew little of the Gauls. Rome was then a rising power on the Italian peninsula – significant, but not without its rivals. Just after the turn of the fourth century BC, it had captured the important Etruscan city of Veii, ten miles to the north of the city, and also subdued the tribes on the surrounding plain of Latium. Other enemies, nevertheless, remained further afield. The Samnites, to the south, were a potential threat, as was the Greek city-state of Syracuse in Sicily. To the north, the Etruscans likewise represented a danger to Rome. It was therefore hardly surprising that the Gauls, even though they had begun to enter Etruscan areas, were little noticed by the Roman authorities. Thus, reports Livy, when a lowly Roman plebeian one night heard a voice more than human near the shrine of Vesta calling 'Tell the magistrates that the Gauls are coming!' – the first, he says, that was known of the Gauls' approach in Rome – the warning was disregarded.

The Gauls' first port of call was Clusium, about ninety miles north of Rome. The sight of the new arrivals, according to Livy, threw the city into alarm. They came in their thousands, arrayed before the gates, men the like of whom Clusians had never seen before – outlandish warriors with strange weapons. Clusium sent for help to Rome. The citizens hoped to be able to deal with the Gauls peaceably, but that the Romans would support them with arms if they could not.

Rome decided against sending any military assistance. Instead, they sent three envoys to warn the Gauls against harming Clusium. Livy muses that things might have ended very differently if the Roman envoys 'had not behaved more like Gauls than Romans'. When all the parties came together to negotiate, the Gauls demanded land from Clusium. They needed land, said a Gallic emissary, and besides, Clusium had more land than it could manage. At this point the Romans intervened, asking what right the Gauls had to demand land, and what they were doing there at all. The Gauls replied that they carried their right on the point of their swords. At that, a fight broke out. One of the Roman diplomats stabbed a Gallic chief with a spear, and began to strip him of his armour. When the Gauls realized what had happened, they turned their anger against Rome. They did not, according to Livy's account, immediately march against the city, but instead sent their own mission to demand the surrender of Rome's envoys, who had breached time-honoured convention by killing their chief while he was engaged on a diplomatic embassy. The Romans, however, not only flatly refused to comply with the Gallic demands, but appointed the men responsible to positions of military command for the following year, thus making them immune to prosecution. The Gauls now gave way to their 'characteristic uncontrollable anger'. Ignoring every other town and city on the way, they marched directly on Rome.

The Roman military preparations to meet the Gallic invasion were lackadaisical. An emergency force was assembled to block the Gauls' advance at the River Allia, about ten miles from Rome. However, it was disorganized and poorly led, and the Gauls swept it away without effort. Rome was thrown into a panic. With its army scattered, the decision was taken that able-bodied citizens and the Senate should retreat into the fortified Capitol and make a stand. The rest of the city was to be abandoned to the barbarian onslaught.

Such was the abiding trauma of the Gallic attack on Rome that it attracted all manner of myth-making to mitigate the reality of what was in truth a catastrophic defeat. Elderly grandees, says Livy, who were too frail to merit a place in the citadel, dressed up in the finery of their past offices and sat, dignified and statue-like, on thrones in the courtyards of their great houses – a sight that filled the Gauls with reverential dread. When the rest of the city had been burnt and the Capitol was under siege, one of the Roman priests, determined that the blockade should not prevent him from celebrating an annual sacrifice that was meant to take place on a particular spot, put on his vestments and walked calmly through the enemy lines to perform the ritual, unharmed. A flock of geese, sacred to the goddess Juno, were also famously hailed as heroes of the siege. The geese, resident on the Capitol, are said to have cackled and hissed as the Gauls attempted a night-time assault. This woke the Roman guards, who were able to repulse the attack.

Yet none of this mythologizing could efface the fact that this was Rome's most grievous defeat: traditionally dated to 390 BC, it was the only time that Rome would be sacked by an enemy before Alaric and the Goths 700 years later, in AD 410. A story Livy tells about the conclusion of the siege illustrates how Rome's shame persisted. After several months, the Romans, starving and hopeless, offered 1,000 pounds of gold to the Gauls to lift the siege. It was a proposal that the Gauls readily accepted. The desire for wealth was likely to have been one of the principal motivations for their attack: they were not experienced in siege warfare, the conditions in the disease-ridden, burnt-out city were not easy for them either, and they were eager to return and secure their northern base in Italy which was under threat from other tribes. A delegation from both sides met to weigh out the gold. As this was happening, the Romans realized that the Gauls were using doctored weights, heavier than marked. When they angrily objected, the Gallic leader Brennus, chief of the Senones tribe, threw his sword into the scales as well and said '*vae victis*' ('woe to the conquered'): 'words intolerable to Roman ears', laments Livy.

The scars of the attack were still present and vivid even in Caesar's time in the first century BC, nearly 400 years later. The destruction of the city, writes Plutarch, led to the loss of the early records of Rome's history. When the Gauls departed, the Romans came close to abandoning the ruins of the city and decamping en masse to another. When they decided not to do so, the work of rebuilding was rushed and ill planned. Old boundaries were ignored. Buildings went up wherever there was space, and no one took measures to ensure that the streets were straight. Old sewers that originally ran under straight streets ended up beneath private property. It was because of the Gallic attack, writes Livy, that the general layout of Rome in his time was more like a squatters' settlement than a properly planned city.

But the scars were more than physical. It took around thirty years after 390 BC for Rome to regain its authority in the immediate vicinity. This time was marked by social unrest in the city, as citizens from the lower plebeian order attempted to seize power from the patricians. All the while, the continuing threat from the newly arrived Gauls of northern Italy weighed heavily on Rome. The following centuries of Roman history are a litany of conflict with the Gallic incomers. On occasion, the latter would offer themselves as mercenaries to the opponents of Rome, including the Syracusians in the fourth century BC, King Pyrrhus in the early part of the third century, or Hannibal – another invader who attacked Rome from the north – in the later years of the second century. Sometimes they would ally with local tribes, such as the Samnites. On other occasions, the Gauls who had settled in the north would be impelled by further waves of Gallic migration to make incursions into Rome's expanding territory in the centre of the Italian peninsula, or join with the latest newcomers in making such attacks. It is a measure of the fear that the Gauls inspired in the Romans that the latter negotiated an early truce with the Carthaginian commander Hasdrubal, Hannibal's brother, in order to deal with what they saw as the more fundamental Gallic menace.

Throughout this period, Roman prejudices vis-à-vis the Gauls seem to have hardened. Polybius, among others, describes the martial customs of the Gauls: they charged into battle with extraordinary shouts, sounding horns and war trumpets throughout their ranks. Some of their number fought naked in the front rank of battle. This made for a terrifying spectacle, the warriors being men of splendid physique and in the prime of life, their bodies adorned with gold necklaces and torques. It was a sight, says Polybius, that did indeed strike fear into the Romans, but when it came to the practicalities of battle, intimidating appearance was to be overcome with strict Roman discipline.

It is a contrast that is pursued ad infinitum by Roman authors. The Gauls were temperamental, volatile, boastful, given to rash displays of boldness at the start of a fight, but were incapable of channelling these qualities into an orderly plan of battle. If their initial – admittedly dangerous – impetus did not produce swift results, they lost heart and enthusiasm; they lacked the discipline necessary to fight a prolonged battle. Frequently, Gallic warriors are seen in the works of classical historians challenging Roman soldiers to resolve battles by single combat. A huge Gaul marches before the battle lines, boasting of his prowess, wielding a long slashing sword. A small and taciturn Roman, with an unglamorous short stabbing sword and a larger shield, comes to meet him. The slashing sword whistles past the Roman, or is rendered useless by its first contact with Roman blade or shield – an analogy between the sword and its Gallic wielder not lost on the Roman authors. The

Roman, hiding safely behind his shield, then dispatches the Gaul with a brief and undramatic stab to the face or torso.

That the Gauls, in the words of Polybius, were swayed by 'impulse rather than calculation' was not just a point of military strategy. It was also a moral judgement. The clash with the Gauls was not only a fight for survival, but also for civilization. The Romans were the representatives of order: a bulwark protecting not only themselves, but also the rest of the Italian peninsular against the perpetual danger of a Gallic irruption with all the chaos that it would bring. The centuries of friction with the Gauls, Polybius suggests, were to some extent responsible for the ever more military character that Rome took on as it developed. They were also at the root of an abiding neurosis that was to play out to the end of the Roman empire: a fundamental terror of what lay beyond the northern frontier.

Fear of the Gauls impelled the Romans to move the frontier northwards, and to take under their control those areas south of the Alps that had been colonized by Gallic migrants. It was a slow, difficult, long-term undertaking, interrupted by the First and Second Punic Wars (264–241 and 218–201 BC). Rome established an early colony in Gallic territory on the Adriatic coast at Sena Gallica (modern-day Senigallia, close to Ancona) in 283 BC after defeating the Senones who had previously settled there. Following the First Punic War, they made further progress in the 220s BC, setting up outposts at Cremona and Piacenza, and settling colonists on the land. These colonists suffered further Gallic attacks; many were captured and sold into slavery by the Gauls in 200 BC. Nevertheless, further colonists were sent and the area was secured by the construction of a road, the Via Aemilia, connecting Piacenza (Placentia) via Rimini (Arminium) to Rome. After the Second Punic War, in which the Gauls had assisted Hannibal's invasion of Italy, Rome moved to take over the rest of the Po Valley. Their forces reached Lake Como in 196 BC, and further colonies were founded to secure the area, including Bologna (Bononia) in 189, and Parma and Modena (Mutina) in 183.

Waves of migration marked the Roman seizure of control. Many of the Boii, a Gallic tribe that had settled around Bologna, returned northwards across the Alps. Yet, at the same time, a different Gallic grouping of migrants including 12,000 armed men, intent on raiding and settlement, attempted to enter the new area of Roman dominance south of the Alps. In 183 BC, they were set upon by the Roman legions, and those who were not killed were turned back north. Henceforth Rome would try to ensure that further such Gallic irruptions – all too reminiscent of the destruction of Rome 200 years previously – were prevented, if at all possible, from penetrating the Italian peninsula. The Alps were by no means a fully defensible border, but, by 180, they seemed a sensible place for the Romans to pause in their northern expansion; they proceeded to consolidate the regions captured by introducing Roman settlers and propagating a Roman way of life. This area, named Gallia Cisalpina ('Gaul-on-this-side-of-the-Alps'), was recognized as a province of Rome a century later, around 80 BC. In the first century BC, this province and its admixture of Gallic tribes and Roman colonists gave rise to three of the most Roman of writers: the historian Livy, and the poets Catullus and Virgil. Some scholars even claim to hear traces of Celtic in their voices.

The Romans themselves were originally migrants. If legend is to be believed – and it is a legend that the Romans certainly *did* believe – they emerged as refugees from the east. In the beginning, they were Trojans. When Agamemnon and the Greeks destroyed the city of Troy, a remnant of its population fled the smoking ruins of the city and the prospect of enslavement, and, huddled in boats, sought a new life in 'Hesperia' – the Promised Land in the west. Led by a surviving prince of the Trojan royal house, Aeneas, they were driven from Asia Minor to the Adriatic, then to the north coast of Africa, and finally to the shores of the plain of Latium and the River Tiber in Italy. Their

journey lasted for several years and was accompanied by deep suffering and privation. Even when they arrived in Italy, the promised
Hesperia, there was no respite from their distress. The local population took exception to these newcomers from the east, and fought a
bitter war against them. The new arrivals, marked by their piety and
self-discipline, were ultimately successful, but as a price of their success they would ultimately have to discard their eastern language and
their Asiatic dress in favour of those of Italy. According to Livy, it was
the descendants of these Trojan emigrants who were to establish the
city of Rome. The traditional date for this, according to the Roman
antiquarian Varro, was 753 BC.

It is perhaps the fact that the Romans and Massalians had in common a shared memory of migrant origins that made for such affinity
between the two peoples. Pompeius Trogus records a legend that the
Phocaeans stopped at Rome on their way from Anatolia to southern
Gaul and contracted an alliance with them even before the foundation
of Massalia. Yet, if a birth in migration forged their affinity, it was not
a feeling either side could extend to the migrant Gauls. Both Massalia
and Rome saw themselves as bringers of civilization from the south.
Trogus, who was of Gallic descent but wrote in Latin from a Roman
perspective, described how the Gauls ultimately learnt a more civilized way of life from their Massalian neighbours: they learnt to lay
aside or soften 'their former barbarity'. The Massalians taught them
to cultivate their lands and enclose their settlements with walls, and
to live according to laws rather than violence. Massalia's government,
writes Strabo, was an aristocracy, and of all known aristocracies theirs
was the best ordered. The Romans, pious and self-restrained, saw
themselves as similarly blessed; they did not believe that good government and civilization – those qualities of the warm south that they
themselves exemplified – would be found among the Gauls. 'Nothing
is more inclement' than the region north and west of the Alps, writes
the Roman historian Florus: 'The climate is harsh, and the disposition
of the inhabitants resembles it.' Romans and Massalians shared a fear

of the Gauls, compounded by their experiences of severed heads and near destruction.

Some authors trace the idea of a Roman and Massalian alliance based on fear back to earlier times. Trogus claims that when news of the Gallic destruction of Rome reached Massalia in 390 BC, the Massalians went into a period of public mourning, and even offered the Romans their personal hoards of gold and silver to help pay for the ransom demanded by the Gauls. Whatever the case, by 150 BC Massalia was certainly appealing to Rome for assistance against their common enemy. The Romans, however, having advanced their northern frontier to the Alps by 180 BC, were reluctant to engage so soon in the complexities of Transalpine Gaul, having only so recently taken Cisalpine Gaul under their control. Yet the calls of their ally in adversity could not be ignored for ever. Thus Rome was led by Massalia into its first engagement with Gaul beyond the Alps.

In 125 BC, the Massalians were coming under increasing pressure from their Gallic neighbours, in particular the tribe of the Saluvii. They repeated their appeal to Rome for help. This time, the Romans agreed to assist them, and their legions were able to score a quick victory. However, once they had crossed the Alps, there was no going back, and they soon found themselves embroiled in further conflict. The king of the Saluvii fled to a neighbouring tribe, the Allobroges, who refused to surrender him. The fight thus widened to include the Allobroges and another tribe, the Arverni, who lived in what is now the Auvergne. The Romans not only demanded that the king be handed over, but also sought retribution on behalf of another Gallic tribe, the Aedui, with whom they had at some point made an alliance. The Aedui, like the Massalians, had complained to the Romans of aggression by the Allobroges and Arverni, and the Romans agreed to take their part.

Although they were the invaders, the Romans had the advantage of military technology. According to Florus, they employed elephants against the Gauls; their ferocity, observed Florus, matched that of the barbarians. The Romans also brought siege weaponry, including stone-hurling ballistas, to break resistance at the Gallic *oppida*, or fortified settlements. Yet, the fact that the Romans had to resort to such weaponry suggests that the Gauls near Massalia were not so sunk in backward barbarity as some Roman propagandists were pleased to portray them. One place where the Roman missiles were found was in the ruins of the *oppidum* of Entremont. Close to Aix-en-Provence, on a rocky promontory overlooking a grand sweep of the Provençal ranges receding into the lilac distance, Entremont is likely to have been the principal centre of the Saluvii. It was not a primitive settlement. Built in about 180 BC, its northern walls on the hillside are about 400 metres long, built of formidable squared-off blocks of stone, relieved every 50 metres by protruding bastions with rounded corners. Only part of the settlement has been excavated, but among the dry shivers of limestone knapped from the living rock of the hill, the lower courses of the walls of the buildings can be still be seen. It must have caused confusion for the Roman invaders when they captured it in 123 BC. Entremont was a settlement of long streets with substantial dwellings, workshops with ovens for melting metals, bakeries, stores of amphorae and stone presses for making olive oil. But at its centre there stood an imposing tower on the site of an earlier shrine: its entrance was adorned with carvings of human heads, and around it were scattered as many as twenty human skulls.

The picture of the Gauls as ferocious and hasty to arms is not fully borne out by the fragments of written accounts that we have of this period. Appian, a historian writing in the second century AD, states that the king of the Allobroges sent an ambassador during the conflict to one of the Roman commanders, Gnaeus Domitius, to sue for peace. The Roman commander was taken aback that the Gauls for the most part used dogs to guard the embassy party, but even more surprised that the greater part of the diplomacy was handled by a magnificently dressed musician. The musician began to improvise a lay on the excellence of the king of the Allobroges, and then the

Allobroges themselves, and then even the Roman commander, praising his descent, his bravery and his wealth. But this early example of the bardic tradition in action availed them nothing. Not only were the musician and diplomatic song chalked up as a manifestation of the empty boasting of the Gauls, but their call for peace was turned down. Between 125 and 121 BC, battles raged along the lower Rhône. Thousands of Gauls were killed, others captured and enslaved, and the hostile tribes were pushed back a distance from the coast.

Massalia and its own possessions were left intact, but before long Rome had taken control of a strip of territory that extended along the Mediterranean coast all the way to the Pyrenees. Since the Romans had acquired colonies in Spain over the previous century, this was a considerable boon, creating a land route that united their newly won international domains. The route from Italy to Hispania, traversing what is now Provence and Languedoc, was traced by Gaul's first Roman road, the Via Domitia. New Roman settlements sprang up across southern Gaul. Entremont was abandoned, but next to it Aix-en-Provence (Aquae Sextius) was established in 123 BC as a replacement,

The walls of Entremont, second century BC.

named after the Roman Consul Sextius Calvinus who was responsible for Entremont's destruction. Roman entrepreneurs rushed in to capitalize on the trade opportunities. Further conflict with tribes along the Rhône as well as the Carcassonne Gap and Garonne in the west led to the capture and re-establishment of further settlements – Vienne, Geneva and Toulouse (Tolosa) – as mercantile depots. Toulouse was connected to the Via Domitia by another new road, the Via Aquitania. Their intersection on the Mediterranean coast by the mouth of the River Aude was guarded by a new colony, Narbo Martius (Narbonne), which gave its name to the new Roman province in Gaul when it finally came to be formally constituted sometime in the early first century BC: Gallia Narbonensis.

The conquest of a large strip of southern Gaul, however militarily and economically advantageous, was no guarantee of safety from the old threats that haunted the Roman imagination. Just a few years after the Romans had entered Gaul, a huge horde of migrants began to move across central Europe. They first made contact with the Romans in 112 BC, when they attempted to enter the land of a Roman confederate tribe through the region of Noricum in the south of present-day Austria. In the process, they came close to annihilating a Roman force tasked with keeping them away from their allies' territory. Only a storm that arose during the battle saved the Romans from complete destruction. The commander of the Roman force, Papirius Carbo, committed suicide out of shame at the defeat.

Although they could have proceeded into Italy, the migrants turned instead west into Gaul. Their presence upset the order that Rome had recently established in and around the newly conquered territory. Tribes such as the Helvetii rose up, and settlements, including Toulouse, rebelled. The legions were ordered in to regain control. It was during this mission that the Romans again came face to face with the migrants at Arausio, the site of modern-day Orange, on the Rhône. This time, the encounter was an unmitigated disaster for the Romans. Divided forces, an ill-thought-out disposition of troops and class-based jealousy between the commanders led to calamity. Livy records that as many as 80,000 Roman soldiers perished in the rout, a figure endorsed even by some modern scholars. Scores of them drowned in the Rhône as, trapped between the river and their opponents, they tried to swim for safety and sank in their armour.

Rome was seized by panic. No one knew for sure who the migrants were. It was rumoured that some of them were called Teutones, and some of them Cimbri. Nor did anyone know where they came from. Some conjectured from the name 'Cimbri' that they were Cimmerians, from the sunless region at the edge of the earth where Odysseus had been to summon the dead from Hades. Others said that 'Cimbri' was simply a Germanic word for 'robber'. There were those who believed they were a branch of the Gauls, or Scythians, or Galloscythians, or a Germanic tribe. Another mystery was the nature of the language they spoke: whether it were a Celtic or Germanic tongue. What *was* known was that the migrants were physically imposing specimens: tall, blue-eyed, and savage in their manner. In the end, the classical geographers including Posidonius and Strabo concluded that they came from the region of Jutland, and had been forced to move because of some convulsion of the sea. It was reported that at least 300,000 people were on the move across Europe – armed men, women and children, their belongings piled in leather-covered wagons. Whoever they were, Rome was agreed on one thing: these were the new Gauls – the latest incarnation of the old threat from the north. It was feared that a repeat of the visitation of 390 BC, with the potential to sweep away Roman cities and Roman civilization, was imminent. On this matter, there was no dissent: the migrants could not be allowed into Italy. There was no room. Land, the Romans pleaded, was now in short supply. Indeed, land distribution had become a matter of contention on the Italian peninsula, with the Romans themselves divided into factions on the issue. They certainly did not want further competition from a group of barbarian incomers.

The Roman people entrusted the mission against the Teutones to the most successful commander of the age: Gaius Marius. The son of a peasant family from a provincial town in central Italy, he rose through the ranks on account of his military genius and Spartan temperament, gaining political offices in Rome as well as military preferment. He made a good marriage into an aristocratic family. Nevertheless, Marius belonged to the populist faction in Roman politics and many in the Senate were uncomfortable with his growing reputation. However, faced by the prospect of a mass incursion by a barbarian horde, they had no alternative but to turn to him in their hour of need. Marius, who had just returned in triumph from Africa leading a rebel king, Jurgurtha, in chains to the Capitol, was immediately despatched to Gaul.

The erratic movements of the migrant column gave Marius some breathing space. When he arrived in Gaul in 104 BC, shortly after the Battle of Arausio, the column veered westwards again and appeared to be heading for northern Spain. Despite this, Marius did not relax his guard. He began preparations to defend the route through southern Gaul into Italy, and readied his men for the conflict. Marius found the Roman legions demoralized, ill-disciplined and unfit. They were, unsurprisingly, terrified of encountering the migrants. Marius set about remedying this state of affairs. He would brook no idleness, leading the legionaries on runs and route-marches, and meting out harsh punishments for the slightest breaches of discipline. Aware of the problems of getting provisions inland quickly from the Rhône, he ordered his men to dig a canal from the port of Fos near Arles to run eastwards across the then marshy land of the Crau* towards St Rémy. As they waited for the migrants to turn back towards Italy, the morale and strength of the legions improved.

By 102 BC, it had become clear that the column of migrants had

---

* The flat area of land at the confluence of the Rhône and Durance rivers.

wheeled round. It had also split into two discrete groups. The group calling itself the Cimbri was to return by a circuitous northern route to Noricum and from there to descend over the Alps into northeast Italy, near Vercellae in the Po Valley. The Teutones, by contrast, were to take the more direct route eastwards across southern Gaul, past Massalia and Aix, and then over the mountains. Marius, meanwhile, had made sure that his troops were generously provisioned, and had established them in a large fortified camp by the Via Domitia, perhaps near the town of Glanum and modern-day St Rémy. The Teutones soon came into view: they had probably crossed the Rhône by the modern-day towns of Beaucaire and Tarascon. Their numbers, says Marius's biographer Plutarch, were limitless; they covered the open plain, and once they had pitched camp for the night, they challenged Marius to battle.

Marius's soldiers, confined in the camp, were desperate to fight. They found the newcomers hideous to look at, their speech and cries outlandish. But Marius restrained his men and ordered them merely to observe the migrants from the ramparts of their camp. When the migrants attacked, they were repulsed. They then decided to strike camp and continue marching eastwards, bypassing the Romans. Such was their number, according to Plutarch, that it took six days for them to file past Marius's camp. As they went by, they shouted 'We're on our way to Rome – got any messages for your wives?' Once they had finally passed, Marius himself broke up his camp and followed them closely, but still kept his men from engaging. His intention was to accustom them to the sight of the newcomers, and by familiarity to remove the aura of invincibility that the migrants had won in their earlier battles with the Romans.

This pursuit continued until near Aix. Marius kept to the high ground, and to positions that were easy to defend but less favourable when it came to finding water. One evening, when his men looked down from the ridge on which they were stationed, they were infuriated to see some of the migrants, after eating their dinner, happily bathing and whooping in a stream fed by warm springs. These were men of the tribe of the Ambrones, who had played a leading role in the defeat of the Romans at Arausio. With some reluctance, Marius allowed his troops to attack, commenting that if they were pre-pared to pay for it with their own blood, they could get some water for themselves. A detachment of his men – indigenous to the area, but now serving Rome – charged down the hill. The Ambrones did their best to form rank and fight, but Marius's troops broke through. They pressed on to the wagons, where the women and children were huddled. The women, reports Plutarch, took up swords and axes to defend their possessions and their children, but many of them were cut down in the skirmish. The Ambrones then rejoined the main col-umn of the Teutones. According to Plutarch, the place resounded all night long with their keening for their dead: '…not like the wailings and groanings of men, but howlings and bellowings with a strain of the wild beast in them, mingled with threats and cries of grief…'

It is likely that Marius was now stationed on the eastern slopes of Montagne Sainte-Victoire, just east of Aix, with his lines arrayed near the modern village of Puyloubier. The narrow valley of the River Arc opens out here into the wide green valley of Pourrières. Apart from the traffic noise from the A8 *autoroute* that now traverses the valley, this is a quiet place. Wild fennel grows luxuriantly from the dry ground; its stems, more often than not, are covered in pearl-like white snails. The air is thick with the aroma of marjoram and thyme. Aleppo pines and oaks with dusty brown leaves cover the slopes, along with vines rich with grapes, deep purple and frosted with bloom. Above, the towering ridge of Montagne Sainte-Victoire rises like an extended fin, sloping at first but then a sheer cliff of chequered rock in its highest register. Beneath the ridge is a band of pinkish-red earth.

Eager to go in for the kill after his successful assault on the Ambrones, Marius turned the valley into a trap. As the migrants debouched through a narrow gorge onto its open floor, he sent a detachment of 3,000 cavalry to gallop all the way round Montagne

Sainte-Victoire and hide behind their rear guard. Marius himself likely drew up his main forces to block their way forward, spanning the entire valley from the modern town of Trets to Puyloubier on the slopes of Montagne Sainte-Victoire.

The Teutones advanced to the Roman lines to do battle. The Romans had the advantage of height, and as the migrants began to tire, the trap was sprung. The cavalry detachment appeared from its hiding place and charged. Confusion overtook the Teutones as Marius responded to the cavalry charge at the rear with his own charge from the heights. Pressed in both directions, the Teutones had nowhere to go. Those who attempted flight were cut down, and defence was impossible in the crush. The Romans showed no mercy. Women and children as well as armed men were killed indiscriminately. A few were spared, to be kept as slaves, but the rest were massacred. It is not known how many died in this battle, named after the nearby town of Aquae Sextiae; some writers suggest as many as 100,000. Rome was saved.

Marius had no time to bask in the glory of his victory. His presence was required elsewhere, to halt the westward progress of the second column of migrants, the Cimbri, which had entered Italy via

The dramatic ridge of Montagne Sainte-Victoire, which stands above the valley of Pourrières.

Noricum. They had overcome a Roman force at the Brenner Pass and reached a place called Vercellae, in what is now Piedmont. These migrants would suffer a similar fate at Marius's hands to that of the vanquished at Aquae Sextiae.

From the moment Marius departed Aquae Sextiae – his last gestures were a grand pyre of the Teutones's wagons and personal possessions offered as a thanksgiving, not to mention the sacrifice of a hundred prisoners thrown down Mont Sainte-Victoire at the prompting of a Syrian prophetess whom he kept in his retinue – he left an enduring reputation as a saviour of Rome. In the aftermath of the battle, the dead bodies of the migrants came to be seen as a blessing. The decaying corpses, too numerous to bury, helped fertilize the fields, and the bones were used by the locals to mark the boundaries of their vineyards. Even the modern French name of the valley, Pourrières, is said to come from the Latin *campi putridi*, the 'fields of putrescence'. The Roman triumph is reflected in the name Mont Sainte-Victoire, where a temple dedicated to Venus Victrix was later cloaked in a Christian guise. In an annual ritual celebrated up until the French Revolution, garland-wearing local villagers danced the *farandole* and ran in procession, brandishing branches cut from box trees, crying 'Victoire!' Marius was a common name in the region until recent times. The Revolutionary leader Mirabeau, who represented Aix at the Estates-General in 1789, cited Marius as his inspiration. He was a friend of the people: the destroyer of the Teutones and the eventual scourge of the Roman aristocracy.

Marius was married to an aristocratic woman named Julia, the sister of a senator. In 100 BC, shortly after Marius's destruction of the Teutones, the senator's wife gave birth to their third child, a boy called Gaius Julius Caesar. The boy's uncle – populist and military hero that he was – had set a fine example for his nephew to follow. And when Caesar, in time, found himself where Marius had put the migrants to the sword, he would follow that example with a vengeance.

An early bust of Julius Caesar, discovered in the Rhône in 2007.

CHAPTER II

Caesar's Command

Homines bellicosos populi Romani inimicos
'A warlike tribe, unfriendly to the Roman people'

JULIUS CAESAR, *De Bello Gallico*, I.2

THE RISE OF CAESAR

·

BEAUCAIRE

·

VIA DOMITIA

·

GENEVA

·

THE RHÔNE

·

COLLONGES

·

PAS DE L'ÉCLUSE

·

THE SAÔNE

·

MONTMORT

·

BESANÇON

·

MULHOUSE

GAUL WAS NOT ALWAYS PART OF Caesar's life plan. There is no sign, either from his own writings, or those of his ancient biographers, that he held the conquest of Gaul as a long-cherished ambition. In his early thirties, Caesar contemplated a statue of Alexander the Great and wept that Alexander, by the same age, had overcome the world while he himself could point to no achievement of note; but his lament, as described by Plutarch, did not extend to wishing he could overcome the old northern enemy of Rome.

Even when he was entrusted with the military command of the Gallic regions for an initial five-year period from 58 BC, Caesar himself confessed that his attention was elsewhere. His command included not just Cisalpine and Transalpine Gaul, but also the province of Illyricum, an area on the eastern coast of the Adriatic corresponding to parts of modern Croatia, Bosnia, Montenegro and northern Albania. Illyricum was wealthy and unstable, a place that offered superb prospects for Roman generals in pursuit of military glory. Moreover, it was one of the strategic keys for the defence of northern Italy. The security of the region towards the Danube is a constant refrain in the military history of Rome, and Caesar well understood its importance and the opportunities it offered. Yet he was to reject Illyricum in favour of the distant wilderness of Gaul. His conquest of that territory was not undertaken by design, nor necessity; nor was it carried out, as was said of the expansion of the British empire, in a fit of 'absence of mind'. What led him to the conquest of Gaul – and thereby irrevocably to change the history and culture of Europe – was his own immediate political requirements: the need for spectacular military success to keep his political enemies at bay, and the need for cash to pay off his debts.

There is much that a citizen of a modern democracy would recognize in the politics of ancient Rome: the opportunity for ordinary people (women, slaves and foreigners excepted) to elect officials and vote on laws; a rigorous system of checks and balances regulated by law and custom to ensure that no part of government became over-mighty; debates in the Senate; the excitement, intrigue and gossip surrounding elections; political factions based on class, money and business interests; a political establishment whose wealthy members assume office from a sense of entitlement, either to use their terms for self-aggrandizement, or else to support their commercial backers; the struggles of brilliant outsiders to break into the cabal of power; long periods of stagnation in which vested interests refuse to deal with endemic problems; and the corruption of a well-meaning but outdated system of government by money and violence.

When Caesar was born in 100 BC, the republican political system of Rome was gasping its last breath. Designed in the sixth century BC, when Rome was a mid-sized market town, it was incapable of dealing with the massive challenges it faced following the acquisition of a world empire. The greatest of these was the inequality of wealth in the Italian heartlands. The conquest of overseas territories from the third century BC onwards – Sicily, Carthage, Greece – led to the concentration of captured colonial wealth and opportunities for trade in a few aristocratic hands. Roman soldiers, however, began to suffer. Drawn from the rural peasantry, they were dependent on farming for their long-term livelihood. Originally, they would return to their small-holdings after short, seasonal campaigns. Now, they could be absent for years. Their farms fell into decay, and were increasingly bought up by the ever more affluent aristocracy who farmed them with cheap slave labour from the provinces. The demobilized soldiery, lacking pensions or any means of financial support, began to look to their individual commanders for their livelihood. The indigent landless

began to fill Rome, with nothing to sell but their votes. At the end of
the second century BC, aristocratic landowners holding the reins of
power blocked moves to break up their great estates, formed from the
old peasant freeholdings, and redistribute them to the Roman poor.
The city became polarized. Loyalties shifted from the Republic to its
successful generals, and party cliques formed behind the aristocrats
(*optimates*) on one hand, and the populists (*populares*) on the other.
At the head of a mass of poverty-stricken veterans and the unem-
ployed urban mob, a successful commander, liberal with his gifts,
could outdo in power any of the grand elected magistrates of Rome.
The stage was set for a prolonged civil conflict.

Caesar's uncle, Marius, lionized after his victory over the Teutones,
was able to dominate politics in Rome at the beginning of the first century BC. He himself was of peasant origin, and made himself the leader
of the *populares*. To the outrage of the *optimates*, he forced through
land laws to favour demobilized soldiers and the landless poor, while
reforming the constitution to break the stranglehold of the old aristocracy on the levers of power. After his death in 86 BC, the aristocrats
fought back. One of their number, Sulla, seized effective control of
the state, reversed the reforms of Marius and enforced his dominance
through terror. He circulated hit lists of his political enemies, declaring
them to be outlaws. Hundreds were killed and their property seized
by informers and speculators. Chief among these speculators was a
financier, Crassus, who made himself one of the richest men in Rome
by buying up the property of the dead at knock-down prices.

Caesar himself and his immediate family were, however, spared.
Although they were on the side opposed to Sulla thanks to their link
by marriage to Marius, they were not prominent or well off and therefore not perceived as an immediate threat. Caesar's father, who had
a government post, died in 85 BC of natural causes. Caesar himself,
then aged about fifteen, had only just put on the *toga virilis*, signifying
his transition from childhood to adulthood, and had not yet entered
public life. Moreover, as Caesar was of an ancient patrician family,

albeit fallen on hard times, it may have been a sense of class sympathy that led Sulla not to proceed against him.

Thus it was in an environment of threat, bloodletting and political decline that Caesar spent his formative years. Little else is known of his childhood. The early death of his father resulted in him assuming a position of absolute responsibility over his family while still a teenager, even having nominal legal control over whether his own mother was allowed to remarry. The indications at the start of his adult life suggest that those around him did not consider he had a career of greatness before him. He married a young woman named Cornelia, daughter of Cinna, another patrician. Cinna arranged for Caesar to assume an ancient and singular priesthood of the god Jupiter, the role of *flamen dialis*. The priesthood was hedged about by a swathe of obscure and ancient regulations. These included rules against the priest having knots in the fabric of his clothing, a requirement for the secret disposal of his nail clippings, and an absolute prohibition against him ever looking on a dead body. The *flamen dialis* was required to remain within Rome at all times, which effectively ruled out a military career or advancement in politics. The priesthood, thus, was often held by those who were bodily weak or suffered chronic illness. Some sources claim that Caesar was afflicted in this way. Even though his taking on the position would have conveniently snuffed out his political ambitions at the outset, Sulla chose to prevent him from doing so, because Cinna, the man who had nominated him, was a supporter of the popular faction. Thus, Sulla inadvertently opened the way for Caesar to pursue a political career.

Caesar's attempt to gain the priesthood appears to have rattled Sulla. Although it was regarded as a dead-end in career terms, the *flamen dialis* was still a prestigious and influential position. When Sulla embarked on a vicious persecution of the *populares*, Caesar – having become son-in-law of one of the most prominent members of the popular party – became a prime target. Sulla issued orders for his arrest, and for a time Caesar had to go into hiding. However, when

Caesar's relatives interceded on his behalf, Sulla relented and Caesar was able to make his first steps in public service. From this point on, the stories that historians tell about Caesar, as well as those he chose to tell about himself, evoke his early promise, energy and ambition. He was posted while still in his teens to the staff of the *propraetor* of Bithynia. There, in a skirmish with the forces of Mithridates, king of Pontus, he saved the life of another Roman citizen, thereby winning the *corona civica*: the wreath of oak leaves that stood as Rome's highest award for gallantry. According to the historian Suetonius, he may have entered into a homosexual relationship with Nicomedes, king of Bithynia. This was, perhaps, for purposes of diplomacy.

After Sulla's death in 78 BC, Caesar, then in his early twenties and back in Rome, began to practise at the Bar. For young men aspiring to high office, this was a quick way to raise their profile among the Roman electorate and political establishment. Caesar took on the private prosecution of two high-profile provincial officials and allies of Sulla – Dolabella and Gnaeus Antonius – charging them both with embezzlement and corruption in the administration of their territories. In neither case was he successful, but he had begun to make his mark on the public scene.

Around this time Caesar travelled to the island of Rhodes to develop his talent for oratory under Greek specialists. On his way there – according to Caesar himself – he was captured by Cilician pirates who held him for ransom on the island of Pharmacussa off Asia Minor. When they informed him that the sum demanded for his release was 48,000 sesterces, he was outraged. He was worth at least 1.2 million sesterces, he told them, and they shouldn't accept anything less. The pirates gave in to his insistence and increased the price on his head. Caesar passed the time by playing games with the pirates, mocking them for their general lack of education and reciting poetry to remedy the defect. He told them that if he were ever released, he would come back and have them all crucified. And when he was finally freed, so Caesar himself relates, this is exactly what he did. After his release he went straight to the coastal city of Miletus, raised a squadron of warships, captured the pirates and eventually had them crucified at Pergamum.

Roman society in the first century BC was not given to reticence or restraint. Those involved in politics knew that prominent public display was a prerequisite for career advancement. But awareness of the importance of their public image did not prevent ambitious politicians from indulging in the pleasures of the flesh. Caesar's early career offers an extreme example of the pursuit of relentless self-promotion in tandem with sensual gratification. According to Suetonius, despite the fact that Caesar was not physically strong – he was tall but slight in build, and given to fits of epilepsy – he possessed almost superhuman energy and firmness of purpose. He could endure hunger as well as any Roman legionary; he could simultaneously dictate several different letters to several different scribes, and compose long poems during the course of extended journeys on horseback. His sexual appetite was prodigious. It was normal for young married men like Caesar to satisfy their sexual desires in the bordello. But Caesar's sex life was not merely about carnal gratification, it was a matter of conquest: he was interested not in prostitutes but in senators' wives. Suetonius lists at least five wives of senior politicians with whom he was connected. The list included Servilia, the half-sister of Cato the Younger, his bitterest rival in the aristocratic party, and mother of Brutus, his assassin.

Caesar was also prodigal in his exploitation of his patrician ancestry. In 69 BC, Caesar's aunt Julia and his wife Cornelia died in quick succession. It was not unknown for aged Roman matrons to receive grand public funerals, but Caesar's decision to accord them both this honour was highly unusual. He may have been motivated by a sense of grief, but the funerals were also an opportunity to display the glory of his ancestry. Despite Sulla's ban on public commemoration of Marius, Caesar included his effigy in the funeral procession of Julia – to widespread popular approval. This was not all. Old legends recorded that the Julian *gens*, or clan, of which Caesar was a part, was descended not only from Ancus Marcius, the second king of Rome seven centuries previously, but also Venus, the goddess of love herself. Caesar may or may not have believed in these old tales, but he was happy to use them to his advantage, and he had no scruples about proclaiming in the funeral orations before the crowds in the forum the especial distinction of his ancestry.

Yet it was his excess in display, and hence in the excess of his spending, that Caesar particularly stood out. Here, he realized, was the way to political glory. Although in the early part of his career he lived in a down-at-heel part of Rome – the Subura, a working-class district full of tottering apartment blocks and seedy brothels – he was fastidious in his own person. He was groomed and coiffed beyond the common run; some accounts say that he kept his body entirely hairless. He cultivated a distinctive sartorial style, wearing his senatorial tunic with long sleeves and an unconventional loose belt. He collected works of art, as well as precious gemstones and *intaglios.** He began to borrow money to fund his conspicuous lifestyle, as well as his political campaigning. Before he achieved his first elected office, that of military tribune in around 71 BC, his debts, according to Plutarch, amounted to more than 31 million sesterces.†

As he worked his way up through the *cursus honorum* (the sequence of public offices held by politicians under the Roman Republic) in the 60s BC, Caesar's appetite for spending borrowed money to enhance his popularity continued to increase. He served as quaestor,‡ a junior official, and was posted to Spain in 69 BC. It was here he is said to have wept at the statue of Alexander the Great. Shortly afterwards, he was elected curator of the Appian Way, the great highway that led from Rome to the southeastern tip of Italy. Caesar lavished money on its repair and restoration, knowing that his name would be associated with its renovation by travellers throughout Italy. This no doubt

---

* Engraved gemstones, often with portrait heads.
† To give a sense of the massiveness of this amount, the average annual wage of a legionary soldier during the first century AD was 900 sesterces per annum.
‡ Quaestors were usually responsible for financial affairs and audits.

assisted Caesar in his election to the next rung on the ladder of governmental offices, that of *curule aedile* in 65 BC. The *curule aediles*, of whom there were two elected annually from the patrician classes, were responsible for the upkeep of the Roman infrastructure – the maintenance of temples, roads, bridges, aqueducts and sewers. They were also responsible for organizing the traditional games in March and September for the entertainment of the Roman crowds – which presented another opportunity for self-advertisement and display. Caesar spent on these games as never before. He erected temporary colonnades in the Forum to exhibit his private art collection. To further boost his reputation, he also manipulated the ancient Roman tradition of staging gladiatorial contests. Formerly, gladiators were only meant to fight to mark the funeral of a famous man; the blood shed in their fighting was supposed to appease the spirit of the departed. Stretching the tradition to breaking point, Caesar announced that gladiatorial games would be held to mark the death of his own father, who had died twenty years previously. These games were on an unprecedented scale: 320 pairs of gladiators were drafted in, each kitted out with tailor-made sets of ornate silver armour.

According to Plutarch, Caesar also used his time as *curule aedile* to put up images of his uncle Marius paired with the goddess of victory on the Capitol. This overt celebration of an individual who had taken power in Rome through military might caused many to fear Caesar's intentions. A number of historians take the view that it was in this year, 65 BC, that Caesar began to emerge as a real contender for a position of power in Rome.

In the following year, 64 BC, a gamble by Caesar allowed him to add to his growing authority. The position of *pontifex maximus*, or chief priest, fell vacant. It was not encumbered by the same taboos as the *flamen dialis*, and was politically a valuable office to hold. Not only did it come with a magnificent official residence for life in the heart of Rome and duties such as administration of the calendar, but the holder was entitled to be one of the first to speak in senatorial debates. There was fierce competition for the post. Senators of much greater seniority than Caesar were determined to win the position, and Caesar was offered a huge bribe by a rival candidate, Quintus Lutatius Catulus, not to stand. But he was set on making the post his own: he borrowed recklessly and paid even larger bribes to the electorate in the hope of securing the necessary votes. As he left his house on the morning of the election, he is said to have told his mother, 'Today, you will see your son as high priest or else an exile.'

Caesar's victory is with us still in the lasting reforms he made to the calendar, yet the immediate consequence was that the traditional governing classes began to grow suspicious of him. The extent of this growing paranoia was revealed the following year, in 63 BC, when Rome was shaken by a conspiracy. A debt-ridden senator, Catiline, had run for the consulship – the supreme office in republican Rome – on a policy of the cancellation of all debts. When his candidacy failed, he organized an armed insurrection to overthrow the state, which ended in his capture and that of his co-conspirators. Cicero, who was then consul, proposed to the Senate that they be summarily executed. Caesar, however, argued against haste. He instead called for the conspirators to be imprisoned until the uprising could be contained, after which their ultimate fate would be decided.

Such was the power of Caesar's appeal that opinion in the Senate seemed to be going his way, until his rival Cato began to accuse the spendthrift Caesar of involvement in the conspiracy. His harangue was for a moment undermined when a messenger brought in a letter for Caesar that Cato ordered him to read, saying it was a clear sign that he was in communication with the remaining conspirators. Caesar cheerfully proceeded to read out a love letter from Cato's half-sister, Servilia. When the laughter had died down, Cato whipped the Senate into such a frenzy of anger against Caesar – who was perceived by many to be manipulating the situation to his own political advantage – that he had to be bundled out of the session under a colleague's toga to avoid being murdered on the spot.

Despite such alarms, Caesar continue his rise up the ladder of Roman offices. In 62 BC, he was elected one of the eight praetors, the most senior rank of official below consul. The next year, 61 BC, he was appointed propraetor of the province of Further Spain. It was in this capacity that he gained his first real experience of a prolonged military command. Over the course of the year, he successfully conducted a campaign in Lusitania, a renegade province that included modern-day Portugal. Caesar's performance entitled him to a triumph: a grand military parade through the streets of Rome where he would be hailed as a victorious commander. The triumph was one of Rome's highest honours, and would leave Caesar perfectly positioned to make a run for the consulship of 59 BC. However, he faced a difficulty. To run for office in that year, he had to forego his military command; but to claim the triumph, he had to retain it. He asked the Senate to relax the rule for him. Thanks to Cato, they refused. Caesar's growing ambition for power overcame his desire to enjoy Rome's most prized honour. He lay down his command and returned to Rome as a private citizen to run for office.

Caesar was not the only magnate to have been thwarted by the Senate and the aristocratic party. The military commander Pompey had for the previous few years been leading a campaign in the east. Over the course of the 60s BC he had conquered a number of territories in the Levant and Asia Minor, covering a large swathe of what is now Turkey, Lebanon, Syria, Israel and Palestine. Pompey needed approval from the Senate for the provisional forms of government he had arranged for the territories. He also needed them to grant land for his veterans to support themselves once they had been demobilized from the campaign. Over all of this, the Senate was dragging its feet.

Crassus, who had been bankrolling Caesar's political career, was likewise in difficulties. One of his principal investments at this time was in tax-farming syndicates. Since Rome did not have the administrative apparatus to collect taxes, particularly in its outlying provinces, the right to collect taxes was auctioned by the state to commercial syndicates, which would then be permitted to keep the difference between the taxes they were able to collect and the sum they paid for the right to collect them. At this time, the investments were turning bad. The tax-take was much lower than the syndicates had expected, and they needed to cut the amount that they owed the state in order to avoid serious losses. Crassus had been trying to negotiate this with the Senate, but had been rebuffed.

It was here that Caesar saw his greatest opportunity. Up until this point, Pompey and Crassus had disliked each other. To achieve their aims, Caesar proposed to them a secret alliance. They would use their support, financial and otherwise, to secure Caesar's election as one of the two consuls for 59 BC. They would also help him to secure a fitting post for the following year – a proconsular command of a rich province, where he could gather up sufficient money to pay off the now vast sums he owed Crassus. In return, he would use his proven political skills to force through the laws that both Pompey and Crassus required.

Once Caesar's candidacy had been announced, the aristocratic party did everything in its power to disrupt his plans. They passed a law that the proconsular responsibility for the consuls of 59 BC, following their year of office, would be no rich province but management of the forests and cattle-paths of Italy. In the end, their machinations were fruitless. Caesar was elected as one of the two consuls at the beginning of January, 59 BC.

Caesar's consular colleague, Cato's son-in-law Bibulus, belonged to the aristocratic party. Such was the nature of the Roman governmental machine that when one consul was in opposition to another, it became impossible to get anything done by legitimate means: each consul was equal in power, and each had a veto over the actions of the other. This had made sense when the constitution had been designed, centuries earlier, with the prime intention of preventing a back-door return to the old monarchy. However, with Rome trying to administer a growing empire, it simply made for paralysis. When Caesar

embarked on his legislative programme, Bibulus refused to co-op-
erate. At first, Caesar was diplomatic with Bibulus and his fellow
aristocrats in the Senate, but in short order he resorted to procedural
trickery and violent intimidation. Bypassing the Senate, he appealed
directly to the people, using stage-managed referenda to approve
bills for land redistribution and the approval of Pompey's eastern
settlement. When Bibulus attempted to veto one of these proceedings, Caesar's supporters smashed his insignia of office and emptied a
bucket of dung over his head. In high dudgeon, Bibulus locked himself in his house and refused to leave for the whole year, relying on his
vetoes and archaic constitutional mechanisms to render Caesar's acts
formally void. Despite this nominal illegality Caesar pressed on, and
by the end of the year had passed the laws he had agreed with Pompey
and Crassus.

When his year of consular office ended, there was still the matter
of Caesar's next job. The Senate was now somewhat more biddable:
Caesar had taken to publishing daily accounts of their proceedings to hold them to closer public scrutiny. Pliantly, they put aside
the cattle-tracks of Italy and offered him an extraordinary five-year
command over the provinces of Illyricum and Cisalpine Gaul. Such
a command meant that Transalpine Gaul, the region beyond which
the Gallic conquest would take place, would not come under Caesar's
sway. Yet at that moment, the incumbent governor of Transalpine
Gaul died suddenly. As an afterthought, the Senate added this province as a bonus to Caesar's portfolio. Caesar's *imperium* now stood
face to face with the unknown hinterlands of unconquered Gaul.

The early Roman colonies of Transalpine Gaul have left little visible
evidence of life there in the half century before Caesar's arrival. But
some traces can be found, and to see them, one needs to search not in
the cities of southern Gaul, but outside them.

Beaucaire stands on the Rhône, close to the point where the Teutones crossed to face slaughter at the hands of Marius. A canal that eventually runs into the Étang de Thau, close to Sète on the Mediterranean coast, begins its course in the centre of this small Occitanian town. From Beaucaire you can take a road west. If you leave the town centre on foot, the path of escape winds through the blank accretions of the modern age, twisting beneath a nicotine-hued railway bridge and past factory silos – ferrous pink as the dust on the earth beneath – before leaving the suburbs behind to reach the fields. Beside the path, in the hedgerows, is a tangle of brambles, their tiny fruit tart and dust-peppered; above them grow blue-black sloes and the bright red berries of autumn. There are Aleppo pines and olives; the coppery seed pods of silk trees jangle in the breeze. After a turn, the track straightens out, departing from its course only to avoid a low farm building. Its surface is neglected gravel, its sole traffic a red tractor. Vines radiate from its margins. Suddenly, the road comes to a bulbous end: a quarry has eaten up the way ahead. On one side sits a mound of rubble and plaster, fly-tipped; on the other, three angular standing stones and the stump of a fourth. They are worn, dust-blasted, lichen-blotted. Looking closely, one can see the ghosts of Roman numerals bevelled into their gunmetal surface. But even when these ancient marks were young, the road was already old.

The Via Domitia is one of the oldest visible Roman constructions in Gaul. It was built in 118 BC by Gnaeus Domitius Ahenobarbus, one of the generals who oversaw the early campaigns in support of Massalia against the Gauls. The four Roman milestones by the road near Beaucaire – the largest group of Roman milestones surviving in France – are not witness to the age of the road; the earliest of them was erected in the reign of Augustus in 3 BC. Yet they do bear witness to its importance. The Via Domitia runs from the Pyrenees to the Alps, providing a land route from Italy and Cisalpine Gaul to the Spanish provinces. It original purpose was military. Rome now possessed a new route – other than the maritime one – for troops to reach the perpetually troubled districts of Spain which, since the time of Hannibal over a century earlier, it had fought to subdue. In the 70s BC, Pompey marched along the Via Domitia to fight his Spanish campaign, and to collect Gallic auxiliaries to assist the Roman cause. Near its western extremity, by the modern-day Pyrenean hill village of Saint-Bertrand-de-Comminges, Pompey established the colony of Lugdunum Conuenarum to mark his Spanish triumph.

As part of its military function, the Via Domitia was probably used for frontier defence. The road, in essence, marked the early character of Transalpine Gaul. This was frontier territory. For the first decades of Roman rule beyond the 120s BC, we are ignorant of the form of its government, but it is likely that it was not highly advanced. In the early years, there may indeed have been no governor, and the administration of the region may have been in the hands of neighbouring provinces. Roman functionaries in the area had to deal not only with the influx of Teutonic migrants culminating in the slaughter by Marius in 103

Roman milestones on the Via Domitia in the countryside beyond Beaucaire.

BC, but also with tribal uprisings and tribal politics. Gallic tribes had to be propitiated, and alliances made with other groupings beyond the formal sphere of Roman influence – the Aedui, for example, in the region south of modern-day Dijon, or the Allobroges near the southern Rhine. Rome had to consider the balance of power between them to ensure stability for the areas within their direct control.

The frontier was also a place to make money. The first person actually known to have been a governor of Transalpine Gaul was Marcus Fonteius. It seems he served in the province from 75 to 73 BC. Sometime after 70 BC, when he was back in Rome, he faced a charge of corruption in his administration. His accusers were Gauls, but his defence counsel was Cicero. Cicero's speech in his defence for the most part survives. Regardless of what we may discern of Fonteius's guilt, the speech allows us a glimpse of life in the early Roman province. 'Gaul', says Cicero, 'is packed with traders, brim-full with Roman citizens.' It was a place where one could go for business and fast profit. Romans of all trades had set up there: 'merchants, colonists, tax-farmers, agri-businessmen, cattle-ranchers'. Veterans from Pompey's Spanish campaigns had also been allotted land confiscated from the indigenous people. Together, they had taken control of the province's economy: 'None of the Gauls ever does any business without a Roman citizen being involved; not a penny changes hands without being marked in the account books of Roman citizens.' The wine-trade was booming, money was being made in the construction and maintenance of roads, including the Via Domitia. But the Gauls were complaining to the court that they were being forced deep into debt while Fonteius milked the province to line his own pockets.

But what weight could one attach to their testimony, asks Cicero? They were Gauls. Not so long ago, Rome had been at war with them. Now here they were, in their cloaks and uncivilized trousers, strutting around the Forum muttering uncouth and unintelligible oaths. Did they understand what it meant to take an oath? What it meant to give evidence in a Roman court of law? These were the same people who, three centuries ago, had burnt down Rome, laid siege to the Capitol and desecrated the shrines of the gods. What was the word of a whole tribe of them worth when weighed against that of a single citizen of Rome? No matter that they were furnishing cavalry to fight for the Romans in Spain and grain to support their troops. One would hardly believe that, a few years later, Gallic ambassadors who had come to Rome to complain about debt would uncover and blow the whistle on the conspiracy of Catiline; or that Cicero would later confess in his philosophical writings that a Gallic nobleman and Druid, Divitiacus, was a close personal friend and esteemed by him as a scholar with a particular knowledge of Greek natural science. No, the whole set of charges brought by these Gauls was nothing more than a perpetuation of their usual blood feuds by other means. Regardless of the testimony brought before the court, Cicero could still play on his audience to devastating effect. Gaul was a place to be exploited, and a place to be feared. Such was the province inherited by Caesar.

Where Lake Geneva empties into the head of the Rhône, in the heart of Geneva itself, the flow of the river is broken by an island. L'Île, as it is referred to in French, is the natural and most ancient crossing-point of the river. In medieval times a great castle was built on the island to control the north–south road. Of this a solitary tower survives, flanked to one side by the glass panels of a watch-shop and adorned with the statue of a Renaissance Genevan patriot, Philibert Berthelier, who strove to keep the city independent of the dukes of Savoy.

On the other side of the tower, lost in the geometry of overhead tram-wires, is a plaque, cream against the old toasted stone, and of much more recent date. It carries a very different message from another plaque across the river that reads *Genève, Cité de Refuge* ('Geneva, City of Refuge'). It states that Caesar mentioned his journey to Geneva at the beginning of his *Commentaries on the Gallic War*, and then lays out several lines of the Latin text to prove the truth of the statement. Among other things, Caesar's commentary tells us that Geneva (Genava) was then a frontier town of the Gallic Allobroges tribe (and hence part of the Roman province of Transalpine Gaul); that a bridge crossed the river – at the site of the modern bridge – to the north bank, where the Gallic tribe of the Helvetii resided; and that in 58 BC Caesar came to the city and ordered the bridge to be broken down. This bridge was probably very close to the tower.

In the first century BC, if a person dwelling on the north bank of the river Rhône in Geneva wished to travel into southern Gaul, their most natural route would be to cross the river and then take a road leading southwest towards Valence, where they would re-encounter the Rhône much further down its course. If the bridge was out of action, however, and it was impossible to cross to the south bank, the only viable route was to follow the north bank westwards out of the city, and after about twenty miles, pass through a narrow defile of the Jura Mountains – the Pas de L'Écluse – and ultimately emerge onto flatter land northeast of the site of present-day Lyons.

Beyond the city limits of Geneva, the northern route is one of great beauty. Travelling along it in spring, one cuts through low white-painted villages, down to the wide meadows that skirt the north bank of the Rhône. Sweet-smelling grasses grow high in the fields; the trackway is starred with flowers of purple sainfoin and yellow gentian. Cows, brown and white, graze contentedly in the rich pastures. Above stretches the Jura range, still snow-capped, a silver bastion embracing a valley of plenty.

But soon the nature of the pathway changes. Below Collonges, the pasture gives way to an ever-narrower strip of woodland clinging to the edge of the river, and the walker has to run the gauntlet of thick branches that sometimes obstruct the way. The pathway is forced down to the muddy edge of the Rhône. There is still a broad expanse of greenery on the south bank of the river, but it is dense and over-grown, more like the Amazon than the Rhône. But even this is soon to be squeezed out of existence as the valley contracts dramatically. The mountains surge upwards to an insuperable height; the river, forced through an ever-diminishing defile between the rocks, funnels and twists, its colour changing to an unlikely and startling cobalt. The path is reduced to a stony ribbon, balanced on the edge, scarcely wide enough for a cart to pass – as Caesar recalls in his account. Soon, the white turrets and crenellations of the Fort de L'Écluse appear above the track, apparently clamped to the mountainside, its purpose to control movement along the pass. But so strait and so vulnerable is the path that the fort seems unnecessary. Any advance along this route could surely be halted by a well-aimed pebble.

This path was witness to the first great migration crisis in European history to be recorded by a contemporary observer. The people on the move were the Helvetii. If the figures recorded by Caesar are to be

The Rhône at the Pas de L'Écluse – route of the Helvetii migration in 58 BC.

believed, they were 360,000 in number. The tribe was moving in its entirety – men, women and children – from its homeland north of Lake Geneva, seeking a new home in the southwest of Gaul, outside Roman territory. The decision of the Helvetii to move was final: they had burnt and demolished their old homes, loaded all their possessions onto carts along with three months' supply of food, and were set for a long journey. Their plan was to take the easy route though Geneva, cutting across the territory of the Allobroges and thus the Roman province of Transalpine Gaul. Their preparations for departure took place in March 58 BC, just after Caesar had been appointed to his governorships of Illyricum and Gaul.

Caesar, as has been said, did not have his mind on Gaul at the time. His plan was to lead an expedition to Illyricum, where armed bands of Getae (Thracian people who had settled on the lower Danube) were making incursions into Roman territory. But when he learnt that the Helvetii intended to cross Transalpine Gaul, he was suddenly transfixed. His plans for a campaign in Illyricum were forgotten. He sent an order for the bridge at Geneva to be broken, to deny passage to the Helvetii. The forces Caesar had at his disposal were minimal (just a single legion in that area of Gaul), but he made arrangements for additional legions to be mobilized and made his way to Geneva.

The Helvetii sent requests to be allowed to cross the river. Caesar, short of manpower as he waited for his reinforcements to arrive, played for time. At his command his available troops threw up a long earth embankment – 5 metres high – and fortifications along the whole of the south bank of the Rhône from Geneva up to the Pas de L'Écluse, a distance of just under twenty miles. He stationed troops along the embankment to prevent any attempts by the Helvetii to cross.

In the middle of April, when his position was somewhat stronger, Caesar gave a definite answer to the Helvetii: they would not be permitted to cross Roman territory. Their response was to ignore his order and attempt to cross the Rhône by means of makeshift rafts and boats lashed together. They took to the water in small family groups, sometimes by day but more often by night. The Romans, however, fired missiles at their boats and thus prevented the Helvetii from reaching the southern shore.

The Helvetii then turned their attention to the only other option available to them: the route following the north bank of the Rhône, through the Pas de l'Écluse. It was a fearsome and daunting prospect: 360,000 people inching their way though a narrow defile along a path scarcely wide enough for a cart. It was also a route that could not be embarked upon straight away, for the path led into the territory of another Gallic tribe outside the Roman province, the Sequani, from whom permission had to be sought. A diplomatic deal was brokered with the assistance of members of the nobility of the Aedui, a tribe allied to Rome but also outside the Roman province. Once the Sequani had granted them permission to pass through their territory, the Helvetii, their worldly goods laid up in carts towed behind them, began to pick their way through the asphyxiating narrows of the Pas de l'Écluse.

We know little about the Helvetii – of their politics, of their intentions, or of the pressures that forced them to move from their original homeland and undertake such a long and dangerous journey. Why were they regarded as such a threat that they had to be prevented from crossing a territory on the periphery of Roman control? Aside from a couple of vague passing references in letters of Cicero, the only witness we have is Caesar. The only surviving comprehensive, first-hand account of the conflict that followed the migration of the Helvetii is given in Caesar's commentaries on the Gallic War, *De Bello Gallico*. There is nothing of substance from any other Roman officer who took part in the campaigns, nor any first-hand accounts that provide a view of these events from the perspective of the city of Rome itself. Despite the fact that they were a literate people, we have no first-hand accounts from the Helvetii themselves; and they left nothing in the way of oral tradition. Nor do the other Gallic tribes involved, the Sequani or the Aedui, supply contemporary evidence. Caesar's victory was so total as to give him – in addition to the victor's laurels – sole ownership of the story of his conquest.

Caesar's account is a masterpiece of the Latin language: he writes in clear and uncomplicated prose, avoiding convoluted phrasing and obscure vocabulary. His text runs to seven books (or long chapters) written by Caesar himself, and an eighth by one of his commanders, Aulus Hirtius, covering the last stage of the conquest after 52 BC. Throughout all of this, his vocabulary extends to little more than 1,300 words. It is this economy of diction, along with its clarity and directness, that has made *De Bello Gallico* a staple for students of Latin for hundreds of years. This straightforwardness of style perhaps suggests – though we do not know for certain – the work's intended audience. Caesar's concentration in the text, when not on himself, tends to be on ordinary soldiers and NCOs. He reports their concerns, their heroism under fire, their loyalty. The deeds of the aristocratic officers receive much less coverage, and what exists paints them less favourably. Whether or not the *Commentaries* were originally intended as annual despatches for the attention of the Senate, or were collated at the end of the campaign by Caesar himself for circulation directly to the public, it is reasonable to assume that his target audience was a popular one, and that the *Commentaries* were intended to reinforce his credentials as a man of the people.

When Caesar describes the Helvetii in detail, he has in mind his Roman political audience and his political position in Rome. He says that the Helvetii were warlike, and that they exceeded all other Gauls in valour. Their original homeland was a region bounded by the Rhine, Lake Geneva and the Jura Mountains – an area of roughly 240 by 180 miles. This area, despite covering more than 40,000 square miles, was not, in the view of the Helvetii, large enough for their population: they felt hemmed in. They were a people who longed for

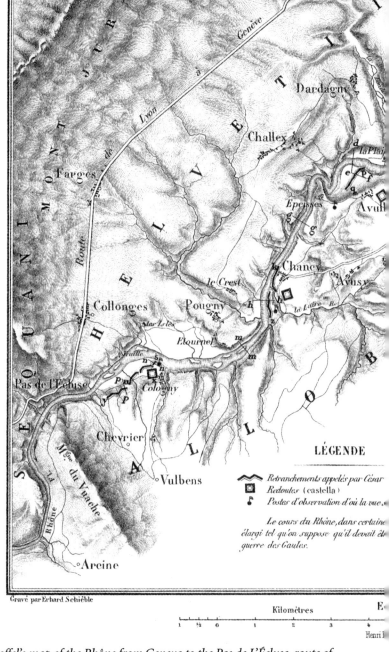

Stoffel's map of the Rhône from Geneva to the Pas de L'Écluse, route of the Helvetii migration in 58 BC.

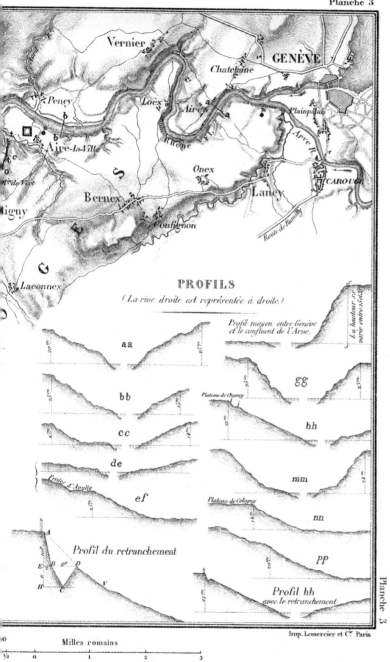

PROFILS
(La rive droite est représentée à droite.)

Profil moyen entre Genève et le confluent de l'Arve.

aa

gg

Plateau de Chancy

bb

hh

cc

de

mm

Pentes d'Avully

ef

Plateau de Cologny

nn

PP

Profil du retranchement

Profil hh
avec le retranchement

Imp. Lemercier et Cⁱᵉ Paris

Milles romains

½   0   1   2   3

war, and they desired to make their home in a place where they could easily make war on their neighbours.

According to Caesar a high-ranking noble, Orgetorix, wished to be king of the Helvetii. He persuaded them that they could become the leading power in Gaul if they simply marched west out of their homeland. He formed a conspiracy with other nobles, and persuaded the Helvetii to embark on a three-year plan to migrate wholesale into the heart of Gaul. The tribe bought extra cattle and sowed extra corn to prepare for the move long in advance. Their leaders, meanwhile, made agreements with chiefs from neighbouring tribes, including Casticus of the Sequani and Dumnorix of the Aedui – who also aspired to rule the whole of Gaul – to facilitate their passage. Even when Orgetorix, who was accused by the Helvetii of intending to become a tyrant, committed suicide, they carried on calmly with their preparations. When 58 BC arrived, the year appointed for their migration, they burnt their dwellings and their towns efficiently and without demur, and were ready for the rigours of their journey.

People such as these, says Caesar, could not be allowed to approach Roman territory. Even if they only passed through it, they would bring chaos and insecurity by robbing and plundering as they went. They would cause harm not only to the Roman domains, but also to the Gallic tribes allied with Rome – even though a number of the latter's factions had pledged support for the migration. Even if they were not intending to settle in Roman territory, it would be intolerable to allow them to make their homes where they planned to do so, near Toulouse. The grain-rich district within the Roman province would be under constant threat.

The situation, as Caesar paints it, is a repeat of that faced by his father-in-law Marius, and in the very same theatre. And if the echoes of the Teutones are not picked out clearly enough at the beginning of the *Commentaries*, the explicit references to the passing of the Teutones through Gaul fifty years previously, and the defeats suffered by Rome as a result, bring the similarities into focus. Caesar writes that when he learnt that the Helvetii wanted to pass through the Roman province, he recalled the crisis of the Teutones, and the fact that the Helvetii had allied with them to defeat the Roman army in the disaster at Arausio (Orange). Later, Caesar met with a Helvetian ambassador named Divico who, according to the *Commentaries*, had been a commander in that same action over half a century earlier. Through the prism of Caesar's reporting, the Helvetii migrants become the Teutones and Caesar becomes the popular hero Marius. Caesar's narrative is as much a monument to Marius as the statue he erected of him on the Capitol several years earlier when he was still *curule aedile*. Whatever Caesar writes of the intentions and politics of the Helvetii migrants cannot be trusted. There is no other substantial witness, and the Helvetii were but manipulable fodder for his relentless campaign of political self-promotion: Julius Caesar was the man who had saved the Roman state from barbarian migrants, and hence a popular leader bound for absolute power.

Another part of the appeal of going to war was the prospect of generating wealth via a successful military campaign, for Caesar's debts were monstrous and pressing. But to wage a war in Gaul against migrants whose character and intentions could be exploited as much as their persons and property was even more attractive: it gave Caesar the political prize of putting himself into the template of Marius. And if Marius's triumph in Gaul is seen as the pattern that Caesar was striving to emulate with the Helvetii, then it provides an explanation not only for his initial dash to Gaul rather than Illyricum, but also for the way in which he chose to expand the campaign. He would be Marius, but, being Caesar, he would be Marius to excess.

When Caesar broke the bridge at Geneva and denied the Helvetii passage through Roman territory, he had a single legion with him (about 5,000 men). On finding out that the Helvetii were minded to take the route through the Pas de L'Écluse, he put his deputy, Titus Labienus, in charge of the situation and rushed back to Italy to enrol two extra legions, and bring three more out of winter quarters at

Aquileia. Curiously, while Caesar was away, the Helvetii were allowed to pass through the Pas de l'Écluse, even though it could have been blocked with the forces at hand; they could have been prevented from advancing further into Gaul without the need for any fighting. But no such efforts were made, a crucial omission for which Caesar gives no explanation in the *Commentaries*. Given that his account speaks of the Helvetii ravaging the lands of the Gallic tribes allied to Rome, despite having brought with them three months of supplies, his failure to prevent their journey through the pass appears even more curious. The explanation that makes sense is that Caesar actually wanted to let the migrants through so that he could meet them on more favourable ground, with several additional legions at his disposal, and defeat them in an eye-catching and triumphant battle. And so it turned out – although Caesar would fight not just one battle against the Helvetii, but two (even if the first was more of a slaughter).

Just as the Greeks of Massalia and neighbouring Gauls had begged Marius, so Caesar's Gallic allies now begged him to take action. Bolstered by his extra legions, Caesar was determined to respond to their entreaties. He came upon the Helvetii as they attempted to cross the River Saône – a river so sluggish, he commented, that you could not tell which way it was flowing. They were making their way over on boats and rafts joined together. One division of them, a quarter of their number, had not yet crossed. It was late at night: the third watch, sometime after midnight. The migrants were heavily laden with their possessions, getting ready to embark. Caesar's troops fell upon them unawares, and set about an orgy of indiscriminate killing. Most of this division of the Helvetii were butchered, though a few escaped into the neighbouring woods. Caesar presents this clash, the Battle of the Saône, as a great victory – not just because he had taken a first and important step to check the Helvetii menace, but because it was an act of vengeance: vengeance on the part of the Roman state, for it was this particular division of the Helvetii, the Tigurini, that had visited disaster on the Romans by aiding the Teutones during their migration fifty years previously; and personal vengeance for Caesar, because the Tigurini had killed the general Lucius Calpurnius Piso, who was grandfather of his own father-in-law.

The second encounter, called the Battle of Bibracte, at least had the character of a proper battle. Caesar met the Helvetii in the gently rolling countryside south of Dijon, most likely on the open fields between the little town of Toulon-sur-Arroux and the village of Montmort. The two sides faced each other in long lines, drawn up on low ridges along a country lane. The women and children of the Helvetii fighters were stationed in a circle of wagons on higher ground to the right of the Helvetii lines, overlooking the battlefield. The Helvetii reeled under the initial impact of the Roman attack. The barrage of Roman javelins pinned together their shields, which they were unable to remove; instead they were forced to throw away their shields and fight without protection. Nevertheless, they maintained their resistance. The two sides fought from midday until after nightfall, pushing backwards and forwards across the gentle valley. The Helvetii were eventually forced to fall back on their wagons and the adjacent heights. From underneath their carts and between the wagon wheels they shot pikes and darts at the Roman legions. But eventually their wagons and baggage were captured, and with them even some of the children of Orgetorix.

Nevertheless, 130,000 Helvetii were able to flee the battlefield. Caesar was in no position to pursue them. His cavalry forces were inadequate, and his men had to tend their wounds in the aftermath of a difficult battle. However, he sent messages to the neighbouring tribes that if they gave the Helvetii any food or shelter, he would do to them what he had done to the Helvetii.

After three days, the remainder of the Helvetii, now starving, approached Caesar and begged to surrender. Having handed themselves over, one 6,000-strong group, thinking that they were going to be slaughtered en masse, panicked and fled. Caesar ordered the neighbouring tribes to round them up. They were brought back and treated, in Caesar's words, as enemies, probably meaning that they were sold off as slaves. Caesar commanded that the remaining Helvetii were to be provided with food, and that they were then to return to their native lands. He told them he feared that Germanic peoples beyond the Rhine would be tempted to occupy their abandoned homelands and hence become immediate neighbours of the Gallic tribes allied to the Romans. The Helvetii did as they were ordered, and thereafter were regarded by Caesar as trusted allies.

Among their captured baggage the Romans discovered the records of a full census the Helvetii had taken before leaving their homeland. It was written in Greek characters, and listed the numbers of fighting men, non-combatant women, children and old men. All in all, says Caesar, the number of Helvetii had been 368,000; the number that returned home was 110,000. Their encounter with Caesar had thus reduced the vast numbers of migrating Helvetii by a staggering two-thirds. Such was the human price of Caesar's political ambition.*

Caesar's narrative of his encounter with the Helvetii makes it so similar to that between Marius and the Teutones that it is difficult not to see it as engineered. And it is similarly difficult to believe many of Caesar's claims about the Helvetii: their intentions, the political state of the tribe, their behaviour, their relatichaptonship with other Gauls, and even their number. The mark Caesar left on Gaul was not merely the blood of thousands of slaughtered Helvetii, but also the conquest and control of the vanquished voices and identities. Caesar says that after his victory ambassadors from nearly all the tribes of Gaul came not only to congratulate him, but also to express their approval of his version of events: namely that the Romans were justified in attacking the Helvetii in revenge for the outrages the Romans had suffered at their hands in Marius's time. What he had done was right for the land of Gaul. The Helvetii had left their homes in a time of prosperity with the intention of making war; they wanted to seize the most fertile part

---

* Their name survives in the modern Latin name for Switzerland, *Confoederatio Helvetica*, which is still to be seen on Swiss coinage.

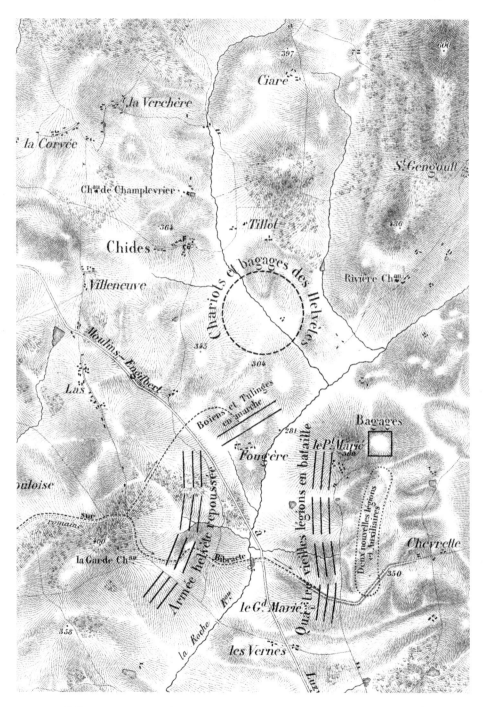

Stoffel's reconstruction of the Battle of Bibracte (58 BC) between Caesar and the Helvetii migrants.

of Gaul for themselves and turn the rest of it into a tributary. Thus did Caesar deftly impute his own intentions to the migrant Helvetii. But even in his own account, there are elements that belie the image of the Helvetii as dangerous warmongers. The Aedui asked Caesar for permission to allow the Boii, a grouping of the Helvetii, to remain and settle within Aedui territory. The Helvetii census, according to Caesar, recorded the number of the Boii as 32,000. The Aedui stated that the Boii were a people of outstanding courage, and happily gave them not only farmland to cultivate, but also full membership of the Aedui tribe. So much for Caesar's claim that the migration of the Helvetii posed a mortal threat, or the suggestion that movements of people at that time would stretch the available resources to breaking point. The settlement of the Boii would set the tone for Rome's quiet policy towards barbarian migrants from outside the empire for generations to come. When, for the sake of manpower, it was advantageous to allow them into the empire, worries about the danger they posed and fears about their barbarism were put aside; land and livelihoods could be found for them without demur.

So plausible had the justification for action against the Helvetii proved to be that it would supply the rationale for immediate action against another people attempting to enter Gaul. The Gallic ambassadors who had come to congratulate Caesar revealed that there was yet another migrant crisis. In Gaul, two rival tribes had been competing for primacy: the Aedui, allies of Rome who occupied territory that is now part of Burgundy, and the Arverni, who lived further to the southwest, in what is now the Auvergne. The Arverni, along with another Gallic ally, the Sequani, tried to get the upper hand by inviting members of Germanic tribes across the Rhine to settle in their territory. The first wave of Germanic migrants comprised 15,000 people, and these fierce incomers quickly developed a liking for Gallic farmland, Gallic civilization and Gallic wealth. Many more of them followed. By that moment in 58 BC, 120,000 Germanic migrants had settled on Gallic territory. With their assistance, the Sequani broke the dominance of the Aedui: they took hostage a number of high-ranking Aedui nobles, and forced them to swear not to ask the Romans for help. But things were even worse for the victorious Sequani than for the conquered Aedui. The king of the Germanic incomers, Ariovistus, ruler of the Suebi tribal confederation, demanded that the Sequani yield one-third of their territory for his followers to settle. He then ordered them to surrender a further third to accommodate yet more Germanic arrivals. Ariovistus was the very essence of a barbarian: rash and quick to anger. It was impossible for the Gauls to endure his presence any longer. Without Caesar's help, they would have to seek out new homes far away from the Germanic incomers, risking everything they had to do so. Caesar hardly had to spell out the implications of all this, though he docs so explicitly in his account: for the second time within a year, a Gallic swarm was in prospect, of just the sort that Marius himself had faced. Now that the Germanic peoples were getting used to crossing the Rhine freely, they would never be content with merely conquering Gaul. They would burst into the Roman province of Transalpine Gaul and then into Italy, just as the Teutones had once intended to do.

In Caesar's account of the negotiations he attempted to hold with Ariovistus, he presents himself in the mould of the populist hero. He goes to meet the Germanic king near Besançon (Vesontio) with an escort of ordinary legionaries, unusually mounted on horseback. One of them jokes that Caesar, by giving them horses, has turned them into knights, thus promoting them up the ranks of the Roman hierarchy. When it comes to the negotiations themselves, Ariovistus warns Caesar that he will be destroyed, and that this would be welcomed by many in Rome, notably the aristocratic faction that has done so much to obstruct Caesar and his party. Thus Caesar deftly implies an unholy alliance: between his aristocratic opponents in Rome and a barbarian horde that wishes to destroy the empire.

But it was Caesar who destroyed Ariovistus. The armies met at the Battle of Vosges in 58 BC, probably near Mulhouse, about five miles from the Rhine. The Roman legions fell into a state of panic before meeting the Germanic forces, just as they had done before they met the Teutones. However, Caesar recalled them to their usual valour, again by reference to Marius. The battle was rapid and fierce. A number of the incomers were chased back to the Rhine, including Ariovistus himself: he was able to cross the river in a small boat, and then escaped to obscurity. Both of his wives were killed, as was one of his daughters; the other was captured.

Caesar had managed, on the pretext of holding back dangerous waves of migration, to provoke and complete two major campaigns within the first year of his command. With the campaigns against the Helvetii and Ariovistus over, he had an excuse to leave Roman forces stationed in winter quarters far beyond the frontiers of the Roman province. The mere presence of these legionaries was a guarantee of further clashes with the Gauls. And of course any suggestion that Roman forces might be under attack by an indigenous people furnished Caesar with sufficient pretext to launch a new campaign against the offenders, to defeat them and then subject them to the Roman *imperium*. The threat of migration had served its purpose for Caesar and would leave its lasting mark. After 58 BC, he could rely on the logic of a spiralling cycle of violence to justify his continuing presence in Gaul.

Statue of Vercingétorix, the Gallic chief who led the resistance to Caesar's conquest in 52 BC. The statue, by Aimé Millet, was erected at Alésia, the site of Vercingétorix's final defeat, by Napoleon III in 1865, and bears the likeness of the French emperor.

CHAPTER III

The Taming of Gaul

Omnes fere Gallos novis rebus studere
'All the Gauls were bent on revolution'

JULIUS CAESAR, *De Bello Gallico*, III.10

GALLIA BELGICA

·

THE SAMBRE

·

ORLÉANS

·

PÉRIGNAT-LÈS-SARLIÈVE

·

ORCET

·

GERGOVIE

·

VENAREY-LES-LAUMES

·

MONT AUXOIS

·

ALÉSIA

·

VERCINGÉTORIX AND CAESAR

I N 57 BC, AFTER THE ROMAN ARMY had spent its first winter in
Gallia Comata ('Long-Haired Gaul', the regions captured by
Caesar), Caesar began to change the justification for continuing
his military action far beyond the established frontiers of the Roman
empire. He no longer implied that he was keeping his forces there as
an emergency response to the migrations of the Helvetii and the Suebi
under Ariovistus. Their business was now outright conquest, a mission that Caesar saw no need to justify nor for which he even troubled
to seek a mandate.

The year 57 BC was dedicated to attacks on the Belgic Gauls in what
is now northern France, Holland and Belgium. These Gauls, claimed
Caesar, were planning a conspiracy. They were fearful that when all of
the central parts of Gaul had been captured they would have to face a
Roman army; some elements, who disliked the idea of the Germanic
peoples under Ariovistus establishing themselves in Gaul, disliked the
idea of a Roman presence even more, and for that reason they were
planning to defy Caesar. On top of this, the Belgic tribes contained a
number of powerful chiefs who habitually recruited warbands with
which to make themselves kings. These chiefs were now disgruntled,
realizing that this would no longer be possible when their territories
were annexed to the Roman empire.

Even though Caesar, without missing a beat, states at the beginning
of the second book of his *Commentaries* that the extension of empire
was now the ultimate purpose of the Roman campaign, he still evokes
the shadow of the Teutones to justify his attack on the Belgic Gauls.
The Belgic tribes were the only Gallic peoples fierce enough to repel
the Teutones and Cimbri. Some of them – Caesar names the Aduatuci
in particular – were even descended from a group of the Teutones and

Cimbri who had pulled out of the long migration southwards half a century previously to make a home in Belgic Gaul.

Caesar raised an extra three legions at the beginning of the year and marched north to the Belgic territories. One of the first tribes he met, the Remi (after whom the city of Reims is named), surrendered immediately, giving Caesar hostages, food and intelligence about the other tribes. Caesar overcame two of them – the Suessiones and the Bellovaci – by force, before meeting the most formidable tribe, the Nervii, at the Battle of the Sambre. It was a difficult battle in which the Romans were hard pressed, but Caesar himself, according to his account, was able to rally the wavering legions by fighting in the front rank with the ordinary men. The Nervii were so badly defeated that when they finally surrendered, they told Caesar the number of their tribal elders had been reduced from 600 to three, and their fighting men from 60,000 to 500. A similar disaster befell the Aduatuci, who surrendered their *oppidum* (possibly modern-day Namur) to the Romans, only to be attacked shortly afterwards. Caesar captured the town and sold all its 53,000 inhabitants, as one lot, into slavery.

Other legions had been sent westwards to demand the surrender of the Gallic peoples of the Atlantic coast, an aim that was achieved with little incident. On the other side of Gaul, messengers from Germanic tribes across the Rhine promised to send hostages to Caesar and follow his orders. At the end of the year, Caesar reported these achievements to the Senate in Rome, stating that the whole of Gaul had been pacified. The Senate responded by voting fifteen days of public thanksgiving in Caesar's honour: an accolade that no one had ever been granted before, boasts Caesar.

Caesar's claim that he had brought peace to Gaul was premature. Many of the tribes, particularly those on the Atlantic coast, had not been expecting the Romans to remain. In 56 BC, when Roman detachments in these areas demanded grain from the local tribes, there was serious unrest. Grain was in short supply, perhaps on account of a difficult winter, but more likely because of the disruption that the war in Gaul had caused to settled agriculture. The Romans' demand for grain at a time of scarcity, combined with a realization on the part of the local tribes that they had lost their freedom, led to revolt among the peoples of the Atlantic littoral. The rebellion was led by the Veneti: they seized two Roman officers who had been sent to them to seek grain, and refused to let them go until the Romans released the hostages they had taken from the Veneti the previous year.

Caesar's attention at this point appears to have been wandering. Having completed the conquest of Gaul – in his own mind at any rate – he was now considering an expedition to his other province of Illyricum, where there were opportunities for new campaigns. However, the news of the uprising of the Veneti forced him to abandon these desires for fresh glory, and he was brought back to the more difficult business of consolidating what he had already won. Caesar portrayed the two captured Roman officers as ambassadors rather than military officials, and thereby claimed that the Veneti had offended against the time-honoured sanctity of diplomats. On these grounds, when he was finally able to overcome the tribe, his retribution was similar to that visited on the Aduatuci. As the year proceeded, the Romans were bogged down in a number of actions more akin to guerrilla warfare then set-piece battles. Caesar himself tried to overcome the tribes of the Morini and Menapii around Boulogne and Flanders, but was unable to flush them out of the swamps and forests into which they had retreated. In addition to these difficulties, Caesar faced an attempt by the aristocratic faction in Rome to remove him from his Gallic command. For a time, he was compelled to leave Gaul for a conference at Lucca with Pompey and Crassus, where he was able to use their influence to extend his command up until 50 BC, and to persuade the Senate to recognise his conquests in Gaul.

Despite this agreement in Lucca, Caesar still faced criticism in Rome. The following year, 55 BC, a group of Germanic migrants, the Usipetes and the Tencteri, crossed the Rhine into the territory of the Menapii. It was a migration, according to Caesar's *Commentaries*, on the same scale as that of the Helvetii. Now that Rome had formally taken much of Gallia Comata under its control, it was more legitimate of Caesar to treat it as a genuine threat. However, when ambassadors from the two tribes began to negotiate an agreement that they should settle on the eastern bank of the Rhine among the Ubii, a tribe allied to Rome, Caesar turned against them. They had asked for a short period of time to take the offer back to their tribes and speak directly to the Ubii. However, Caesar accused them of intending to use this time to prepare attacks against Gaul. Showing the same disregard for diplomatic convention for which he had criticized the Veneti, Caesar had the two envoys seized and bound. The Usipetes and Tencteri, who had evidently been expecting the results of diplomacy rather than battle, were then put to the sword. For this, Caesar was lambasted by Cato, his leading opponent in the Senate, who accused him of bringing the Roman reputation for good faith into disrepute and called for him to be handed over to the Germanic tribes for punishment.

Caesar was not, of course, delivered to the Germanic tribes, but the fact that he soon made attempts to launch new and eye-catching campaigns of conquest suggests a desire to deflect criticism in Rome, and to distract attention from the less glamorous and more difficult work of securing the Gallic conquests. In 55 BC he crossed the Rhine, the first Roman general to do so, but his expedition ended up being little more than shadow-boxing with the Germanic tribes. Frustrated by the lack of any concrete gains, he then made an expedition to Britain. Again, he was the first Roman general to do so, but it was a reckless move, since it was late in the season and he had not prepared adequately. The near-disaster of the British invasions of 55 and 54 BC are dealt with in another chapter (see pages 121 to 143). Suffice to say in this context that Caesar managed to spin these expeditions as great successes in Rome.

Caesar's crossing of the Rhine and the English Channel, which were little more than military displacement activities, did not succeed in placing Roman rule in the Gallic territories on a more secure footing. In 54 to 53 BC a sequence of chaotic uprisings broke out, particularly in northern Gaul. One chieftain, Ambiorix, was able to lure a Roman detachment of fifteen cohorts into a trap, destroying it outright, and then subjecting another legion, under the command of Cicero's brother, Quintus Cicero, to a gruelling siege. It was only with difficulty that Caesar could save the situation, and he resorted to ever-increasing brutality to suppress the disorder. Villages and fields were burnt. Large groups of tribespeople were captured and led into slavery or simply left to starve. Noble Gauls involved in conspiracies faced agonizing deaths at the hands of the Roman forces.

One such event at the end of 53 BC – the execution of a rebel chieftain named Acco, who was cudgelled to death (a method chosen by Caesar for its archaic viciousness) – led to a wider and much more organized revolt. At the beginning of 52 BC, when Caesar's attention was distracted by the murder of his ally Publius Clodius Pulcher in Rome, the Gauls fell on the Roman population of Cenabum (modern-day Orléans) – in territory recently captured by Caesar – and slaughtered them. As with the original province in the south, an adventurous group of traders and their families had moved into a new area of opportunity created by Roman control. None escaped the massacre, and news of it travelled fast across Gaul. When any event of importance occurred, it was the custom to spread the news by shouting it in relays from field to field. Thus the massacre at sunrise in Cenabum was reported 160 miles away in the territory of the Arverni, around their chief *oppidum* of Gergovia, by sunset. There was a signal for a general uprising.

In this situation, there was one Gallic chief who was able to rise to the challenge of leading a united resistance against Caesar. His name was Vercingétorix. Our primary source of information about him is, as with much else, Caesar himself. Only a few coins minted with his name, found scattered around the *oppidum* of Alésia (about which more in due course), bear contemporary testament to his rule. Vercingétorix was a noble member of the Arverni tribe; at the time of the uprising of 52 BC he was at the Arverni *oppidum* of Gergovia, in the heart of what is now the Auvergne. Caesar tells us that his father was named Celtillus, and that he had been put to death in the previous generation for aspiring to the kingship of the whole of Gaul (a claim that may well be a projection of the native Roman fear of kingship onto the Gallic peoples). Vercingétorix was a young man of 'supreme influence', and he had the good fortune to be in such a position at the turning of the tide of history.

Vercingétorix seized on the massacre at Cenabum as a call to arms. According to Caesar, he summoned his tribal dependants and urged them to join the revolt. The other chiefs in Gergovia, including one of Vercingétorix's uncles, did not consider it safe to attempt such a rebellion and expelled him from the city. Undeterred, he went into the countryside, where he raised an army of 'beggars and outcasts'. With their support, he returned to Gergovia and seized it. He was hailed as 'king'. Vercingétorix then sent messengers to other tribes to seek pledges of loyalty in the form of men, weapons and hostages. In a vote, he was chosen to be the overall commander of the revolt. He was, says Caesar, a brutal leader: serious infringements of discipline were punished by burning or torturing to death, while lesser punishments included the severing of ears or gouging out of eyes. By such measures Vercingétorix ensured allegiance and loyalty.

The uprising caught Caesar off guard: he had to raise new forces, then rush back from Cisalpine Gaul to confront the rebels. As the Romans attempted to catch up with the main body of Vercingétorix's forces, Caesar captured a string of Gallic *oppida*. Vellaunodunum and Noviodunum – their sites now unknown – were taken; Cenabum was plundered and burnt. Vercingétorix, aware of the dangers of a battlefield encounter with Caesar's forces, called for greater sacrifices to halt the Roman advance. Cities and territories were no longer to be defended. Instead, the Gauls were to burn their own villages and crops that stood in the way of the Roman advance to deny them forage and stretch their lines of supply. The Gauls accepted the command, but pleaded for Avaricum (Bourges) – 'the fairest of all their cities' – to be spared. Vercingétorix, against his better judgement, relented. The subsequent fall of the city to the Romans, the loss of 40,000 people and the Roman capture of the city's food supplies, merely served to prove Vercingétorix's strategic sagacity.

Roman detachments throughout the Gallic territories, particularly in Lutetia (Paris), struggled to deal with the uprising. The rebels, by spreading apparent misinformation over Caesar's intentions, managed to peel off a number of his Gallic tribal supporters, including many of the Aedui. At an assembly in their capital, Vercingétorix was hailed as the commander-in-chief of all the Gallic tribes. A cat-and-mouse game with Caesar ensued before the two armies met in Vercingétorix's native territory, at Gergovia.

Gergovia is to be found south of the old tyre-producing city of Clermont-Ferrand in the Auvergne. It sits high on a flat plateau in a wide, green landscape of dark, volcanic plugs. There is no easy or direct route to it. I approach Gergovia through the suburban village of Pérignat-lès-Sarliève. It stretches along a straight, quiet road, untroubled by cars and lined with geometric houses in various shades of beige and cream, their facades draped with honeysuckle. Telegraph wires beat a languid rhythm, hanging from post to post.

Gergovia was besieged by Caesar in 52 BC, and was the site of one of his few defeats. I find myself wondering whether it was across Pérignat that the Aedui cavalry, as described by Caesar, charged to assist the Roman legions; or whether the route of their charge lay outside the village, across the vineyards that reach down to the A75, roaring at the bottom of the valley.

I make my way round to a point south of the plateau before embarking on the ascent. Caesar mounted his siege by building a Great Camp at the nearby town of Orcet on the other side of the A75. Later, he captured a height about two miles to the west, above the village of La Roche Blanche, and established a smaller camp there. Between the two camps he had two parallel trenches dug – each of them 3.5 metres wide and 3,000 metres long – to provide security for his forces going between them. Crossing and recrossing the modern suburbs of La Roche Blanche, there are no sign of these works beneath the neat gardens and vegetable patches planted with rows of onion and lettuce.

I turn left and cross a bridge over the A75, through a maze of traffic lights, to reach Orcet. Caesar's Great Camp here was excavated in the 1860s by Napoleon III's archaeologist, Colonel Stoffel, and he laid down stone markers to mark the corners of its ramparts. One of them is easy to find, sitting demurely on one side of a residential street. Engraved in grubby nineteenth-century lettering on a slate-grey stone against a wall are the words *Camp occupé par Jules César, L'an 52 avant J.C.* ('Julius Caesar's camp, 52 BC'). Some of the others are more difficult to locate. I run the second marker to earth along a broken track on the edge of town, lined with nettles and brambles, behind a veil of undergrowth. The next lies hidden in high grass behind a mangled green wire fence, doing its best to protect a small factory producing agricultural metalwork. On the land itself there is no sign of a rampart, but the markers at least preserve Caesar as a once-recovered and half-forgotten memory.

Turning back to climb to the plateau of Gergovia, I take a road that Caesar's crack 10th Legion may have marched up in their attempt to assault the Gallic stronghold. The road skirts the edge of the hill as it heads upwards. On one side, sometimes cut into the rock, are chiselled doors and windows that lead into abandoned troglodyte chambers. In gardens by the wayside, vines are trained high upon trellises; two men sit motionless with a bottle of wine outside a shed in the afternoon shade. Firebugs, armoured with their red and black escutcheon wings, toil over fragments of dry bark in the gutter.

On the slope some distance below the top of the plateau, the road passes through the village of Gergovia. In in its lower reaches there are

One of the pillars set up by Stoffel in the 1860s to mark the corners of Caesar's
Great Camp at Orcet for the siege of Gergovia.

capillary-winding culs-de-sac; its centre is ancient and stone-built. Large barn dwellings stand like cattle in a stall along a narrow, winding main thoroughfare. Honey-coloured lintels are carved with dancetty coats of arms staring out into the street. A Romanesque church sits on a promontory above a small and irregular village square. Cockerels squawk. Two boys play at a fountain, lashing the water with sticks. Above, a plaque records the visit in 1862 of Napoleon III, great searcher for Caesar and the Gauls in France. The plaque records not just the emperor's visit, but also his munificence. The name of Gergovia had been lost to the village generations before his visit. By then, it rejoiced in the name of Merdogne – 'Shit-hole'. By his command, the older and more dignified name was to be restored in the modern French form of Gergovie.

Plaque above the fountain at Gergovie recording Napoleon III's visit and his change of the village's name from the less decorous 'Merdogne'.

Through the village, and off a country road, a stony track slippery with cow-dung leads to the top. It was on this part of the slope below the plateau, if Caesar's commentary is correct, that his legions met an array of Gallic warriors camped behind a hastily built wall of stones. Despite an order from their commander to retreat, the Roman troops made a sustained attack. The ground was against them and their lines were severely extended. Many were killed, and the attack was repulsed. I wonder if there is a sense of the sudden slaughter in the air, or if it can be read upon the gorse-fringed stones on the track. But if I do sense a frisson, a quickening of the pulse, I conclude it comes from the connection of Caesar's text to the place, not the place itself.

After reaching the summit, the path leads first to the footprint of vanished building. Only a low ziggurat of a few stone steps remains. The steps are characteristic of a temple base, with a few stumps – the remnants of columns – ranged on top of them. Grass pokes through the corners and cracks. The rest of the structure has disappeared. This is not the remains of a temple but of accommodation built before the Second World War by a group of archaeological students from Strasbourg University who were studying the site. Nearby stands a memorial: many of them were executed by the Nazis.

The plateau of Gergovia extends, green, wide, level as the flat of a knife. The plain of the Auvergne below, broken by the dark fists of volcanic plugs, ebbs into the powder-blue horizon. Caesar wrote of how, when the legions fought the cordon of Gallic warriors just below the plateau, the women in the town of Gergovia threw their clothes and silver from the walls, baring their breasts and begging the Romans to spare them and their children. Now there is a quiet open space where children stride with coloured kites across the meadow-flowered grass. At one end of the site stands a café, admittedly Gallic-themed. Behind it, a wedding is in progress. The wind blows and whips around ribbons tied to green chairs. A memorial rises to the Gallic chieftain Vercingétorix, three bluff columns like a pile of millstones topped with a vast, empty winged helmet. The inscription is in Latin, the language of the Gauls' enemy. The edge of the plateau is fringed with the sparse remnants of ramparts, black basalt cubes, built against the Romans at the time of Caesar. In the centre of the plateau, more low barrows of basaltic rubble lie like little grave cairns, hardly showing their tops above the grass. There was a Gallic shrine here before the Romans came. It was remodelled after the conquest, while the rest of the town around it withered in the first century AD and was abandoned for Augustonemetum (Clermont-Ferrand), the Roman foundation on the plain. The shrine itself was forgotten by the third century, and the plateau sank back into oblivious green.

This was a place where Caesar was defeated. But still, he had his victory, for the Gallic past was effaced, even after his departure. The place fell into nothing. Even its name was lost, degenerating to 'Shit-hole' until it was recovered via reference to Caesar – the only real gateway to the memory of old Gaul. We cannot know in truth what Gaul was, and the only sight of its existence is Caesar's note of its passing.

Gergovia is a flat wasteland. Bibracte, capital of the Aedui and another great Gallic *oppidum* – near modern Autun in Burgundy – was abandoned and reclaimed by the forests of Morvan. Caesar destroyed the Gallic town of Avaricum (modern-day Bourges), the 'fairest in the whole of Gaul' in Caesar's own words, in 52 BC, allowing his men to kill the population of 40,000; a mere 800 escaped. He killed around 160,000 of the Usipetes and Tencteri in 55 BC, by the streams of the Waal and the Maas in the east of the Netherlands. The Belgic tribes – the Nervii, the Senones, the Menapii – received similar treatment. On the southern coast of Brittany, Caesar executed the entire nobility of the Gallic tribe of the Veneti in 56 BC, and sold the whole of its male population into slavery. The Veneti were a long-established seafaring nation who controlled much of the ancient trade across the Channel into the British Isles. They built ships specialized for the rough conditions and tides of the Atlantic coasts, flat-keeled and high-prowed; Roman vessels paled by comparison. When Caesar stormed their strongholds on the rocky Armorican coast, they took to the sea in defiance. But when Caesar's men discovered a way of disabling the Veneti ships by cutting the rigging of their sails, their resistance came to an end. Scarcely any of their fleet returned to land. A people and a tradition were brought into the light of history by Caesar only through his account of their destruction.

Writing in the century after the conquest of Gaul, the Roman historian Pliny the Elder records that Caesar, during his campaigns there, had caused the deaths of around 1.2 million people. Although many Roman historians would have marked this to Caesar's credit, Pliny does not. 'I am not going to put it down as a mark of his glory, what was really an outrage committed against humanity.' Along with all those who died, or were marched into slavery (each Roman legionary who served in the Gallic campaign received a Gallic slave), the Celtic culture of pre-Roman Gaul, and the Gallic testimony of that culture, was simply erased. The Gauls were not able to give an account of their own culture, unfiltered by a Roman lens. Beyond Caesar's dismissal of the Gauls as a boastful, garrulous people who were unable to see a plan through to its conclusion, we know nothing of the actual Gallic character. The true nature of the Gallic Druids, their philosophy and their gods, remain a mystery. After their obliteration in Gaul, they became nothing more than an empty vessel into which the modern age poured notions of picturesque savagery and a romantic longing for a wise and magical past. As Lucan, a Roman epic poet of the first century AD described them, the Druid priests dwelt in ancient, sunless groves, pallid with decay, where giant stones were smeared with the blood of human sacrifice, and effigies of the gods hacked out of rotting wood struck terror into the uninitiated. And of Gallic society, its history, its stories, we know little beyond what Caesar wanted them to be; there are just a handful of other Roman and Greek accounts, some fragments of archaeology, and a distant, refracted vision of what they might have been in the medieval writings of their Celtic kindred in

Stoffel's reconstruction of the Battle of Gergovia between Caesar and Vercingétorix in 52 BC.

Orignat

379

Route

Impériale

352

347

ANCIEN LAC DE SARLIÈVES

Pᵗ Sarlièves

368

445

393

de

Gergovia

363

395

Marche des Éduens

Grand camp

Paris

395

Marmant

434

413

Double fossé

397

Pᵗ Orcet

Auzon Rᵘ

Orcet

en

Espagne

Puy de Chignat

Rᵘ

par

Ireland. Caesar made his profoundest impact on history by bringing Gaul fully into the sphere of Rome and Mediterranean culture, but in doing so he drew an impenetrable veil over centuries of indigenous Gallic culture. In its absence and loss we feel Caesar's continuing presence to this day.

But where Caesar destroyed, he also laid foundations for the new. And this was true as much for the identities of the people he had eclipsed as for the cities and territories he had razed.

The railway station of Venarey-les-Laumes, a small town in the luxuriant hilly countryside northwest of Dijon, is, on brief inspection,

View of the hilltop of Gergovie from beyond Pérignat-lès-Sarliève.

an unremarkable place: a quiet ticket office, gravelly walkways across the dusty tracks, an entanglement of sidings winding among greying locomotive sheds. It is only on reaching the platform, or pulling into the station as a new visitor by train, that one notices something rather striking.

Beyond the tracks, by a factory, stands a large warehouse. The factory is grubby and dishwater beige, but the slatted walls of the warehouse are bright and freshly painted. However, what they advertise is neither a product of the factory, nor a car nor a chemical, nor an agricultural feed. On a cream-white background, picked out in blood red, are the towering head and shoulders of a man. His hair and moustache are long, his torso sturdy and heroic, his brow furrowed; he gazes over his back, as if in level contemplation of the future and of suffering to come. On a red band above his head is the word 'Alésia'. The man is Vercingétorix. And it was here, at the settlement of Alésia, on an almond-shaped plateau not far from the station, that he led the climactic battle against Caesar and the Romans in 52 BC. It was his defeat at this spot that led to Caesar's ultimate victory over Gaul and its incorporation into the Roman world.

After his confrontation with Caesar at Gergovia, Vercingétorix somewhat unaccountably chose to retreat north. Instead of maintaining his earlier scorched-earth guerrilla campaign, he fell back on Alésia, the hill-top *oppidum* of the small tribe of the Mandubii.

Alésia sits on a great hill, Mont Auxois, surrounded by an amphitheatre of other hills – the Montagne de Bussy and the Montagne de Flavigny, among others. Only to the west and southwest, where Venarey-les-Laumes is sited on a plain around the scanty waters of the River Brenne, is there any relief from the heights. Vercingétorix had stationed his army, around 80,000 strong, within and around the *oppidum* on the hilltop. As at Gergovia, he had strengthened the *oppidum* with a ditch and an embankment 1.8 metres high.

Caesar settled down for a long siege. The scale of the Roman siegeworks at Alésia, as described by Caesar, defies belief, until one learns that archaeology and aerial photography confirm his account, revealing the scars he left on the land itself. He constructed a 17-kilometre (11-mile) encirclement of Mont Auxois. Two trenches, one filled with water, were backed up by a rampart, around 3.6 metres high, topped with wickerwork battlements and crowned with wooden watchtowers every 15 metres. On the plain, earth was used to build the rampart. But as the trenches climbed undaunted over the surrounding heights, they had to be cut into the limestone rock of the hills, and in these places the limestone spoil was used to construct the ramparts.

Between the two trenches were placed devices to rival the barbed wire of a First World War no-man's land. Caesar cut the boughs of trees, and then sharpened and entangled the branches. These he set into the earth facing towards Alésia, so that any force that approached would be impaled. Beyond these were pits a metre deep with stakes as thick as a man's thigh, tapering to a fire-hardened point, all concealed with brushwood to trap the unwary. And in front, logs embedded

Full-scale reconstruction of Caesar's 52 BC siegeworks around Alésia at the MuséoParc Alésia.

with sharp iron hooks pointing upwards were planted in the ground. Caesar revelled in the rough humour with which his men named these contrivances: the entanglements of branches were called *cippi*, meaning both 'boundary-marker' and 'tombstone'; the concealed stakes, on account of the resemblance in form, were called *lilia* – 'lilies'.

Before Caesar had completed these siegeworks, Vercingétorix had been able to despatch an appeal to the other tribes of Gaul to send a relief force to attack Caesar in his rear. Caesar, conscious of this danger, took action to guard against it. The same defensive works he had constructed to face in towards Alésia, he also constructed, over a 22-kilometre (14-mile) circumference, to face out towards any relief army that might attack him. He was therefore both besieger and besieged. His own force of about 60,000 men was concentrated in a narrow ring around Alésia, no more than 120 metres across at its widest. Discreet stone markers set in the pavement by the railway sidings at the station record where the lines of each fortification were later rediscovered.

The siege was protracted and brutal. With so many civilians and fighters clustered on the hilltop, grain was in desperately short supply. Vercingétorix made himself personally responsible for allotting the rations. However, after a month in which there was no sign of the Gallic relief army, the Gauls decided to take desperate measures. The chiefs in the city held a council of war. Caesar claims to record the speech of one of the Gallic war-leaders, Critognatus. He argued, according to Caesar, that their parents had faced such a situation when the Teutones had invaded, and had left an example of the sacrifices that were necessary under such extreme circumstances: namely that useless civilians – women, children and old men – should be fed to those who were strong enough to bear arms. With Caesar at the gates, they should do the same again.

The Gallic defenders of Alésia chose not to eat the civilian population, but decided to expel them from the city towards the Roman lines. They assumed that Caesar would admit them to his camp, and at least save their lives by selling them into slavery. The women, children, old men, numbering in their tens of thousands, were hustled down the hill, most likely via the road that descends from the summit towards the west, and which is now lined by modern bungalows and pleasant gardens. They reached the plain, and came upon Caesar's lethal entanglements, the snares and the traps arrayed before the Roman trenches. Caesar merely remarks that he ordered that they were not to be admitted to the Roman camp, but neglects to speak of their fate. Critognatus's savagery conveniently diverts the reader from Caesar's cruel decision to use the starving civilians of Alésia – abandoned in no-man's land – as another weapon to put pressure on the Gallic army to surrender.

Soon after the Mandubii civilians were left to their fate between the lines, the Gallic relief force arrived from the west. A series of intense battles was fought around Alésia, as the Gauls struggled to break through weak points in the Roman defences. However, after the second round of substantial fighting, it became clear to the Gauls that they did not have the capacity to break the siege. A further council of war was held within Alésia, and Caesar again reports its proceedings. Vercingétorix told his assembled commanders that it was not for himself that he had taken up the campaign against the Romans, but for the sake of their common liberty. As they now had to yield to fortune, he offered himself up for whatever they should choose: they could placate the Romans by killing him, or hand him over alive.

The council sent messengers to Caesar, who ordered the Gauls to surrender their arms, and to bring their chiefs to him. Caesar took his seat among the defences in front of his camp to await the leaders' arrival. When Vercingétorix appeared, he cast his arms down before his Roman enemy, and Caesar ordered him to be bound and taken away. There would be sporadic uprisings for the next year or so, but effective Gallic resistance to Rome was over. Little more is heard of Vercingétorix. He spent six years as a prisoner in Rome, and last saw the light of day in a triumphal procession celebrating the conquest of Gaul. After his appearance before the cheering crowds of Rome, a chained acolyte for Caesar's glory, he was silently and ritually executed, his purpose fulfilled.

In a clearing of tattered oaks and beeches on the western height of Mont Auxois, above the village of Alise-Sainte-Reine, stands a statue of Vercingétorix, looking down over the scene of his defeat. The clearing is empty and silent when I visit, and the peaks of the surrounding hills where Caesar camped are hidden in cloud. Rainwater has washed seawatery green stains from the metal body of the statue into the limestone plinth, and the mass of it lours dark against a leaden sky. The statue has stood here since the 1860s, when it was commissioned by Emperor Napoleon III. Its inscription, adapted from the commentaries of Caesar, bespeaks the power imputed to its subject: *La Gaule Unie, formant une seule nation, animée d'une même esprit, peut défier l'univers* ('Gaul, united, forming a single nation, animated by the same spirit, is able to defy the universe'). Caesar had defeated and captured Vercingétorix, imprisoned and executed him, and appropriated the record of his deeds for his own benefit. And yet Caesar, for all his self-glorification and destructiveness, had laid sufficient foundations for a new identity for Vercingétorix – and for Gaul – to emerge in years to come.

For many centuries of the modern age, the Gauls remained in the shadows where Caesar had left them. They had no place in the identity of the developing state of France. They were the defeated and malleable pagan masses, barbaric and obscure, who only took form when worked on by the magic of conquest. The Gauls before Caesar were of no moment. Even after the decline of Roman rule, ordinary Gauls were but pliant material to be moulded into civilized order by the Franks and the Christianizing King Clovis in the late fifth century AD. Vercingétorix remained unknown from this time until the late eighth century, when a manuscript of Caesar's commentaries was rediscovered in a monastic library. But even then he excited little interest. France took its identity and legitimacy from the Catholic Merovingians, and for antique glory traced its origins, like Rome, to refugees from ancient Troy. The French kings wished to be compared to Caesar rather than to any indigenous Gallic chief. For example François I (r. 1515–47) was dubbed a 'Second Caesar' and 'Conqueror of the Helvetii' after his victory over the Swiss at the Battle of Marignano in 1515. Even with the stirrings of the Renaissance, Vercingétorix continued to attract scant attention. Writers from the Auvergne, his native territory, extolled him as a regional hero, but scholars from Paris looked down on him as a mere provincial leader. If anyone from the legendary past of Gaul mattered to them, it was Brennus, the purported leader of the Gallic attack on Rome many generations before Caesar.

But at the end of the eighteenth century, the atmosphere changed. With the emergence of the Romantic aesthetic, there was a surge of interest in the notion of a Celtic past. A fabricated collection of ancient epic verse, attributed to a Celtic bard named 'Ossian' and 'collected' from Gaelic-speaking Highlanders by the Scottish poet James Macpherson, took Europe by storm. In France itself, the overthrow of the monarchy, and the succession of different forms of government that followed, prompted a reassessment of the foundations of French national identity. Likewise, the invasion of France and the occupation of Paris by the Prussians and Cossacks in 1814–15 led to an intellectual debate as to how France should respond. Caesar's invasion of Gaul and the example of Vercingétorix offered a template to follow.

By the beginning of the nineteenth century, the time was ripe for a reconnection with the Gallic past. An early stirring in this direction was made during the French Revolution itself in 1789, when the political writer Abbé Sieyès characterized the Revolution as an indigenous Gallic population throwing off the shackles imposed by a noble class of Frankish invaders; but the idea did not gain immediate traction. The first real and influential attempt to develop this idea was made a little later by two historians, the brothers Augustin and Amédée Thierry. It was Augustin Thierry who, in 1820, at the age of twenty, fulminated at the centuries of darkness into which the Gauls had been cast by the historians of France. 'It is absurd', he writes, 'to make just the history of the Franks the starting point for a history of France. Such a choice consigns to oblivion the memory of a vast number of our ancestors, of those who, I would venture, have a just claim on our filial veneration.' France, he observes, is made up of much more than the Île-de-France and Paris. The hallmark of a well-written national history, he argued, was one that left out no one as it ranged over the whole mass of the national territory, as well as the entire scale of time. In ignoring the Gauls, the histories of France written up to that point had failed entirely to do this.

His younger brother Amédée took up the cudgels. Contrary to the received notion that French history began with the Franks, Amédée saw a continuum. The roots of France stretched back to the Gauls. 'Descendants of the soldiers of Brennus and of Vercingétorix, of the citizens of Carnutum and Gergovia, of the nobles of Durocortorum and of Bibracte, have we nothing left of our fathers?' He saw the Gauls as the ancestors of the French. The nature of France and the French, he maintains, is to a greater or lesser extent thanks to the legacy of the Gauls: 'I have concluded that our qualities, both good and bad, did not come into being yesterday in this land.' For Amédée Thierry, Vercingétorix is a romantic hero, a 'young chief' endowed with 'virtues and brilliant qualities', 'grace' and 'courage'. And, as such, he offers a noble and virtuous contrast to the mediocrity of the present. After the final defeat of Napoleon at Waterloo, the Bourbon monarchy had been reimposed on France in the person of Louis XVIII. For Amédée, the shabby image of the restored Bourbon monarch returning to his homeland in the baggage train of the Duke of Wellington's army only serves to burnish the heroism of the ancient Gallic chieftain further: 'Vercingétorix was too patriotic to owe his elevation to the humiliation of his country, and too proud to accept a throne from the hands of a foreigner.'

Amédée's writings were republished several times throughout the nineteenth century and exerted a notable influence on French culture and intellectual life. Other academic historians who persisted in arguing for the discontinuity between the Gallic period and the modern French nation, or who maintained the older idea that Rome was the bringer of civilization to a barbarous wasteland, never attained the same level of popularity as Amédée Thierry. Vercingétorix, the hero bequeathed by Caesar, allowed nineteenth-century France to develop a different notion of the origins of its identity. The Frankish background was decried on account of its association with the monarchy and old nobility: they were invaders who had imposed their will on a captive indigenous population. Indeed, the invasion of the Germanic Franks in the late fifth century seemed merely to presage the invasion of the Germanic Prussians in Amédée's own century. France's Roman imperial pedigree was likewise out of favour, given that it was held responsible for Napoleonic Caesarism and the legacy of clericalism. Only the Gallic past – painted as heroic, egalitarian, a time of liberty – was able to meet the terms required for a redefinition of French origins. Vercingétorix, moreover, was perfectly suited to be a hero in the face of adversity: a symbol of resistance, struggle and necessary sacrifice. Yet his defeat could also be seen as the beginning of hope: it signalled rejuvenation, a restoration of status and a new civilization that would be brought by Rome.

As the nineteenth century proceeded, the life of Vercingétorix became a major subject for French literature. Dozens of plays, poems, novels and histories and works of art appeared, extolling the virtues of the newly remembered hero. These included Eugène Sue's novel *Les Mystères du peuple* (1842–3), which evokes Vercingétorix as the 'chief of a hundred valleys', and Henri Martin's five-act verse drama *Vercingétorix* (1865). So scanty is Caesar's account of his life that Vercingétorix was open to a multitude of conflicting interpretations; indeed, the absence of biographical certainty may have been a large part of his appeal. Some called on him as a republican hero, standing defiant against Caesar. One trope taken up by a number of writers was the idea that Brutus, in killing Caesar, was acting to avenge the death of Vercingétorix. Yet others, particularly apologists for the Roman Catholic Church, saw Vercingétorix as a kingly figure, even treating him as a prefiguration of Christ himself. In Vercingétorix's surrender to Caesar, only cursorily treated in the *Commentaries*, they discerned a Christ-like self-abnegation: for the sake of his friends, he was meekly obedient even unto death; and his sacrifice was necessary and blessed, because via the conversion of Rome, France would later come to the Christian church. Some, by contrast, saw his defeat as marking the disastrous end of the liberty enjoyed by an indigenous civilization, overtaken by the Roman culture that, rather than Gaul, was truly barbarous. Caesar was held up in wretched contrast to Vercingétorix: he was 'vile... an assassin' (Henri Bernard); 'The bloody author of so many vile atrocities' (Pascal-Louis Lemière). Alexandre Soumet, who wrote a verse tragedy (1831) depicting a Druidess, Norma, during the time of the Roman conquest of Gaul – which would very soon inspire Bellini's opera *Norma* (1831), with a libretto by Felice Romani – puts outspoken views in the mouth of his heroine: 'How I hate the Romans! They are cruel, perfidious, sacrilegious, deceitful / And by parricidal sermons / They place their crimes under the guard of heaven.'

Vercingétorix himself was elevated to the highest rank of the French national pantheon. Even a member of the French house of Bourbon, Henri d'Orléans, the duc d'Aumale, could extol the virtues of the Gallic chief, so often held up as a republican hero. In 1859 he wrote:

> I often remember the emotion stirred in me in my childhood by the story of Vercingétorix's struggle against Caesar. Although the passage of time has changed my ideas about it on many points, and although the Roman conquest does not stir in me the same indignation and I recognize everything that it has given to our modern French nation, I have kept the same warm enthusiasm for the hero of the Auvergne. For me, it is in him that is

personified for the first time our national independence; and if it is permitted to compare a pagan hero with a Christian virgin, I see him, in his successful end, as a precursor to Joan of Arc. He is not even without the halo of martyrdom. Six years of captivity followed by death… is worth as much as death at the stake at Rouen… And since… he devoted himself to the salvation of his companions, I salute him as the first of the French.

Others took up this cry. As the writer Adolphe Bréan commented in 1864, for the three ages of French history, there were three great heroes. In the Middle Ages, there was Joan of Arc; in the modern age, Napoleon; but in antiquity there was Vercingétorix.

The contradictions in the French response to Vercingétorix and his defeat by Caesar came to a head with Emperor Napoleon III. He had come to power initially as the only president of the Second Republic following the final collapse of the Bourbon Monarchy in 1848. When, in 1852, the terms of the constitution prevented him from continuing in presidential office, he staged a coup, positioning himself as a popular modernizer, not dissimilar to Caesar. In the 1860s, when he eased some of the repressive measures designed to secure his position following the coup and his declaration of himself as emperor, he began to show a deep interest in the early history of France and the Roman invasion. He ordered wide-scale searches to take place to discover the locations of battles and sites described by Caesar in his *Commentaries*. He also embarked on the project of writing the life of Caesar in three volumes. The work was never completed, but the use to which the emperor wished to put Caesar and his victory over the Gauls are made entirely clear in the two volumes that were published.

The emperor attacks the denigration of great men: 'Too many historians find it easier to lower men of genius, than, with a generous inspiration, to raise them to their due height by penetrating their vast designs.' Too often, 'paltry inspirations' were imputed to Caesar's 'noblest actions'. Thus 'if he throws himself into Gaul, it is to acquire riches by pillage or soldiers devoted to his projects; if he crosses the sea to carry the Roman eagle into an unknown country, but the conquest of which will strengthen that of Gaul, it is to seek there pearls which were believed to exist in the seas of Great Britain'.

The emperor presents himself as a saviour of the French people, who had a vision for redevelopment of the country. Indeed, Haussmann's redevelopment of Paris, the first department stores, the great railway stations of Paris, and movements for gender equality all belong to his age. Julius Caesar, suggests the emperor, was also a man of vision – a vision that locked together the fortunes of Rome and Gaul in the development of European civilization. It was nothing less than 'civilization at stake' when the Gallic and Roman armies faced each other across the 'hills and fertile plains, now silent, of Alésia'. While one must admire Vercingétorix for his spirit of independence, says Napoleon III, 'we are not allowed to deplore his defeat'. Had Caesar failed to overcome the Gauls, the penalty paid by the people would have been much worse. 'The defeat of Caesar would have stopped for a long period the advance of Roman domination which, across rivers of blood, it is true, conducted the peoples to a better future... let us not forget that it is to the triumph of the Roman armies that we owe our civilization; institutions, manners, language, all come to us from the conquest. Thus are we much more children of the conquerors than the conquered...' Without Caesar, the barbarous peoples of Gaul would have likely overrun Italy and extinguished the light of Mediterranean civilization. Rule by a benevolent and popular despot, therefore, was the only salvation for a society that wanted to progress. It was unnecessary to labour the modern parallel.

Yet it was Napoleon III who commissioned – and paid for out of his own funds – the statue of Vercingétorix at Alésia that stares pensively over the site of his defeat. No equal monument stands there in commemoration of Caesar's salvation of French civilization. And looking closely at the face of Vercingétorix, his brow furrowed against the ashen sky, one sees, behind the shock of hair and the drooping moustache, the face of Napoleon III himself. This fact caused the politician Henri Rochefort to remark that the emperor had celebrated Caesar by the pen, but Vercingétorix by the statue. And the historian André Simon, among others, suggests that this contradiction still runs through French society and identity, even today: rejoicing in the benefits brought by Roman colonization, but paying a spiritual allegiance to the stubborn resistance of Vercingétorix.

The loss of Alésia was evoked as a response to the French defeat in the Franco-Prussian War of 1870. Léon Gambetta, who led the French resistance to the invasion following the defeat of Napoleon III, was cast as a new Vercingétorix, opposed to a German Caesar, Bismarck. To the republican left following the conflict, ancient Gaul was ceaselessly evoked as a political model, with the suggestion that its chiefs were democratically elected by the people; this heritage, it was suggested, stood in contrast to the crowned governments of the rest of Europe. New monuments arose to the democratic Vercingétorix, such as in Clermont-Ferrand and on Gergovia itself, now erected not by an emperor, but via public subscription.

However, it was after a graver defeat, at the hands of the Nazis in 1940, that Vercingétorix and Alésia were more thoroughly pressed into service. The situation was far worse than in 1870, and authority in France was divided between German occupiers, the Vichy administration under Marshal Pétain and the exiled Free French Government under de Gaulle. Again, Vercingétorix was used to provide a light and direction to the vanquished population of non-occupied France. For commentators in the press, Pétain, who had led the French armies successfully against the murderous German attack at Verdun in the First World War in 1916, was the Vercingétorix of the age. He had taken up arms, like Vercingétorix, for the liberty of all. Like Vercingétorix he had given, as René Giscard d'Estaing (uncle of President Valéry Giscard d'Estaing) remarked, the gift of his person to France. In order to bring a longer-term victory out of defeat, there were lessons to be learnt from Vercingétorix: the need to avoid lassitude, hopelessness and a withdrawal from the world; the need for self-sacrifice and the creation of a sense of national unity. Beyond this, the Pétainists even equated the German victory with that of Caesar: a new civilization had conquered France, but – if the French collaborated with their conquerors in the wake of defeat – a brighter future was believed to be in prospect.

The symbolism of Vercingétorix was remorselessly exploited by Pétain to lend credibility and lustre to his government. Gergovia, rather than Alésia, was the focus of this effort. Close to Vichy and the Auvergne, which many saw as the ancient heart of France, Gergovia was cherished as the site of the Gallic victory over Caesar. Soon after the surrender to Nazi Germany, Pétain oversaw the establishment of the Légion Française des Combattants ('French Legion of Combatants') for military veterans. This organization was to be a movement for 'moral renewal', a 'National Revolution', based on the principles of self-sacrifice and unity that Alésia was held to embody. It provided practical assistance with harvests and food shortages, and also filled the ideological and social space created by the outlawing of political parties. In 1942, on the second anniversary of its foundation, a grand ceremony was held at Gergovie designed to foster a sense of national unity and loyalty to one's leader, values that were said to have been upheld by Vercingétorix in the face of Caesar's invasion. Urns of earth were brought to Gergovie, purportedly gathered from 'every commune in France' as well as the 'French empire', including Djibouti, Madagascar and even the French possessions in the Far East. In front of the massed ranks of 30,000 legionaries, Pétain mixed the earth and buried it in a crypt on the Gergovian plateau to signify the indivisibility of France (despite its occupation and the different claims to its government) and also a communion between the France of 1942 and the Gallic realm at the time of Caesar's conquest.

In the aftermath of the German defeat in 1945, Caesar's victory over Vercingétorix was again reinterpreted to illuminate the new

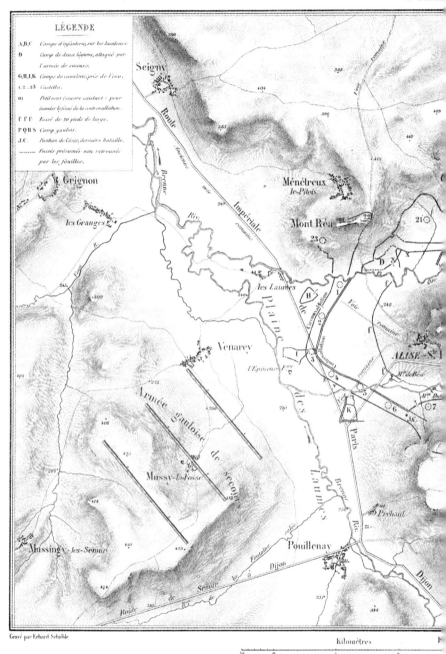

PLA

LÉGENDE

Stoffel's reconstruction of the siege of Alésia, 52 BC.

Marche de l'armée gauloise de secours

Milles romains

Imp. Lemercier et Cⁱᵉ Paris.

political reality. An alternative approach, which also existed in opposition to the official Pétainist doctrine, is neatly summed up on a marble inscription, erected in 1949, at the railway station close to Alésia: 'In this plain 2,000 years ago, Gaul redeemed its honour by leading its people, at the command of Vercingétorix, to face the legions of Caesar: but after the defeat of its arms, reconciled with the victor, together they defended against the Germanic invasions: open to the lights of Greece and Rome, it knew three centuries of peace.'

Following the war, General Charles de Gaulle offered a further corrective to the dogma of Pétain. Vercingétorix was, for him, the '*premier résistant de notre race*' ('the first resistance fighter of our race'). His Gaullist ideology – his 'certain idea of France' – treated the country as a timeless and eternal person in itself, with whom a 'mystical dialogue' was possible throughout the course of history. Although the origins of the *French state* were to be found with Clovis and the Merovingians, the origins of *the people* were to be found before Caesar, with the Gauls themselves. The character of the Gauls, as he saw it, had been transferred to the French: courageous, demanding and mercurial, with the propensity for revolution and civil conflict, for which a strong state was the antidote prescribed by historical experience. Such was the importance of Vercingétorix to de Gaulle that he visited Alésia every year between 1947 and 1957 on 5 September, the date recorded by Caesar for the capture of Vercingétorix.

Vercingétorix and his conflict with Caesar have continued to exercise an influence even on more recent generations of politicians in France. François Mitterrand, president of the French Republic from 1981 to 1995, cited Vercingétorix as one of the leading historical characters to have influenced him, since he had been able on occasion to defeat the Romans although the Gauls had been in no state to resist 'the Roman machine'. He regarded Bibracte, where Vercingétorix had been voted the supreme war leader against Caesar, as the birthplace of the first stirrings of French unity. Mitterrand made major speeches at the site on two occasions, including an appeal for national unity. He also expressed a wish, which remained unfulfilled, to be buried there. The Gaullist politician Jacques Chirac, Mitterrand's presidential successor, used the plateau of Gergovia in 1989 as a site to launch the campaign for the European elections, with a call for French identity to be safeguarded. Chirac made reference to the inscription on the base of the statue of Vercingétorix, saying that they were a 'singular people, in the first rank when united'. He even played on Vercingétorix's worsting of a Roman centurion, Lucius Fabius; one of Chirac's political opponents was the socialist Laurent Fabius.

The contradictions in the story of Vercingétorix and the Roman invasion still provide fodder for political conflict. The former Front National leader Jean-Marie Le Pen made a speech at Alésia in 1990, calling for France to resist invasions and return to its roots. Vercingétorix was an 'unfortunate hero' and a symbol for the French people whom Le Pen judged to be 'menaced in their substance and security by other types of invasions… I do not question the immigrants themselves, but the criminal policy of immigration'. By contrast, a demonstration held in Clermont-Ferrand against discrimination at the same time was able to claim Vercingétorix for its own; as one of the organizers said, 'it is fitting that our march against racism ends in front of the statue of Vercingétorix, that is to say the hero of liberty and of liberties'. In November 2016, Nicolas Sarkozy, in his (failed) presidential bid, evoked Vercingétorix in the debate over migration and French identity. He declared that 'Whatever the nationality of your parents, at the moment you become French, your ancestors are Gaul and Vercingétorix,' thereby demanding that immigrants fully accept the French way of life as a prerequisite for receiving French nationality.

But although Vercingétorix has continued to be used by politicians as an idol and lesser cousin to Joan of Arc, since 1959 his potency as a serious political symbol has been somewhat reduced thanks to his appearance in the *Astérix* series of *bandes dessinées* (comic books), written by René Goscinny until his death in 1977, and illustrated by Albert Uderzo. To be sure, the habit of lightening the treatment of the

Gauls did not appear with *Astérix*. Since the end of the nineteenth century, the Gauls had been used in advertising as the French population became ever more familiar with their idealized images in cheap and widely distributed school textbooks and popular history pamphlets. Gallic chiefs found themselves not in Roman captivity, but corralled into selling cigarettes, strange varieties of liqueurs, petrol and pneumatic tyres. It was in this atmosphere that *Astérix*, gently satirizing the French way of life in the twentieth century, came to be conceived. The paradoxes inherent in the conflict between Rome and Gaul are fully on display – the cities and towns rebuilt and flourishing under Caesar, with amphitheatres, temples and aqueducts, but counterpointed by the invincible and resistant rustic village with its communal life, jollity, contrariness and constant quarrels. The contrast finds its fulfilment in the portrayal, in *Le Bouclier arverne* (*Asterix and the Chieftain's Shield*, 1968), of the surrender of Vercingétorix at Alésia. After the event Caesar describes to his followers how the defeated Gallic chief meekly laid his weapons at the feet of his conqueror, while Caesar looked on – majestic, cold and impassive. It is an emotive scene treated frequently in nineteenth-century French art. In the comic-book telling, however, certain members of Caesar's entourage remember the event differently. Vercingétorix does not lay his weapons humbly at Caesar's feet, but, riding up to his Roman adversary, drops them from a height on Caesar's spindly toes.

Sign at the entrance to Devil's Dyke, Wheathampstead, thought to be the site of a battle in 54 BC between Caesar and the British resistance leader Cassivellaunus.

CHAPTER IV

Tales of the Imagination

Neque enim temere praeter mercatores illo adit quisquam
'Nobody except traders journeys thither without good cause'

JULIUS CAESAR, *De Bello Gallico*, IV.20

BOULOGNE

·

DEAL

·

WALMER

·

ROMNEY

·

CANTERBURY

·

BIGBURY HILL

·

ARTHUR'S-HOVEN

·

WALTON-ON-THAMES

·

WHEATHAMPSTEAD

·

RICHBOROUGH

·

CASSIVELLAUNUS

D URING HIS MILITARY CAMPAIGNS of the 50s BC, Caesar twice invaded Britain, once in 55 BC and again in 54 BC. His footprints on *terra Britannica*, however, are rather less easy to discern than those he left on the French side of the Channel.

It is unlikely, as Suetonius suggests, that he was drawn to the island in the belief that it offered a vast supply of high-quality pearls (other Roman authors knew that British pearls were of particularly low quality). However, it is difficult to accept Caesar's claim that he went there merely to stop the Britons sending assistance to the Gallic tribes in their uprisings against him. He makes only one glancing reference before his first invasion of Britain to such external help, and it appears unlikely that the Britons posed a grave enough threat to the security of Roman forces on the continent to justify the extraordinary risk of launching an amphibious attack on the island of Britain.

Seen in the wider context of the conquest of Gaul, a more credible motivation becomes apparent. By 55 BC, Roman troops had made their presence felt across the whole of Gaul. Caesar's work was shifting from the exciting business of conquest to the more mundane work of consolidating the new territories or suppressing dissent. Since his proconsular mandate over the territory still had several more years to run, it is likely that he wanted to continue to present the Senate – and more importantly, the people of Rome – with eye-catching victories to consolidate his reputation and justify the unusual length of his command.

The first symptom of this desire was his construction in 55 BC of a bridge across the Rhine to pursue the Germanic tribes on its east bank and deter them from making incursions into the newly Roman areas of Gaul. The expedition, despite its pioneering nature – it was the first Roman incursion across the Rhine (and, it would no doubt have occurred to the Roman audience, towards the putative source of the Teutones) – consisted more of shadow-boxing than any real military engagements. The tribes that Caesar sought to chastise were nomadic in character, and were able to melt away into the far recesses of their territory, keeping such a distance that it would have been suicidal for Caesar to have extended his supply lines far enough to reach them.

Lacking a new enemy to fight, Caesar turned his attention westwards. Although it was late in the campaigning season and there were threats of revolt in Gaul, and despite the fact that he lacked not only intelligence about the ancient Britons but a navy that was fit for purpose, Caesar had made up his mind. He marched his legions from the Rhine to the Channel and prepared to make a crossing. He billed the first expedition as an information-gathering exercise, which was not an unreasonable quest this late in the season. However, the beauty of sailing for Britain, in contrast to crossing the Rhine or campaigning elsewhere in Gaul, was that victory was not a prerequisite for glory. Britain, for the Romans of the time, was less of a place and more of a myth. Many saw the English Channel as the occidental boundary of the known world. Whatever lay beyond – Britain, Hibernia, Ultima Thule on the edge of the disc of the world, where the land was bound with ice and the sun was said never to set – was the stuff of tales told by eccentric travellers. A sailor, Pytheas, who had set out from Massalia in the third century BC, claimed to have circumnavigated the British Isles; but his account, the remains of which suggest he was true to his word, was savaged by ancient geographers. Many of them, however, could not even agree as to whether Britain was an island. Given such scepticism, merely to set foot in Britain with an army as witness would match Hercules's exploit of reaching the underworld; military success would be an agreeable addition, but by no means a necessity.

Under these circumstances, it is of little surprise that Caesar's preparations were rushed and inadequate. He sought information about the island from Gallic merchants who made regular voyages there. Given his earlier massacre of the sea-going Veneti, however, and their likely fear that any expedition of Caesar's would disrupt their trade to the island, they told him nothing of use. It is also unsurprising that they forewarned the British chiefs of his intended voyage. The chiefs, hoping to forestall an armed invasion, sent envoys across the Channel offering to submit. Caesar took these messages at face value, and interpreted them as a sign that the indigenous population was well disposed rather than hostile, thus deceiving himself as to the level of risk involved in an expedition.

Having discovered little of the geography from local sources, Caesar was compelled to gather the information himself. He sent out scouts in a reconnaissance boat, but their work was slapdash. They failed to find any suitable anchorages for large vessels. They were able to locate Dover – a site the British could easily defend – but they did not search far enough around the coast to find the nearby haven of Richborough, which would be used in the Roman conquest of Britain a century later. They also made no attempt to explore inland. Thus, they returned with a dearth of useful intelligence, but their presence had acted as a further warning to the Britons of Caesar's imminent arrival.

In his haste to depart, Caesar ordered transport ships to be gathered at Portus Itius (Boulogne). He was able to assemble eighty vessels. For his purposes, this was barely sufficient, as he wanted to carry two legions (12,000 men, a small number in itself for an expeditionary force) with their equipment across the Channel. Each vessel was probably no more than 20 metres long, but each had to carry up to 150 soldiers. The men were packed in tightly. Their heavy equipment had to be left behind and their rations were kept to an absolute minimum. They would have to rely on foraging once they arrived, adding to the vulnerability of their meagre headcount. The nature of the ships also made their task more difficult. They were high-sided, and unsuitable for a beach landing. If Caesar were able to find a suitable harbour, this would not present a difficulty; but failing this, his ships would have to disgorge his legions into deep water to fight their way onto shore. Although he could have waited over winter until he had built enough suitable ships and gathered helpful intelligence, none of these considerations troubled him. He set out at midnight on 24 August, 55 BC.

The view from the end of Deal pier, looking back towards the land, reveals a grand sweep of the Kent coast. The shore rolls from Ramsgate in the north, hazy in mist as it reaches into the sea, down through the gentle curve of Sandwich Bay to Richborough and the mingled seafronts of Deal and Walmer. Then the land turns and rises suddenly into the white wooded cliffs of South Foreland, where the coastline wheels out of sight and runs southwest towards Dover.

The pier is modern and spartan; unornamented barrel-iron legs march unevenly, bearing the concrete and girders of a bare walkway back to the shore. The coast lies low and flat behind a grey sea, the peaks of the skittering waves teased into silver points by the reluctant light of a pewter sky. The level expanse of the seafront is toothed with high, narrow houses, Dutch in aspect, and as muted in colour as the sea before them. The beach below is a high bank of sandy pebbles, mottled where the sea has drawn back over them, wrinkled by the pulse of the surf at high water mark.

It is here, where the steepness of the beach levels slightly between Deal and Walmer, that Caesar is believed to have come ashore. His intention had been to put into Dover, but on reaching it in the morning he saw the cliffs about the harbour lined with armed men, ready to throw projectiles at his ships should they approach the land. He ordered the fleet to follow him round the coast, and where the cliffs sank into a flatter beach he decided to disembark his men. Drawn up on the beach in their chariots, daubed with woad and festooned with gold torques, were the British warriors who had followed the Romans round the coast to their landing point.

It was a daunting task for the legionaries to jump from the high sides of the ships, heavy with weapons and battle dress, into the deep water where the Roman ships had dropped anchor. In his *Commentaries*, Caesar could at least divert the reader's attention from the consequences of his impetuous behaviour by praising of the bravery of his men. He made a point of lauding the standard-bearer of the 10th Legion, his favourite, who leapt into the water, proclaiming that he was doing his duty to Rome and Caesar. Nevertheless, Caesar managed to save the situation by good generalship, calling down fire from the ships' catapults, slingers and archers against the right flank of the Britons. Advancing through the water under this cover, they were at least able to secure a beachhead and construct a camp, and to haul the ships up on shore to keep them under guard.

Where Caesar made his beachhead camp on the coast at Walmer, a sprawl of fishing boats and their gear now sits sequestered behind metal barriers. The slate-heavy air is relieved by bright blue tubs and tarpaulins, stacked green crates, the winding of ropes and nets and waving ensigns. A man at a trestle table by the shore path hacks at the fat body of a skate with an instrument fearsome as a machete. The wind rattles the antennas and masts. This has always been a coast that has dreaded invasion. Behind the fishing boats stands the compact roseate form of Deal Castle, which has warded off a succession of enemies – the French, the Dutch, the Germans. But this is a construction of the Tudors, not Caesar.

Imagination and tradition invoke Caesar's presence in this place, where real traces of him are lacking. Wishful local tradition attaches evidence of Caesar to anything that might have suggested his presence. The Tudor antiquary, John Leland, records that in his own time, Deal boasted 'a fosse or great bank artificial betwixt the towne and se, and beginneth about Deale, and renneth a great way up toward S. Margaret's Clyfe, yn so much that sum suppose that this is the place where Caesar landed *in aperto litore*'. Many liked to think that this bank was created by Caesar. An Elizabethan traveller and mapmaker,

William Lambarde, makes such a record in verse: 'Renowned Dele doth vaunt itselfe,/ With Turrets newly rais'd:/ For monuments of Caesars host,/ A place in storie prais'd.' Some of the locals even called the bank 'Romesworke'. But in reality it was just a result of the coast inching forwards into the sea, which Leland concedes was the most likely explanation: 'Surely the fosse was made to kepe owte ennemyes there, or to defend the rage of the se; or I think rather the casting up beche or pible.'

It is not difficult to find real traces of the Romans near Deal. They can be found at Richborough Castle along the coast. One can visit Canterbury and descend below the streets to see subterranean mosaics rumpled by slow movements of the earth, or trace the line of Roman arches in the stonework of the city walls. There is a building

The Church of St Martin of Canterbury. The walls of the chancel, pictured above, are thought to have stood since late Roman times.

here whose walls are substantially Roman – the small church of St Martin's, whose sanctuary was built before the fourth century, and which sheltered St Augustine when he returned to bring Christianity to Britain in AD 597. But this is the inheritance of the invasion of Claudius in AD 43, and not of Caesar. One may say that Caesar paved the way for Claudius, but that aside, Caesar's own presence after his two abortive invasions is felt more in story, tradition and myth. The locations of his landings, his camps, his itineraries and his battles are speculative best guesses. At the beginning of the twentieth century, following much scholarly debate, the shore between Walmer and Deal was agreed to be the most plausible landing site for Caesar's forces.

But myths placing his arrival elsewhere remained stubbornly embedded in popular tradition and literary sources. The town of Romney, for example, much further west in Kent, claimed Caesar's landing for itself. The Elizabethan herbalist John Parkinson links his landing there with the ancient presence of *Urtica romana*, the common Roman nettle. William Camden, the Elizabethan historian, though disagreeing with Parkinson's story, records it for posterity:

> It is recorded (saith he) that at Romney, Julius Caesar landed with his soldiers, and there abode for a certain time, when the place (it is likely) was by them called Romania, and corruptly therefore Romeney or Romney. But for the growing of the Nettle in that place, it is reported, That the soldiers brought some of the Seed with them; and sowed it there for their use, to rub and chafe their Limbs, when through extreme cold they should be stiff and benumbed; being told before they came from home, that the Climate of Britain was so extreme cold, that it was not to be endured without some friction or rubbing to warm their blood, and to stir up their natural heat: since which time, it is thought, it hath continued there, rising yearly of its own sowing.

The site of Caesar's first battle when he returned to Britain in 54 BC, having scarcely escaped safely to Gaul after the winter storms of 55 BC, is placed by archaeologists at Bigbury Hill Fort, a few miles' walk northwest from the centre of Canterbury. The fort was an Iron Age stronghold of several hectares, a palisaded keep on the side of a hill framed by the River Stour and an ancient track whose route would later be followed by the Pilgrims' Way. It is the only encampment of this sort in the vicinity, and the best academic guess as to a site described by Caesar where the troops of the 7th Legion had to fight their way into a wooded hill fort whose gates had been sealed with pyramids of logs. The archaeological record suggests that habitation there came to an end around the middle of the first century BC. Excavations from the end of the 1800s found indigenous weapons – spears and axes – as well as agricultural and cooking gear – coulters, ploughshares and pot-hooks. They also found a set of human shackles, showing that

Bigbury Hill Fort, by the Pilgrims' Way near Canterbury. This was the most likely site of Caesar's first battle during his second invasion of Britain in 54 BC.

the place had some sort of involvement in the Roman slave trade. But that Caesar was present here is only a guess. Legends place his engagements with the local tribes elsewhere. Camden suggests the battle was fought southwest of Canterbury at the village of Chilham. The locals, he records approvingly, believed the name of their settlement to be a corruption of '*Julham*, as if one should say, *Julius's station, or house*; and, if I mistake not, they have truth on their side'. The place was imbued with magic, and Camden could not resist adding his own speculations to the local legend of the Romans:

> Below this town is a green *barrow*, said to be the bury-
> ing place of one *Jul-Laber* many ages since; who, some
> will tell you, was a *Giant*, others a *witch*. For my own
> part, imagining all along that there might be something
> of real Antiquity couch'd under that name, I am almost
> persuaded that *Laberius Drusus* the Tribune, slain by
> the Britains… was buried here; and that from him the
> *Barrow* was call'd *Jul-Laber*.

On his first invasion, Caesar was unable to progress very far from the coast. In his haste, he had ordered his cavalry to set sail at a different location from his infantry. The two forces were separated and the cavalry, because of adverse winds, were not able to reach Britain. This hampered him from moving inland. The itinerary of his second invasion is likely to have been a route from the coast at Walmer, past Canterbury, crossing the Thames at some unknown ford; then penetrating beyond St Albans to confront a local chieftain, Cassivellaunus, who, as Vercingétorix would do in Gaul, had managed to unite the disparate local tribes in resistance. But legend has expanded the scope of Caesar's travels and achievements. Although he had failed to make his landing at Dover, local tradition holds that he left his mark there. During the Middle Ages, a Roman lighthouse inside the precincts of Dover Castle was turned into the bell tower of the adjacent church of

St Mary in Castro. It was built around AD 50, following the invasion of Claudius, but legend gave it to Caesar. The pre-thirteenth-century *Chronicle of St Martin of Dover*, compiled at Dover Monastery, states that the tower was his, built as a treasury, and that Dover Castle beside it was built by Arviragus, the son of Cymbeline. Leland in Elizabeth's time says that he saw a Latin inscription in the church to this effect; and Lambarde remarks that in the Castle itself 'certeine vessels of olde wine, and salte' were kept in Caesar's memory 'whiche they affirme to be the remayne of suche prouision as he brought into it'.

Caesar's achievements as a builder go far beyond Dover. The castles of Canterbury and Rochester, both Norman, had accrued a Caesarian origin by the Tudor period. The twelfth- century Anglo-Norman poet Wace and later chroniclers state that Exeter owed its origins to Caesar after he built a camp on the River Exe. The Tower of London was also similarly honoured; in Shakespeare, it is 'Julius Caesar's ill-erected tower'. Across the country, there are a number of Iron Age forts and other early earthworks, entirely innocent of association with Caesar or the Romans, to which folk accounts have accorded the name of 'Caesar's Camp'.

Caesar was not only a builder, but a bringer of amenity. The twelfth-century chronicler William of Malmesbury attributes the hot springs of Bath to him. Such achievements could be brought about by magic; a fourteenth-century Anglo-Norman chronicler, Nicholas Trivet, records that Caesar also built Chichester. On completing it, he realized that it lacked running water. To remedy this, he sent a painting of the city, along with opulent gifts, to the poet Virgil (who at that time was in Greece), asking for the magical provision of a source. Virgil sent back an enchanted serpent sealed in a box, with instructions that it should only be opened where the source of water was desired. The messenger was curious to see what Virgil had sent; so, just before reaching Chichester, he opened the box a little to peek inside. The serpent sprang out and buried itself in the ground, and there the River Lavant welled up and found its course to the city.

If Chichester was out of Caesar's way, Scotland was even more so, but this did not prevent legends of him from taking root there. In medieval times, on the banks of the River Carron near Stenhousemuir, there stood a curious cylindrical stone building topped with a dome. It was called Arthur's-Hoven, for some locals said that King Arthur, when visiting Scotland, used to visit it for recreation. However, others, adhering to a more ancient tradition, called it Julius'-Hoff. The Northumbrian Chronicler, Sir Thomas Grey, writes in the 1350s that it was a pavilion erected by Caesar. John of Fordun, writing in the following generation, records various popular theories about Caesar's purpose in building the tower:

> He wanted to build this little house as a sort of extreme goal in the circus of Roman possessions, at the end of the world, and as a lasting sign of his famous soldiery, just as Hercules, in memory of his eternal fame and long labours, once fixed columns in the island of Gades at the western limit of Europe. Another version, particularly among the common people, is that Julius Caesar had this little house carried about with him, stone by stone, by his troops, and rebuilt each day wherever they camped, because he could rest more safely in it than in a tent; but that when he returned to Gaul he was in such a hurry that he decided to leave it behind, with the stones just laid together, as can be seen to this day.

A sixteenth-century historian, John Leslie, confirms the more popular account. Each stone was numbered, so that 'the place quahir euerie stane sould be sett mycht esilie be knawen and discernet frome vthir.' Later antiquaries theorized that the monument was a trophy set up in the second century AD by Quintus Lollius Urbicus, a Roman general of Berber origin, in the campaign that led to the establishment of the Antonine Wall, which ran close by its site. However, it is a question

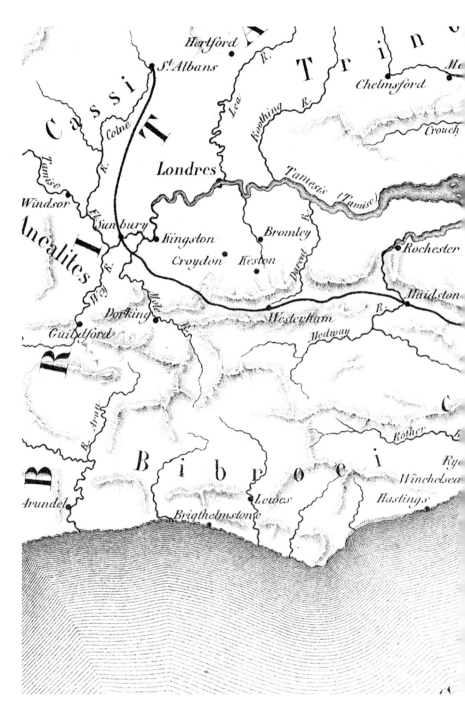

The routes of Caesar's invasions of Britain in 55 and 54 BC, according to Stoffel.

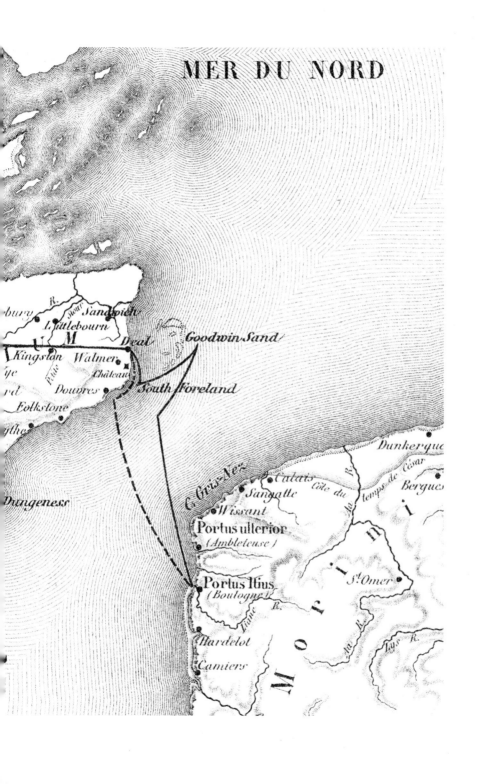

MER DU NORD

bury
R. *Stour*
Sandwich
Littlebourn
Deal
Goodwin Sand
M
Kingston
Walmer
Château
ye
Blue
Plue
rd
Douvres
South Foreland
Folkstone
the

Dungeness

Dunkerque
Côte de César
G. Gris-Nez
Calais
Bergues
Sangatte
Côte du
temps de César
Wissant
Portus ulterior
(Ambleteuse)

Portus Itius
(Boulogne)
St. Omer
Liane R.
M
O
R
I
N
I
Hardelot
au R.
Lys R.
Camiers

that will never be resolved. The tower was torn down in 1742 by an industrialist, Sir Michael Bruce, to provide material for a dam at the nearby Carron Iron Works.

But it was Caesar's Thames-side confrontation with Cassivellaunus that proved the most fertile source of myth. As has been briefly described above, Caesar pursued his forces from Kent to the Thames. Somewhere along its banks, Caesar records, Cassivellaunus attempted to prevent the Romans from crossing the river by positioning stakes below the water. Caesar negotiated this obstacle, only to be harried by the Briton's forces as he pressed northwards into their tribal

Arthur's Hoven, depicted in an eighteenth-century engraving shortly before its destruction in 1742.

heartlands. Cassivellaunus, however, lacked the diplomatic skills of Vercingétorix, and Caesar was able to exploit divisions in his alliance, securing the loyalty of various British chiefs by offering them protection. Cassivellaunus then attempted to raise the Kentish chiefs to Caesar's rear, but the tactic came to nothing. Caesar and Cassivellaunus met in a final battle at the latter's stronghold: a place, says Caesar, 'fenced with woods and marshes' in which the Briton had assembled a considerable quantity of men and cattle. Caesar was not especially impressed by his efforts: 'Now the Britons call it a stronghold when they have fortified a thick-set woodland with rampart and trench', but although it was 'particularly well-fortified by nature and handiwork', with a vigorous assault the Roman legionaries were able to overcome it without difficulty. Many of the British warriors were captured as they fled and put to death, perhaps because Caesar did not have the means to transport them back to Gaul as slaves.

Cassivellaunus's placing of stakes in the Thames – as well as the possible location of Caesar's crossing – held a particular fascination for later writers. The Venerable Bede, writing in the eighth century, says that the stakes were still visible in his day, 'the thickness of a man's thigh, and being encased in lead, stuck immovably in the depths of the river', though he omits to say where they were. King Alfred, in the translation he made of the late Roman imperial historian Orosius, said that Caesar had crossed the river at Wallingford (now in the southern part of Oxfordshire). Other writers, from the Renaissance to the present day, have suggested such locations as Teddington, Brentford, Southwark, Windsor and Kingston-upon-Thames. William Camden fixed the crossing at a place called Coway Stakes, not far from the present bridge at Walton-on-Thames, convinced by the name and by the fact that the river was easily fordable at this point, being, he claims, just a couple of metres deep. Others offered the same story as Camden, but in greater detail. In the anonymous thirteenth-century French romance, *Li Fet des Romains* ('The Deeds of the Romans'), Caesar managed to destroy the stakes by burning them down to the river bed with Greek fire.* John Weever, writing in 1767, suggests that there were elephants in Caesar's army: 'for I have heard that he terribly frighted the Britons with the sight of one at Coway Stakes, when he passed over the Thames'.

Similar uncertainty surrounds the location of the stronghold of Cassivellaunus, fortified with 'rampart and trench'. The *Chronicle of Dover Monastery* fixed it nowhere near St Albans, but rather near Bridge on Barham Downs in Kent. The battlefield, states the *Chronicle*, was to that day covered in mounds under which were concealed the bodies of those who fell. In following centuries, writers identified it with St Albans, Cassiobury in Hertfordshire (whose name, it was argued, preserved the name of the Catuvellauni, a tribe loyal to Cassivellaunus), Wendover, Pinner or Harrow, and even the City of London itself. In 1932, the archaeologist Sir Mortimer Wheeler excavated Devil's Dyke, an old earthwork on the edge of Wheathampstead, and suggested this as the site of Cassivellaunus's last stand. The Dyke, an abbreviated gully overgrown with brambles and shaded with canopies of beech, preserves such a brooding and numinous sense – despite being hemmed in on one side by semi-detached houses of the 1950s in orange brick – that it would be easy to believe it the site of Caesar's climactic battle. Although no hard evidence could be offered of Caesar's presence, in 1937 the dyke's new-found historical status led to its being given to the nation by its owner, Lord Brocket, to commemorate the coronation of George VI. An inscription was placed by its entrance stating that 'It was probably here that Julius Caesar defeated the British King Cassivellaunus.' As François Mitterrand looked to Bibracte, where the united Gallic chieftains acclaimed Vercingétorix as their war leader, as the first capital of France, so Wheathampstead – a small, agreeable Hertfordshire town – now plumes itself with the title 'First Capital of Britain'. No British politician, however, has attempted to exploit this modern myth.

---

* A flammable liquid substance that could burn on water, developed by the Byzantines for use in naval warfare. Its use by Caesar is a delicious anachronism.

Although the supposed locations of the battle between Caesar and Cassivellaunus have given rise to many myths, it is those that grew out of the confrontation itself that have the greatest power. In 1136, Geoffrey of Monmouth, a cleric of Welsh origins, completed a new work intended to shine some light on the early history of the British Isles, a period shrouded in darkness. Geoffrey claimed to have acquired an ancient book in the 'British tongue' (i.e., Welsh) that provided a detailed history of the islands from the dawn of the British nation through to the Saxon conquest. This ancient book formed the basis of his own work, the *Historia Regum Britanniae* ('The History of the Kings of Britain'). For all his claims about this 'ancient book', Geoffrey's account is, in fact, a weaving together of credible historical sources, including Caesar's *Commentaries* and the writings of Bede, with strange and fantastical stories whose likely source was his own vivid imagination. Geoffrey's probable design was to further the claims of the post-conquest Norman kings of England, and Rome plays an important role throughout his narrative. The Britons, like the Romans, owe their origins to Troy. The kingdom was founded by Brutus, the grandson of the Trojan prince Aeneas, who came to Britain as a refugee and gave it his name. He established London, originally with the name of Troia Nova ('New Troy') and later Trinovantum. His descendants, according to Geoffrey, turned Britain into an advanced and civilized culture: it was Roman before the Romans. The British developed cities, roads, even amphitheatres. Two early rulers, Dunvallo Molmutius and Queen Marcia, laid down laws for the people to follow. Later, there is a civil war. One of the rival kings, Brennius, is presented as being the Brennus who went to sack Rome in 390 BC, though in Geoffrey's account he is a Briton, not a Gaul.

Thus, when Caesar came, Britain was a nation as civilized and ancient as Rome, and with an equal claim to dignity and dominion in Europe. Because of their descent from Aeneas and Brutus, Caesar considered the British and the Romans to be kinsmen, but he saw the British as degenerate, 'living beyond the deep sea and quite cut off from the world'. It would be an easy matter, he thought, to force them to pay tribute to Rome. However, he wished to do this by sending them a simple order, as he did not wish to spill the blood of a kindred people.

He therefore despatched a letter to Cassivellaunus, seeking the submission of the British. Cassivellaunus wrote back a contemptuous reply. Pointing out their kindred descent, he stated: 'It is friendship you should have asked from us, not slavery... We have become so accustomed to the concept of liberty that we are completely ignorant of what is meant by submitting to slavery... we shall fight for our liberty and for our kingdom.'

Caesar thus made the first of his attacks on Britain. He came ashore at 'Dorobellum', perhaps a distant corruption of Deal, to face a fantastical array of the British nobility: Androgeus, duke of Trinovantum, and Tenvantius, duke of Cornwall, Cassivellaunus's nephews; the sub-kings Cridous of Albany, Gueithaet of Venedotia and Brittahel of Demetia; there was also Cassivellaunus's brother, a prince named Nennius. The Britons fell on Caesar's army as it came ashore. In the vicious combat that followed, Nennius and Caesar came face to face in the mêlée. Nennius had the chance to land a decisive blow, but Caesar struck him on the helmet and wounded him. When the Roman attempted to deal him a second and fatal blow, his sword stuck in Nennius's shield, and in the confusion he abandoned it. The sword was magic, named *Crocea Mors* ('Yellow Death') and its touch was fatal. Nennius took it and raged about the battlefield, killing Caesar's deputy Labienus and many others. By the end of the day, thanks to the heroics of Nennius, the Britons were masters of the field, and Caesar was forced to return to Gaul. Nennius, however, wounded by Caesar's sword, died fifteen days after the battle and was much lamented by his brother Cassivellaunus. He was buried at the north gate of Trinovantum, Caesar's sword beside him in his coffin.

The defeat brought Caesar to a sorry pass, according to Geoffrey. On his return to the continent, a rumour swirled around the subject

Gauls that Cassivellaunus had launched a fleet to pursue Caesar across the Channel. A revolt was brewing. Caesar, fearful of having to fight a war on two fronts, 'opened his treasure chests' to bribe every chieftain in turn to remain at peace: 'To the people he promised freedom, to those who had been disinherited he promised their lost possessions, and he even went so far as to promise liberation to the slaves.' Geoffrey of Monmouth is contemptuous: 'He who had once raged like a lion, as he took from them their all, now went about bleating like a gentle lamb, as with muted voice he spoke of the pleasure it caused him to be able to give everything back to them again.'

Two years later, once he had calmed the Gauls, Caesar attempted a second invasion of Britain. He launched a vast fleet carrying a huge army and sailed up the Thames towards Trinovantum. However, his ships cruised fecklessly into the famous stakes. 'Thousands of legionaries perished as the river water flowed into the holed ships and sucked them down.' Caesar did his best to get his bedraggled troops onto dry land and rally them for battle, but they were outnumbered three to one by the Britons on the river bank. Once again Caesar had to turn tail and flee back to the continent with the remains of his army.

According to Geoffrey of Monmouth, it was only by treachery that Caesar was able to triumph over the Britons. After defeating the Romans for a second time, Cassivellaunus ordered all the British leaders to assemble at Trinovantum for a feast to honour the gods who had given them victory. The day began with sacrifices: 'They offered forty thousand cows, a hundred thousand sheep and so many fowl of every kind that it was impossible to count them. They also sacrificed three hundred thousand wild animals of various species which they had caught in the woods.' Having feasted, the people turned their attention to games and sports. A wrestling match between Cassivellaunus's nephew and a man who was loyal to Androgeus ended in disagreement over who had won. A fight broke out, and Cassivellaunus's nephew was killed. Cassivellaunus was enraged, and the quarrel escalated to the point of civil war between himself and Androgeus.

Androgeus realized that his only chance of success was to appeal to Caesar for support; and Caesar jumped at the opportunity to avenge his own failures in Britain. This time, he landed at Richborough, and Cassivellaunus duly arrived to do battle with him. The fight was evenly poised. However, at the vital moment, Androgeus, hiding in a forest glade with 5,000 men, emerged to attack Cassivellaunus from the rear. Cassivellaunus's men were forced to retreat to a hilltop redoubt, but continued their dogged resistance. Caesar settled down to starve the British into submission. Androgeus, satisfied that Cassivellaunus had been humbled but not wishing to see him perish, begged Caesar to have mercy. The Roman, fearful of Androgeus's intentions, acceded to his request. Cassivellaunus agreed to pay an annual tribute to the Romans of 3,000 pounds of silver, and in return would retain his throne. Remarkably, Caesar and Cassivellaunus then became friends. Caesar wintered peacefully in Britain before returning to Gaul to gather an army together 'from every source and every race of mankind' and marching to Rome to attack Pompey.

The *Historia Regum Britanniae* was immensely popular throughout the Middle Ages and into the Renaissance, across Europe as well as in Britain. Its portrayal of the authority of the crown as stretching back to the ancient past and being equal in antiquity and dignity to Rome made it a favoured chronicle of the English and later the British monarchy. As late as the seventeenth century, kings and queens relied on Geoffrey of Monmouth for proof of their prerogatives. In Cassivellaunus's resistance to Caesar, and indeed in Brennius's earlier victory over Rome, the *Historia* also asserted British precedence over the continental powers.

Yet the appeal of the *Historia* was not solely down to this. Geoffrey also popularized the story of King Arthur, who before then was a shadowy figure who had only appeared briefly in a couple of early chronicles. Geoffrey, as he had done with Cassivellaunus, fleshed out the story of Arthur, such that he became one of the staples of European literature. Caesar and Cassivellaunus, being thus predecessors and players in the Arthurian myth, also entered by this route into the great canon of medieval European romance. The story of Caesar's invasion and Cassivellaunus's resistance echoes across Europe in English, French, Latin and Welsh retellings. Continental writers are prone to make Caesar a more dignified figure than does Geoffrey of Monmouth. Wace, writing in French, makes him a wise, courageous and generous leader, whose motives for attacking Britain – revenge for the earlier destruction of Rome by Brennius – are nothing but lofty. In surviving Welsh literature, Caesar does not appear in such an honourable light: for summoning Julius Caesar to Britain, Afarwy son of Lludd (perhaps a corruption of Androgeus) is reckoned in the *Red Book* to be one of the 'Three Dishonoured Men' of Britain. Cassivellaunus, under the name Caswallawn, is shown in a better light. He was, among other things, a maker of golden shoes. He took an army of 60,000 men to Gaul to rescue Fflur, the daughter of

Remains of the Roman fortifications at Richborough.

Mynach the Dwarf, from Mwrchan, a Gallic prince. He defeated the Romans who came to Mwrchan's aid and settled in Gascony where, according to the *Myvyrian Archaiology*,* his descendants were still known in medieval times.

In the fifteenth-century French prose romance *Perceforest*, Caesar invades Britain because one of his knights, Luces, is in love with a mythical queen of England. Luces has hatched a plot with the queen to destroy her husband's kingdom, and persuades Caesar – who has already been repulsed from the island once – to launch an attack on Britain in support of their conspiracy. In the course of his second invasion, Caesar destroys the British nobility and lays waste to the island. Thereafter, it is possible to wander for six months without finding 'city, town, borough or house'; the survivors of the invasion are reduced to living 'like dogs', and dressed only in deerskins. One Briton, Ourseau, vows revenge. He is able to acquire Caesar's lance, which has been cursed to the effect that it will be the instrument of Caesar's death. Ourseau's brother, Orsus Bouchesuave, fashions the lance into twelve daggers and gives them to Brutus and his co-conspirators in Rome. The plotters, together with Ourseau's brother, then use the daggers to stab Caesar in the Senate.

Caesar also made appearances in German literature. In Enikel's *Weltchronik*, written in the late thirteenth century, Caesar drives out 'cyclopes' and the 'monstrous flat-feet' from the German lands, before bestowing special honours on the German peoples for helping him to overcome the Senate and take absolute power. Only they, along with Caesar, are to be addressed with the honorific pronoun *Ihr*, and he ordains that anyone failing to do so will have their tongue cut out. This is but a prelude to their receiving Caesar's ultimate legacy: the Holy Roman Empire, the *imperium* of Rome, which would in future ages be passed down to the German peoples.

---

* *Myvyrian Archaiology* is a compilation of Welsh literature from the medieval period.

Caesar reports that his exploits in Britain – two quick invasions, both of which nearly led to his destruction through over-hasty preparation and failure to take the danger of revolt in Gaul seriously – earned him a twenty-day public thanksgiving in Rome at the command of the Senate. It was granted not so much for his military achievements, which were meagre, but for that fact that he had been able to reach the far and mysterious land of Britain. So it is perhaps fitting that his footprints in Britain are hidden in obscurity, and that his traces are to be found more in imagination, story and myth.

Mausoleum of the Julii, Glanum. Built around 40–20 BC,
it appears to be a tomb dedicated to a family of Gallic aristocrats
who were Romanized soon after Caesar's conquest, even
taking the name 'Julius'.

CHAPTER V

When in France

Unum illud propositum habebat, continere in amicitia civitates
'He had one purpose in mind, to keep the tribes friendly'

JULIUS CAESAR, *De Bello Gallico*, VIII.49

SAINT-RÉMY-DE-PROVENCE

·

GLANUM

·

MARSEILLES

·

COLONIES OF CAESAR

·

ROADS OF AGRIPPA

·

GALLIA: *'PARTES TRES'*

·

DIVIDING THE TRIBES

·

LYONS

·

CONDATE

·

ALTAR OF THE THREE GAULS

E AST OF BEAUCAIRE, not far from Saint-Rémy-de-Provence, a slip road from the Via Domitia leads towards the Gallo-Greek settlement of Glanum. It is a confusing road to follow, criss-crossed as it is by modern pathways and occasionally rerouted around newly built properties. But contemporary rustic villas are not the only distractions for those who walk this route.

The road to Glanum is surrounded by memorials to past suffering and the displaced: one of them commemorates 250 political refugees from Spain who assisted in public works during the Second World War; another remembers 10,000 French members of the International Brigades who went to support the Spanish Republic during the civil war of 1936–9. Nearby, behind a high stone wall, is a graveyard over-grown with brittle grasses, oak saplings and Scots pine. This ancient Jewish cemetery, used intermittently over the centuries, received its first dead in the 1400s, was abandoned when the Jews were expelled from Provence by King Louis XII in 1500, and then came back into use after the French Revolution. But in the twentieth century the site was closed again for good. A sign by the gate declares a verse of the Psalmist: *L'Eternel m'a châtié sévèrement, mais il ne m'a pas livré à la mort* – 'The Lord hath sorely chastised me: but he has not given me over unto death.'

But persistence will bring its reward: the track passes along an old gully, where the powdery ground is relieved by the dappled orange of marsh fritillaries basking in the heat, and then up on to a plateau where the first Roman monuments come into sight. They stand alone, brilliant against the lapis lazuli sky, an arch and a tower over 15 metres high, isolated from the rest of Glanum by the modern road that cuts across from Les Baux to Rémy. Their isolation does not detract from their dignity. They are locally known as Les Antiques ('The Antiquities'). The ancient slip road from the Via Domitia would have passed beneath the arch into the town. The principal role of the arch was to demarcate the territory of the settlement – considered not just civilized but also sacred – from the profane and dangerous hinterland beyond. Although the arch has suffered the ravages of time – the upper storey is missing and large portions of the carved marble facings have been pulled down – it still retains a sense of its original function as a holy portal.

However, this is not the only role of the arch. It is also a preserver of memories. As is inevitable for anything related to Caesar, many of these memories are imagined. It was widely believed in the nineteenth century that the arch and adjacent tower were the work of Caesar himself, thrown up shortly after his campaign to commemorate not only his own conquest, but also the earlier victories of Marius. Indeed,

The Arch of Glanum, built around 20 BC and decorated with burgeoning fruits and reliefs of Gauls in chains.

an embankment at the site is still called the 'Wall of Marius'. But the style of the arch suggests a later date, around 20 BC, similar to monuments being built in Rome under Augustus. Thus the arch reflects not so much the immediate moment of conquest, but a memory of the early period of Roman control: a reflection of how the Roman empire, having itself endured the trauma of the long-running civil war and the triumph of Augustus as the first emperor, attempted to digest and assimilate the newly conquered territory of Gaul.

The arch has two, somewhat contrasting, stories to tell. The immediately striking thing about it, whether one approaches it from the ruins of Glanum or via the slip road from the Via Domitia, is that each side is framed by two tall fluted columns. In each of the four panels made by these columnar frames are two figures, more than life size. Some are better preserved than others, but their common subject matter is clear. At least one of the figures on each panel is male: strong, muscular, mostly naked, standing with a firm and determined contrapposto. These are Gauls. Each of them is in chains: chained at the neck, bound at the wrists, arms tied behind the back. Next to certain of the figures are piles of Gallic arms, captured and stacked as trophies of victory. For good measure, the men are chained to these also. On top of these trophies sit women. One appears to be a Gaul, weeping for her lover from whom she is soon to be separated. Another, more richly dressed but now lacking a head, may be a personification of Rome, guarding the arms – forever forfeit – of vanquished rebel tribes. Yet the male figures in chains are not all presented in their habitual indigenous innocence. One wears a Gallic coat, a *sagun*, but not in the normal fashion. Instead, it is draped around him in the manner of a Roman toga, as if he had been touched by the civilization of Rome, but had then foolishly chosen to turn away from it.

This is not the only time that a Gaul in chains appears in Roman imagery. A statue of a defeated Gallic warrior, kneeling and bound, was found in a fountain in Glanum itself. Captive Gauls also appear on the arches of Carpentras and Orange, and they featured as a motif on contemporary Roman coinage. Gaul was a land in chains, held by the might of Rome: this was a primary fact, not to be forgotten.

But on the arch at Glanum these images of Gaul held in bondage are counterbalanced by something very different. It appears when one comes closer to the arch and finally passes underneath it. The lip of the arch and the vault underneath do not share the quiet flat surface of the greater part of the monument; they are covered with carvings of flowers, plants and fruit. In this, there is nothing lightly ornamental, polite or reserved. There are vines, bulging clusters of grapes, pomegranates, apples, bundles of oak rich with acorns, laurels bearing berries, pine cones – all winding and writhing about each other, enmeshing, threatening to burst out of the narrow channel allotted to them.

The theme continues beneath the arch. Flowers erupt from the stone, and every corner and crevice of the vault is alive with tendril

Detail of the Arch of Glanum, showing the lush fruits, flowers and vegetation suggestive of Rome's beneficence.

and leaf. There is a dizzying canopy of abundance, making the very stone seem more animate and vital than the dusty ground of the plateau round about. And all this bounty, this vigour and renewal springs from the touch and the domination of Rome.

With the conquest of Caesar, Gaul was everywhere in chains. However, the tightness of the bonds varied. They developed over time and changed in nature from place to place. Sometimes they expressed themselves in violence and the destruction of cultures and lifestyle. In other ways and at different times they took the form of nudges and inducements, rewards offered, reputation and proximity to power in return for supporting the Roman machine.

Caesar departed Gaul in 50 BC. Following his victory at Alésia the threat of another full-scale revolt against the Roman presence had been virtually eliminated. However, this did not prevent the continuation of low-level unrest. Caesar and his commanders therefore spent their remaining time in Gaul engaged in mopping-up actions of spiralling brutality. The Carnutes, dwelling between the Seine and the Loire, were driven from their homes in midwinter and left to starve without shelter in the freezing storms of the season. In the northeast, the Bellovaci were crushed following a persistent guerrilla campaign. The fighting men of Uxellodunum (Puy d'Issolud, near Cahors) who held out in a siege but later surrendered, had their right hands cut off as an exemplary punishment.

Caesar, having won his grand victory in the provinces, was getting impatient with these engagements. His term of office was coming to an end, and he did not want to be tied down in policing activities. His concern was now with Rome, with his opponents in the Senate and his rivalry with Pompey for control of the empire. It seemed that under these external pressures, Gaul could be pacified with remarkable speed. During the winter of 50 BC, his last full year in office, Caesar, having used violence, turned to kindness to secure Roman dominance. Aulus Hirtius, who completed the last book of Caesar's *Commentaries*, briefly notes that Caesar 'addressed the tribes in terms of honour, gave very considerable presents to the chiefs, and imposed no new burdens'. By this sudden display of comradely gentleness after so many years of ruthlessness, the Gallic chiefs, worn out by conflict, were easily kept in peace 'under better terms of obedience', notes Hirtius.

These few comments of Hirtius summarize most of what can be known about the first attempts of Rome to develop a political settlement for Gaul. There were no immediate signs of a grand plan in the immediate aftermath of the Gallic campaign. Rome expressed power by destroying implacable opponents and co-opting the tractable chiefs via financial incentives and the confirmation of their own authority in Gallic society. In the first instance, Caesar used the hierarchies already in place to carry out the functions of government on behalf of the Romans. In reality, he had little choice. Rome was on the verge of being convulsed by the penultimate round of its long-running civil war; confrontation between Caesar and Pompey was looming. The time and resources required to develop formal mechanisms of government and the grand manifestations of Roman power in the far-flung frontier regions of Gaul were lacking. Besides, given the scale of the devastation, it would not have been practical to impose in short order the elaborate institutions of Roman government on the newly captured territories.

Thus for the first few years following the conquest, Gallia Comata was administered as part of Transalpine Gaul. Comata was under the authority of the same governor, and there is no sign that Rome attempted to make any changes there during this period. It was the question of security throughout Gallia Comata that weighed most on the Roman mind; it has been suggested by some modern historians that the region was subjected to some form of martial law at this time. Gallic discontent continued to manifest itself. In 46 BC, the first governor after Caesar, Junius Brutus Albinus, was compelled to put down a further uprising among the Bellovaci, who had been one of the last people to fight Caesar. In 44 BC, it was a matter for great relief in Rome that the Gallic tribes made a promise to Aulus Hirtius, by then governor of Gaul, that they would not cause any difficulties following the assassination of Caesar, who two years before his death had assumed supreme power in Rome. However, this peace of mind was short lived. The following year, the general Lucius Munatius Plancus was called to campaign on the Rhine against the Raeti (a tribal federation originally based in the Alps). Such disturbances were to continue for another three decades.

Roman intervention following the conquest of Comata was more pronounced in Transalpine Gaul than in the newly captured areas. This was partly as a result of the civil war; Caesar looked to Gaul to supply him with men and resources during his battle with Pompey. In 49 BC, when Massalia – still an independent Greek city in the midst of a Roman territory – refused to support Caesar in the war, his forces besieged the city and, after an artillery bombardment, captured it. It was stripped of all of its remaining territories and was left with only nominal independence. As Massalia was brought more firmly under Roman influence, so the Roman presence was made more strongly known in the wider hinterland of Transalpine Gaul. Following Caesar's victory over Pompey in 46 BC, many of his veterans were settled in the transalpine colonies of Narbonne, Béziers, Fréjus and Orange. The settlements of Nîmes and Vienne on the Rhone were also given 'Latin Rights' which endowed their inhabitants with a number of liberties and allowed those in positions of authority to claim Roman citizenship.

It might have been that the foundation of these colonies in Transalpine Gaul was part of a wider plan that Caesar himself had conceived for the long-term settlement of Gaul. Had he escaped assassination in 44 BC, the subsequent developments in Gaul (later attributed to the agency of others) might in fact have been shown to be Caesar's initiatives. However, this will never be known. We can only guess as to whether Caesar had a grand scheme for establishing a proper government in Gallia Comata; it is possible – given his reforms in Rome itself in 46 BC, including changes to the calendar and to the institutions of central government – that putting Gaul in order could well have been on his mind. However, in the absence of any proof, the credit for fully incorporating Gaul into the empire must fall not to Caesar but to others.

The first permanent Roman institutions on the fringes of Gallia Comata were founded shortly after Caesar's assassination. In 43 BC, Plancus, who had defeated the Raeti, established two colonies: Lugdunum (Lyons) and Augusta Raurica, a forerunner to Basel. These colonies, in the first instance, served the purpose of defending the transalpine region against the potential instability of Comata. They also allowed troops to be levied who might then participate in the civil war.

It was when authority over the empire was divided between Octavian (later known as Augustus; Caesar's nephew and adopted son) and Mark Antony in 40 BC that closer attention was paid to the newly captured lands. Mark Antony took charge in the east; the west was Octavian's domain. Gaul, as a fresh and substantial part of Octavian's sphere of authority, demanded his particular consideration. The need to make it secure both against Gallic uprisings and external incursions was one question; the placing of Comata's government on a more regular footing was another. The new lands, as they had done for Caesar, also provided Octavian with an opportunity. Given their size and potential for generating wealth and manpower, he would have seen that they might supply him with a powerbase and a well of resources – an important consideration should he come into conflict with Mark Antony in a further round of civil war, as indeed would come to pass.

Octavian made his first visit to Gaul in 39 BC. He appointed one of his most capable and trusted lieutenants, Agrippa, as his governor. It was becoming clear that, in the future, the real areas of unrest were likely to be the northeast and the southwest of Gaul. Both regions bordered on areas either uncontrolled by or not fully under the control of Rome. The northeast looked towards the Rhine and the tribal lands of the Germanic peoples. The southwest lay next to the Spanish provinces, where the authority of Rome was still weak. In both cases, the unruly neighbouring populations would encourage revolt in the adjacent parts of Gaul. Bearing this in mind, Agrippa began to develop an infrastructure that would allow for its defence and security.

The development of a road network was a top priority. This was, in the beginning, a military undertaking. It had to allow for the swift movement of troops from the Italian heartland to the colonial towns in Gaul, and then on to the unsettled frontiers in the northeast and southwest. It is obvious that roads had existed in pre-Roman times, and were in some cases substantial enough to withstand reasonably heavy wheeled transport. Indeed, Caesar would never have managed his conquest without such infrastructure. However, nothing built before Agrippa's governorship of Gallia Comata would have equalled the Roman constructions for sturdiness or safety: all-weather, stone-clad and regularly policed.

Agrippa was meticulous in his work. It appears that he undertook a survey of Gaul, giving both a figure for the length of its coastline as well as the distances from coast to coast. Armed with this information, he laid out the skeleton of Rome's first road network in Gaul, probably between 39 and 27 BC. As the geographer Strabo observes, he took the recently founded colony of Lyons as the hub of his network, since it was 'in the centre of the country: an acropolis, as it were, not only because the rivers meet there, but also because it is near all parts of the country'. From Lugdunum, a number of roads radiated outwards. One branch led to the Roman towns on the Rhône, including Arles, Nîmes, Orange and Vienne, linking to the earlier Via Domitia. A western arm led to Saintes in the region of Aquitaine on the western coast, allowing access to the southwest. A northwestern branch led to Boulogne, thus facilitating trade with Britain and laying the groundwork for any future attack on the island. An eastern branch connected Lyons to Augusta Raurica and the regions near the territory of the Helvetii. A final branch proceeded northeast, running to Cologne (then called Oppidum Ubiorum, a stronghold founded by the Ubii tribe in 38 BC).

Once Rome's physical presence could be seen on the ground and its will enforced by the easier movement of troops, the administrative division of the land could proceed. The unwieldy entity of Transalpine Gaul, which had ingested the vast new territories of Gallia Comata, was broken up. The original Roman province of Transalpine Gaul became Gallia Narbonensis, named after Narbo (Narbonne), one of the leading colonies on its southern coast. Gallia Comata,

A well-preserved section of the Via Domitia outside Ambrussum, complete with chariot-wheel ruts.

approximately following Caesar's own division of Gaul at the beginning of his *Commentaries*, was divided into three parts. The southern part, from the Seine to the Garonne, was Gallia Lugdunensis, or Lyonese Gaul. The northern part, from the Scheldt to the Seine, was Gallia Belgica, Belgic Gaul. The southwestern part, from the Garonne to the Pyrenees, became Gallica Aquitania, Aquitaine Gaul. These three new provinces were known as the Tres Galliae, the 'Three Gauls'.

In this apparently innocuous process of administrative division, it may be possible to detect traces of Caesar's own manipulation of identities. Some have argued that 'Gaul' as a geographical concept among the Romans and perhaps among those living in the territory bounded by modern-day France, only applied to Lyonese and Narbonese Gaul. Culturally and linguistically, although there was a certain communion of language and culture across the regions, Belgica and Aquitania were distinct regions that were never thought of by Romans or the indigenous peoples as being Gaul. When Caesar starts his *Commentaries* with the famous statement '*Gallia est omnis divisa in partes tres*' ('Gaul as a whole is divided into three parts'), he is guilty of misrepresenting the idea of Gaul. He appropriates the term and applies it to different areas of Europe – Belgica, Aquitaine – as a justification for his conquests. If Belgica and Aquitaine went under those names, there was little reason for Caesar, as a governor of Transalpine and Cisalpine Gaul, to stray into them. If, however, they were indeed to be seen as part of Gaul, albeit more distant, Caesar could more easily argue that he had business there as a governor of the southern regions of 'Gaul'. The result of this was a new foundation for the idea of Gaul – a formerly fragmented region that extended across a large part of Europe, generated by an imperial idea from the Mediterranean world, and later to be inherited by the successors of Rome: the French.

The problem of geographical division applied at a lower level: how should the Gallic tribal states be classified and incorporated into a regular Roman system of government? As entities, they did not fit easily into the Roman mindset. The Romans were well used to dealing with small-scale Mediterranean city-states, each consisting of its own city with a hinterland but no other intermediate towns or settlements of political weight. This did not gel easily with the Gallic tribes extended over large tracts of land, which might possess a number of different *oppida* of unclear political function. It was only by an ingenious legal fiction that Rome was able to digest the tribal structure into its own imperial hierarchies. Each tribe was labelled a city-state (or *civitas*); the whole territory of a tribe was designated, in essence, as a city in itself. One foundation in the tribal region would be seen as the *civitas* capital, from which the functions of local government would be administered. From these centres, the ways and commands of Rome would be projected more widely across the Gallic peoples and landscape.

The arrangement of the *civitates* bore signs of the trauma of the conquest. It was an opportunity for the Romans to rationalize the arrangement of Gallic tribes. Many tribal names that had existed before Caesar's time now vanished. The Mandubii, who had been caught in the middle of the siege of Alésia, disappeared as a separate tribal entity. Other tribes found themselves amalgamated. In Belgica, the Aduatuci, the Eburones and the Condrusi, along with a number of others, were now lumped together as the Tungri. In Aquitaine, thirty original tribes were now merged into nine. These amalgamations were not only for the sake of administrative convenience; they pointed to the number of Gauls who had died, been taken as slaves, or migrated as soldiers since Caesar's arrival in Gaul. Individual tribes, shrunk by the turmoil, simply ceased to be viable. More than this, the frontiers of the three new Gallic provinces were arranged so that the three most powerful tribes in the heart of Gaul – the Aedui, the Arverni and the Sequani – were separated, none of them sharing the same new province.

With the reordering of the tribes came a census of the Three Gauls in 22 BC, a process that was to be repeated every fifteen to twenty-five years. And with the census came the development of the tax system. To be sure, Roman taxes had been imposed on the conquered territories since the beginning. However, their organization had been vague. All conquered peoples had to pay a tribute to Rome as a mark of their nominally captive status. Tribute money was in essence a substitute for service as a slave, to which any people conquered by Rome were technically liable in the first instance. However, Caesar had left everything far from consistent. Before his departure he had used remission of the tribute as a tool to pacify a number of the tribal chiefs to prevent disorder after his return to Italy. These individual privileges appear to have been clawed back from various tribes over the course of time. The system developed so that all had to pay the *tributum soli*, a land tax of probably 10 per cent, and the *tributum capitis*, a poll tax at an unknown rate. There was also the *quadragesima Galliarum*, a 2½ per cent customs tax on goods passing through land or sea frontiers; the *centesima venalis*, a sales tax of one percent; and the *vicesima libertatis*, a 5 per cent tax on the freeing of slaves.

With taxes came oppressive officialdom. The historian Cassius Dio preserves the story of one administrator, Licinius, who came to prominence early in the emperorship of Augustus, around 15 BC. So overbearing was his behaviour that the gods even sent a portent to warn the Gauls when he assumed office: a giant sea monster, six metres wide and eighteen metres long 'resembling a woman except for its head', was washed up on the shore. Licinius was himself a Gaul, captured by Caesar and taken as one of his personal slaves. However, Caesar later freed him, and – thanks presumably to his knowledge of Gaul and his connections – he was able to secure a high position in the new Gallic administration. Licinius, writes Cassius Dio, 'with his combination of barbarian avarice and Roman dignity, tried to overthrow everyone who was ever counted superior to him and to destroy everyone who was strong'. He was prolific in schemes for lining his pockets and those of his friends. One of his most brazen made use of a system whereby people paid the tribute on a monthly basis; he told them that there were in fact fourteen months in the year, saying that December (as its name suggested, and as had been the case long ago) was in fact only the tenth month, and that there were four months beyond it. Dio suggests that Augustus turned a blind eye to Licinius, and even accepted a vast bribe of Gallic treasure in return for ensuring that the administrator faced no punishment for his corruption.

Such oppression could even come directly from the emperor himself. According to Cassius Dio, in AD 40 the emperor Caligula had exhausted the revenue of Italy. He therefore proceeded to Gaul on the pretence that he was going to make war across the Rhine, but in fact to extort money from the province. He marched off with a train of 'many actors, many gladiators, horses, women, and all the other trappings of luxury'. Having made a feint first towards the Rhine and then towards a new invasion of Britain, he settled down to seek forced gifts from the wealthy populace, not without the occasional murder to encourage them to comply. He then hit on the idea of selling off antiques and curios of the imperial family to the Gauls of Lugdunum in a strange charade of an auction. He sold each item off by citing 'the fame of the persons who had once used them. Thus he would make some comment on each one, such as, "This belonged to my father," "This to my mother," "This to my grandfather," "This to my great-grandfather," "This Egyptian piece was Antony's, the prize of victory for Augustus."' His rapine went to finance grand military parades at Lugdunum to commemorate victories that he had not actually won.

It is surprising that there was little in the way of open unrest in direct response to taxation and such behaviour from imperial elites. A revolt in AD 21 by two Gallic noblemen, Florus and Sacrovir, was attributable, according to Tacitus, to heavy taxation and indebtedness at high rates of interest. However, such debts may have been caused not only by the need to borrow to pay the taxes, but because Gauls were tempted to spend more money on new building and newly available Roman accoutrements. Perhaps on this account, the rebellion was poorly supported by the Gauls, and was quickly snuffed out and forgotten.

On top of Roman oppression via taxes came oppression of culture. The practices of Druids, whom Caesar states carried out vast human sacrifices, burning convicted criminals or even scores of innocent victims encased in giant wicker men to appease 'the majesty of the immortal gods', were repellent to the Romans. It is possible that the Romans also saw them as a potential focus of opposition to their rule: a venerable order that acted as the repository of law, philosophy and ritual religious practice transcending many of the tribal divisions across Gaul, they might well have been able to act as a unifying force to stand against the new imperial masters. Whatever the reason, the Romans progressively clamped down on the Druids. Augustus forbade any Roman citizen from engaging in Druidic activity. Two later emperors, Tiberius and Claudius, took measures to ban the Druidic order in the first century AD. 'Such being the fact,' remarks Pliny the Elder, 'we cannot too highly appreciate the obligation that is due to the Roman people, for having put an end to those monstrous rites, in accordance with which, to murder a man was to do an act of the greatest devoutness...'

Thus in religion, in taxes, in government, in the organization of their tribes, after Caesar's departure the shades of the Roman prison house closed in on the ancient life and order of the Gauls.

The flowers on the arch of Glanum, however, were not set up to mock the conquered Gauls. The Romanization of Gaul may have come at a fearful price, but it would lead, in time, to a rich cultural flowering.

Anyone departing from Glanum in the midsummer of 12 BC and journeying north would have found ample evidence for this. It was not only the town of Glanum itself that had by this time been largely and lavishly rebuilt, along with the similarly flourishing colonies on the route – Orange (Arausio), Vienne with its grand new walls – but also the new metropolis at the radial point of Agrippa's road network, Lugdunum (Lyons).

It is not for nothing that Strabo uses the word 'acropolis' to describe Lyons. In the heart of the old town, the Fourvière Hill rises in a meander of the Saône, a huge limestone crag that then slopes down gently northwestwards to merge into the flat panorama of the new city. Here it was that the Roman colony was founded in 43 BC. Around the open ruins of the original Roman town, the succession of whitewashed alleys and stone staircases feel heavy with the ennui of a long civilization.

The Roman theatre and the odeon* near the peak of the hill, both originally an endowment of Augustus, offer support for this idea of a cultural flowering. So do the forum and original grid of streets, laid out by the city's founder, Plancus – now hidden, but suggested by the row of shops behind the theatre, their square-stone walls still standing, looking out over a well-laid street of lozengey granite slabs undercut by arched sewers and concealed terracotta water-pipes.

But the strongest evidence for the notion is found beyond the acropolis and the heart of the old Roman city. Descending the streets and recrossing the Saône, one comes to a wide and flattish plain between the Saône and the Rhône, before the land tails into a narrow peninsular. Here on the plain was the original site of a Gallic village, Condate. The name itself may mean 'confluence', and the village would have been a prosperous entrepôt for trade and portage between the two rivers. Now it is fully a district of Lyons. Some parts of the suburb, although busier than the Fourvière Hill, preserve their otherworldly air. The buildings of the Montée de la Grande-Côte, one of the gently curving narrow medieval lanes, appear candy-coloured, pearl-dusted, their irregular facades both benevolent and louring, pierced with stone arches and high mullioned windows. The area, later called the Quartier Croix-Rouge, was home for centuries to the silk workers of Lyons, and was regularly wracked by their uprisings. Their cry was 'Vivre libre en travaillant ou mourir en combattant!'

---

* A Roman odeon was a small roofed theatre intended primarily for performances of music and poetry.

('Live free working or die fighting!'). A plaque there even commemorates the founding in 1835 of the first French workers' co-operative store. But the absence of their uproar and the noise of their factories seem to add to the heaviness of the peace.

Then, if you turn a corner into the Rue Burdeau, the peace and lightness suddenly disappears. The street is regular, straight, oily in patina; the windows are regular above, the shops shuttered; signs plead for tenants. The graffiti becomes more direct, more political: 'I hate the invader'; *Angleterre avait Maggie Thatcher – Aujourd'hui La France a Maggie Hollande, Maggie Valls et Maggie Macron...* ('England had Maggie Thatcher – today, France has Maggie Hollande, Maggie Valls and Maggie Macron'). The sullen and discontented Rue Burdeau shows nothing of its Roman past; but it was arguably here that, in 12 BC, one of the most important endowments was made to Roman Gaul, going to the heart of the nature of its government and also its very identity.

Fourvière, the theatre and odeon complex in the heart of Roman Lyons.

What disturbances there were in Gaul after the rise to power of Octavian were concentrated, as Agrippa had foreseen, in the northeast and southwest. The northeast was the more troublesome of the two regions, and military campaigns were launched there in 30–29 BC and again in 19–17 BC. In 16 BC Germanic tribes beyond the Rhine captured and crucified a number of Roman citizens who were travelling in their territory – presumably merchants – and then pressed on to attack deep into Gaul. A detachment of Roman cavalry was despatched to repel the Germanic fighters, but they were ambushed by their enemies. The Roman governor, Lollius Paulinus, was himself present at the defeat, which counted as a serious humiliation for Rome. The emperor Augustus was troubled at the setback and made an extended visit to Gaul, lasting for three years, from 16 BC. He was not only able to oversee the final conquest of the difficult and independent high Alpine passes to secure the route between Gaul and Italy (marking the victory with the building of the Tropaeum Alpium at La Turbie near Monaco), but also began to prepare for a more major assault against the Germanic tribes in the northwest, to be led by his stepson Drusus. The prospect of such an operation was not something Augustus would have treated lightly. The large-scale movement of troops and their concentration in a particular area could provoke local unrest, or even rebellion on the part of the troops themselves. Moreover, the preparation of such an expeditionary force would have necessitated an extraordinary levy of taxes. A new census to facilitate the levy was planned for 12 BC and threatened to cause further discontent. Under these circumstances it would have been especially prudent to take measures to ensure the loyalty of the Gauls.

In 12 BC, before Drusus left for the new campaign, he invited a representative from each of the sixty *civitates* in the Three Gauls to assemble together at Lugdunum. The occasion was the inauguration of an altar, which stood where the Rue Burdeau now runs. It was a grand affair. Its base was marble, about 50 metres long. Strabo records that it bore 'an inscription of the names of the tribes, sixty in number' and also 'images from these tribes, one from each tribe', although the images may have come later. On either side there were tall Ionic columns in rich red Egyptian porphyry, each topped with winged statues of the goddess of victory. Beside it was a small amphitheatre in which the representatives of the *civitates* could gather. Its dedication was to Rome and to Emperor Augustus. The date chosen for the representatives to assemble annually thereafter was 1 August: the anniversary of Augustus's defeat of Cleopatra at Alexandria in Egypt.

The altar grew more elaborate as the empire went on, but disappeared afterwards. The only visible remains are the porphyry columns, which were recovered in the eleventh century, sawn in half and used in the nearby basilica of Saint-Martin d'Ainay. Its appearance is known from literary accounts, inscriptions and coins. But the altar's disappearance belied its long-term importance. Worship of the imperial cult by the leaders of defeated Gaul appears at first to be the most abject form of self-degredation; inviting a subject people to abase themselves before the imperial genius would hardly seem the most effective way to secure their abiding loyalty. However, although the altar was a way of demanding a display of fidelity, it was by the same token a means of enfranchising the peoples of the Three Gauls.

Lugdunum was by no means unique in the empire, or indeed in Gaul, in having an altar dedicated to the worship of the imperial genius. However, it was distinct from the others in a number of ways. Before long, the priesthood and its establishment had become unusually elaborate. There was not only the *sacerdos* (priest) himself, but also the *iudex arcae Galliarum* and the *allectus arcae Galliarum*, not to mention the *inquisitor Galliarum*, the *tabularius Galliarum* and the *iudex arcae ferariarum*. It seems that each of these officials (whose titles are not easily translatable) had a role in collecting and disbursing the funds for the altar, financing its business and the festivities surrounding the annual assembly. Their roles might also have included involvement in the civil administration at Lugdunum. Although Roman citizens, they were necessarily of Gallic origin; the *sacerdos* himself at least (and perhaps the others) was elected by the representatives from the Gallic *civitates*.

The names of many of these priestly officials survive in inscriptions. A large number are held at the Gallo-Roman Museum in Lyons. It is possible to wander in the museum's cool subterranean vaults, passing by countless proud marble blocks that advertise to posterity in elegantly chiselled lettering the careers of this host of Gauls who took on a Roman mantle and wallowed in the glory of imported clerical offices. 'To Caius Ullatius... son of Ullatius Priscus, Priest of the Temple of both our Caesars within the Temple of Rome and Augusti at the Confluence of the Saone and the Rhone, the first of the Segusiavi to be so honoured'; 'To Quintus Licinius Ultor, son of Licinius Taurus, who, at the age of twenty-two was entrusted with the administration, after that of his father, of the Altar Priesthood, the Three Provinces [of Gaul] have raised this statue...'

The role of the imperial altar's priesthood was to praise Rome and foster the loyalty of the Gauls. But it also created a position and a

The Altar of the Three Gauls, as depicted on a dupondius coin issued during the reign of Augustus.

hierarchy of great prestige that was Roman in appearance, but peopled and controlled by Gauls. An imperial overlord that was lacking in confidence would never have created such an alternative centre of power and potential focal point for discontent. But imperial Rome was not unconfident in this way. It was its business to create such positions of prestige and alternative centres. Up to and well beyond the time of Julius Caesar, the apparatus of provincial government was tiny in relation to the areas it had to administer and the duties it had to carry out. Only a handful of officials and administrative staff were ever available to be sent from Rome. It was thus the case in Gaul that most of the work of government was passed on to the Gauls themselves. Although the manner of internal government within the *civitates* was nominally a matter for the Gallic tribes, the Gauls developed their own institutions modelled on those of the Roman provincial centres and colonies, staffed by Gauls who imitated Roman custom. The Gauls began to boast of their *aediles*, their town councils and *duoviri*, or *magistri pagi*. Prestige conferred by blood feud, the size of a warrior retinue or the number of heads on display on the lintel of one's front door quickly became a thing of the past. Now status largely came via the possession of these offices, much as it would for a Roman noble; and their holders probably wielded much more effective, intricate and stable power over their own peoples than was ever possible under the old pre-Roman dispensation.

Such emancipation went back to the very time of the conquest. The more fortunate of the subject peoples were offered not only positions at home, but also the chance to participate in the life of the wider empire. Julius Caesar offered citizenship to Gallic nobles who assisted him. Noblemen such as Togirix, an Aeduan chief, added Caesar's name to his own – Gaius Julius Caesar – to create his own Roman name: Gaius Julius Togirix. A number accompanied Caesar to fight on his behalf in the civil wars against Pompey. Many members of the Gallic warrior class joined the Roman army as auxiliaries, thus gaining the opportunity to travel widely, give vent to their warlike ambitions, accrue wealth, learn the Latin language and acquire the privileges of citizenship, before returning with the cachet attached to a military career and an inclination to adhere to Roman ways in their Gallic homeland.

The opportunity of association with the imperial family likewise added to the sense of the importance of the Three Gauls. Many of the colonies and settlements were named or renamed in part after members of the royal family: Augustodunum (Autun); Augustonemetum (Clermont-Ferrand); Colonia Claudia Ara Agrippinensium (Cologne). Augustus spent many years in Gaul. The emperor Caligula was brought up as a child among the soldiers on the frontier, and Claudius was born in Lugdunum on 1 August 10 BC, the second anniversary of the dedication of the imperial altar. When Claudius came to the throne, he was responsible for the highest level of Gallic emancipation possible, a capstone to the development of civic offices and priesthoods within Gaul itself: he gave citizens from the Three Gauls the right to seek membership of the Senate and to run for the highest offices in the Roman empire. A speech he gave on the subject was engraved on a large bronze tablet and hung in the precincts of the altar. It was rediscovered near the Rue Burdeau in the sixteenth century. It is no wonder that the Gallic priesthood chose to memorialize his words in this way. He had to overcome deep opposition to the move in the Roman establishment, but he based his decision on what he saw as being the essential nature of Rome:

> What was the ruin of Sparta and Athens, but this, that mighty as they were in war, they spurned from them as aliens those whom they had conquered? Our founder Romulus, on the other hand, was so wise that he fought as enemies and then hailed as fellow-citizens several nations on the very same day. Strangers have reigned over us... United as [the Gauls] now are with us by manners, education, and intermarriage, let them bring us

their gold and their wealth rather than enjoy it in isolation. Everything, senators, which we now hold to be of the highest antiquity, was once new… This practice too will establish itself, and what we are this day justifying by precedents, will be itself a precedent.

Just as Claudius did not see the admission of Gauls to Roman offices as a threat to Roman identity, neither did the Gauls taking up Roman offices see this as an extinction of their Gallic identity. They may have Romanized their names, taken on Roman citizenship and carried out their duties in Latin – rhetorical speaking schools quickly sprang up, most notably in the new Aedui capital of Augustodunum (Autun) – but this made them no less Gallic. Many of the surviving inscriptions declare careers within a particular *civitas*, proclaiming the membership and contribution of the official to that group: 'Priest of the Aedui'; 'the first of the Segusiavi'; 'Julius Severinus, of the Sequani, distinguished in his city by every honour…' The identities are complimentary. The officials existed in a Roman cultural milieu, but their allegiance also belonged to their tribe; the honour conferred by the Roman office brought them prestige among their own people. *Romanitas* ('Romanness') and Gallic culture thus found a means to cohabit.

Beyond the priesthood of the altar and the many like positions created by the Roman presence, another aspect of the cult at Lugdunum was of similar importance. The veneration of the Three Gauls was conveyed not only by the priest and his officials, but by the representatives of all the Gallic *civitates*. Collectively, they were known as the *concilium Galliarum*, or Gallic council. Gallic tribes are known to have held such councils before Roman times – such as the one at Bibracte that elected Vercingétorix as war leader – and this Roman creation was perhaps in imitation of this tradition. Its presence at the annual festival on 1 August was not an empty show; its effective duty went beyond the election of the *sacerdos* and participation in the rites surrounding the yearly ceremony. There was certainly much in the way of frivolity surrounding the occasion. Caligula instituted a competition in Latin and Greek, where 'the losers gave prizes to the victors, and were forced to compose eulogies upon them, while those who were least successful were ordered to erase their writings with a sponge or with their tongue' unless they preferred to be beaten with rods or thrown into the Saône. A later *sacerdos*, Titus Sennius Solemnis, spent 332,000 sesterces on gladiatorial shows in the adjacent amphitheatre. But aside from these festive amusements, the council had real business. It was vested with no formal powers of government, but, being an assembly of the most prominent Gauls from throughout the Tres Galliae, it could not help but be a bellwether for the mind of the provinces. The assembly could send formal messages of congratulation or condolence to emperors, but also loyal expressions of complaint. Information in cases against corrupt governors is likely to have been collated at the instigation of the council. It is even attested that Solemnis, as well as spending so lavishly on gladiator shows, used his influence to deflect the council from having a Roman governor charged with maladministration.

Such an occurrence showed what the council was capable of doing, and that it ultimately became a force to be reckoned with. Again, Rome was not afraid to enfranchise its subject peoples even if it gave them the scope to use that power against Rome itself. The establishment of the council also assisted in the development of a collective identity. It is difficult to believe Caesar's claims that particular chiefs had, before his time, aimed at ruling all of Gaul, or had ruled all of Gaul (unless he meant by 'Gaul' just the provinces of Narbonne and Lugdunum). But under Roman tutelage, Caesar's vision of a wider Gaul came closer to reality.

Among the grand inscriptions at the Lyons Museum there is a set of large, wordless marble fragments. Instead of another report of a glittering official career, they merely bear the carving of an oak wreath. But even in this, there is no restraint. The wreath is a fat, rich festoon, luxuriant in foliage and dripping with acorns. It has the same riot and unbounded wealth as the display on the arch at Glanum. Yet, despite the similarity, the model for the wreath is not the Glanum arch. They both draw ultimately from the same original. Shortly before the construction of the Lugdunum shrine, an altar was inaugurated in Rome. This was the *Ara Pacis*, the Altar of Peace. It was erected mainly to commemorate the end of the civil wars that had plagued Rome for over a century, and exalted Augustus, the first emperor, as the bringer of a golden age of peace and tranquillity to the empire. The luxuriance of the fruits and foliage are a sign of the new abundance of the age, under Augustus's divinely inspired leadership. But this luxuriance, suggests the altar, is not simply the product of a brutal victory. Another scene on the walls of the *Ara Pacis* represents the imperial family in a sacrificial procession. Despite being imperial, there is no ostentation about them. Their dress is restrained, understated, strictly traditional. They are not broadcasting their status, but their piety. All is owed, as the poet Horace put it, to the gods: it is humility before them and their will – not ostentation or the rapacious accumulation of wealth – that will ensure their favour and success on earth.

The *Ara Pacis* reflects a new mood; Augustus acceded to the imperial throne under the guise of a 'restored republic', where he managed to hold supreme power in the state under a constitutional form by assuming a combination of republican magistracies. There was no merit in seeking vast self-enrichment at the cost of the common good, as had happened during the civil war. The old Roman virtues of simplicity, frugality and hardiness were to be revived and cherished. Such virtues had brought Rome its empire, as had adherence to the will of the gods. And the vesting of Rome with empire was not a divine caprice. In the words of the epic poet Virgil, who at this time wrote the *Aeneid* – which defined what it was to be Roman – Rome throughout history had a mission, ordained by Jupiter, king of the gods, to 'rule the peoples of the world with [its] power… to crown peace with law, to spare the conquered and to bring down the proud'. To be Roman was not to think of self, but to be dutiful both to the gods and to the subject peoples in one's charge.

This signature justification for imperialism – which formed the view of modern imperial administrators such as Lord Macaulay in India – seems to have been entirely absent from Caesar's own motivation for conquering Gaul. But Gaul's conquest, and the consequent sudden growth of the empire by 30 per cent in landmass between 58 and 50 BC, must have been one of the spurs that caused Romans to ponder the justification for their possession of such extraordinary power, and to condone it via a sense of duty. The apparent building of a replica or partial imitation of the *Ara Pacis* at the very focal point of Gallic loyalty to Rome suggests not only that Rome was willing to emancipate the Gauls, but that they wanted it to be believed – even if they were not sincere in this – that Rome acknowledged its duty to Gaul, just as much as Rome demanded loyalty from it. Such was the revolutionary message of the garlands that hung on the monuments of Glanum, Lugdunum and elsewhere.

However sincere the message of give and take and ultimate equality, over time it appears to have had its effect. The worst moment of instability in Gaul, and the empire more broadly, during the first century AD was the 'Year of the Four Emperors', 68–69. This was a brief period of civil war, which arose in response to the tyrannical behaviour of the emperor Nero. It had its spark in Gaul. The governor of Lugdunensis, Gaius Julius Vindex, was descended from a line of Gallic chieftains. Given his name, it is possible that his family was enfranchised in the time of Caesar. He himself was a member of the Roman Senate, and had likely been admitted thanks to the reforms of Claudius. He would have visited Rome, worked there with other Roman citizens and passed his way up the *cursus honorum*. When Vindex rose up against Nero, it was not to establish a separate empire for himself, nor to allow Gaul to break away from Rome; he did not give into any revanchist fantasy, despite his patrician Gallic heritage. His revolt was as a dutiful Roman senator, decrying the shameful unRoman excesses of Nero, and seeking a better man to take the imperial place. He supported no Gaul to take the throne, but rather the governor of one of the Spanish provinces, Galba, an elderly man who was the very image of a traditional Roman senator. Thus, within a century of the conquest, Gauls fought to ensure the *Romanitas* of the empire that ruled over them.

The same period of turmoil even brought an attempt by a Romanized leader of a Germanic tribe, Julius Civilis, to stir the Gauls to revolt and to seek an *imperium Galliarum*, an empire of the Gauls. Despite some initial successes, the Gauls for the most part sided with Rome. The historian Tacitus quotes one of the Roman commanders responsible for crushing the uprising addressing two of the Gallic tribes:

> There were always kings and wars throughout Gaul until you submitted to our laws. Although often provoked by you, the only use we have made of our rights as victors has been to impose on you the necessary costs of maintaining peace; for you cannot secure tranquillity among nations without armies, nor maintain armies without pay, nor provide pay without taxes: everything else we have in common. You often command our legions; you rule these and other provinces; we claim no privileges, you suffer no exclusion... Therefore love and cherish peace and the city wherein we, conquerors and conquered alike, enjoy an equal right.

The ideals expressed on the imperial altar at Lugdunum had become a commonplace. And they were being manifested not only in this official presentation of the Roman regime, but in the way that the cities, countryside and culture of Gaul developed over the following centuries. The age of Gaul had passed with Caesar. A Gallo-Roman future lay ahead.

View of the interior walkways, amphitheatre of Arles.

CHAPTER VI

High Life and City Chic

ea quae ad effeminandos animos pertinent
'The commodities that make for effeminacy'
JULIUS CAESAR, *De Bello Gallico*, I.1

ARLES

·

'CITY OF THE LION'

·

FORUM

·

CARDO AND *DECUMANUS*

·

CRYPTOPORTICUS

·

AMPHITHEATRE

·

THEATRE

·

'TOUR DE ROLAND'

·

THEATRE OF ORANGE

·

BATHS OF CONSTANTINE

·

ARCH OF SAINTES

·

VAISON-LA-ROMAINE

HUMANS ARE NO LONGER KILLED for sport in the amphitheatre of Arles. The age when gladiators fought to the death and criminals were torn apart by wild beasts to satisfy the blood-lust of the crowd has long since passed. And yet, for the most part, the amphitheatre continues to serve the original function that Rome intended for it.

The streets of Arles are heavy with the nobility of age. Light aslant in an evening sky picks out the granular detail of its weathered stone: the arms of knightly and monastic orders above the gates of decayed commanderies; the apostles in grey marble around the porch of St Trophimus, haunted in their gaze with the repeated knowledge of heaven; the palimpsest of silver-dappled medieval walls, topped with corbels and crenellations, facing with stately unconcern the last turn of the exhausted Rhône before it loses itself in the marshy delta of the Camargue.

The nobility of the city has long transfixed the artists and writers who have visited. Vincent van Gogh, resident in the Maison Jaune, painted again and again the square by the Porte de la Cavalerie, the area once given over to the Knights Templar. Frédéric Mistral, the great poet of nineteenth-century Provence and the Provençal language, hailed Arles as 'the city of the Lion, seated on the banks of the Rhône like a venerable and majestic queen, in the shadow of your glory and your monuments'. Mistral and Dumas both insisted that the women of Arles were the most beautiful in France. This came to be attributed to the isolated nature of the city after the fall of the Roman empire, the idea being that the indigenous genetic inheritance of its ravishing classical inhabitants had been preserved undiluted. This idea became a commonplace for nineteenth- and twentieth-century writers. Cecil

Headlam eulogized 'these splendid creatures, who walk like goddesses and look like ancient Romans', with their 'large eyes and handsome nose, straight as the Greek, perhaps, or curved in the Roman arch; her beautiful Greek chin and delicately modelled ear... The superb regularity of her features is balanced by a proud gait; her mien is as haughty as his carriage, and she seems to challenge you to refuse her the homage due to a worthy descendant of the noblest imperial race.' Lawrence Durrell, unsurprisingly for him, approved this sentiment even as late as 1990, the year of his death, but still went beyond it to describe Arles as 'outstanding in its beauty and sadness'.

But there is no need for such doubtful – and possibly lascivious – theorizing to see the imprint of Rome on the city of Arles. Its monuments are still open to view. To see the amphitheatre of Arles for the first time, rearing up suddenly in the gap between buildings on turning the corner of the street, its arches as bright as a fanfare of trumpet bells raised to the sky, is to experience, as did the inhabitants of Roman Gaul, the power of the empire.

With cities such as Arles as examples to the rest, Gaul would be changed. It would turn from being a land dominated by the rural, and a chaos of inchoate settlements scarce half made, to an organized set of provinces in the image of the Mediterranean city-state. Governance would flow from Romanized institutions in Romanized colonies, and such colonies would advertise the commerce, order and permanence of Rome.

Arles was not born with the conquest. A settlement of sorts is known to have existed here since around 550 BC. It is mentioned by Greek geographers under two names. The first, Theline, perhaps comes from an ancient Greek word meaning 'fertile'. This may point either to the fertility of the land at the mouth of the Rhône, or else the potentially lucrative nature of the spot, situated at the start of the riverine trade route to the Gallic heartlands. The other name, Arelate, is more clearly of Celtic origin, meaning 'the place by the marsh' or 'place by the waters'.

However, it was at the hand of Caesar that Arles came into its own. When he attacked Massalia during the civil war in 49 BC, the settlement at Arles became a vital base for his forces. It was here that he ordered the construction of twelve 'long vessels' to assist in the siege. Three years later, he ordered it to be made a Roman colony for the settlement of veterans of the Sixth Legion. Such was the importance he placed on the city, it was named after him in its official title: Colonia Iulia Paterna Arelatensium Sextanorum – 'The Ancestral Julian Colony of Arles of the Men of the Sixth Legion'. Caesar likely had it in mind to make Arles a counterweight to disloyal Massalia: and he knew that, thanks to its position by the mouth of the Rhône, it was excellently placed not just for military purposes but also for trade and agriculture. The Romans, recognizing the fecundity of the soil, followed the Greeks in giving Arles the epithet *mamillaria* (best translated as 'breast-bearing' – i.e., 'milk-giving'). But the city, not the fields, was their real achievement. A later poet, Ausonius, called it *Gallula Roma* – the Gallic Rome.

As with a number of other Roman settlements of the time, much of what went before seems to have been cast aside in an effort to start again with a standardized civic plan. The first step in the creation of the city was to lay out a centre around a crossing of two main roads: the *cardo*, which ran from north to south, and the *decumanus*, which ran from east to west. Such was also the custom when laying out a military encampment.

It is possible to follow what would have been the course of the *cardo* along the modern Rue de l'Hôtel de Ville up to the meeting point with the Rue de la Calade, which is closest to the old *decumanus*. Boutiques cluster in the narrow street with impromptu cafés. The sun is kept at bay by high Renaissance façades, broken at some of the corners by statues of the Virgin Mary or the saints. By this crossroads was laid out the monumental heart of the colony, the forum: a vast colonnaded square, 3,000 square metres in area, embracing not only the ceremonial buildings at the heart of civic life – a temple for honouring the gods and the imperial cult, a basilica or meeting place for courts and business, and a *curia* for the assembly of local officials – but also shops and eating places.

The buildings of the forum were most likely built under the reign of Augustus, by around 25 BC, and later altered under his successor Tiberius at the beginning of the first century AD. They were also places for display of statuary relating to the imperial family. It was not only at the altar of Lugdunum that the genius of the emperor would have been praised, or the stories of Caesar and his house retold. Pieces of sculpture found at the forum of Arles each tell a part of the imperial myth, and it is possible to follow the family from generation to generation. A slab of yellow Tunisian marble, the capital of a pilaster, chased with a dolphin whose eye is a comet, proclaims the tale that Caesar, after his murder, ascended to the heavens, his fiery soul shooting up to Olympus as a star; a round shield in fine Carrara marble, engraved with an inscription stating that it had been given by the Senate and people of Rome to Augustus in token of his 'virtue, clemency, justice and piety towards the gods and the *patria*' was a copy of such a shield in gold erected in the Senate house in Rome in 26 BC, shortly after Augustus chose to be so known instead of Octavian; there are busts of Augustus's grandchildren, Gaius and Lucius, both of whom predeceased their grandfather, as well as Tiberius. The heart of the city served to display to the colonists and Gauls alike the glory of the imperial name.

It was a message to which some of the local Gauls responded. Also found by the forum were inscriptions, like those at Lugdunum, recounting the lives of local men who had made the priesthood of the local branch of the imperial cult the capstone of their glorious Romanized careers. One example is Titus Julius, whose name suggests that he was of a Gallic family given citizenship by Caesar. A plaque inscribed with his offices is dated to the beginning of the first century

AD. He was appointed to the equestrian order, and also served as a senior centurion, military tribune, prefect of the camp, maritime prefect, *duumvir* (official of the town council) before attaining the priesthood of the imperial cult. The fact that Rome offered such item-ized glory to those Gauls who were loyal – easier, cosmopolitan and more agreeable than seeking it by head-hunting raids on neighbours – was thus displayed to the crowds.

There still is a Place du Forum at the heart of Arles, a busy but serene square shaded with plane trees and set out with tables and chairs for the café-goers and boulevardiers. It reflects but a fraction of the original Roman complex. Two columns supporting the corner of a pediment are all that can still be seen of the original, incorpo-rated into the wall of a later building. The columns in grey marble with their lacily drilled Corinthian capitals, and the pediment with its intricate maze of foliage, sit uneasily next to the garish fluorescent signs of the neighbouring hotel, picked out in electric blue.

There are still enough remains uncontaminated by modernity for the original scale of the forum to be appreciated. In one of the council buildings of the Hôtel de Ville, there is a staircase that leads down to a grand series of subterranean chambers. They are damp and cool, a dark and agreeable escape from the bright afternoon sun. A vaulted tunnel runs for several hundred metres, tracing three sides of a square. On one side of the tunnel there is an arcade, low and sturdy, built of heavy blocks, carefully cut and cleanly squared. In places, the arches turn into mighty rectangular piers, and a small warren of chambers lead off from the original tunnel to unnerving dead ends. Water chan-nels picked out by white stone blocks and inexplicable low walls curve around the piers. Piles of broken marble fragments lie about, fluted column drums, capitals, entablature. The beauty of each carving, quatrefoil, scroll, and acanthus leaf can be seen close up, waxy and smooth after centuries concealed. The marble shield of Augustus was found here, as were a number of the royal marble portrait heads and inscriptions of the imperial priesthood. They lay broken, heaped in one of chambers, ready to be burnt up in a lime kiln, but abandoned and forgotten even for that.

These subterranean chambers are called the Cryptoporticus. Built before the forum itself, they were a necessary response to an engineering problem. The *cardo* and *decumanus* crossed on the side of a hill. The site of the forum was therefore on a slope. To get a level surface for the great square, so that all the columns around it might be the same height, it was necessary to raise the level of the ground on three sides. The Cryptoporticus was the solution: a giant reinforced arcade below ground, which would provide the level surface needed as well as support for the grand buildings and colonnades above. It is likely to have served a secondary purpose as a warehouse for the goods sold in the shops of the forum, or even, as some have argued, as sleeping quarters for slaves. The work in itself is a marvel of surveying and engineering, almost dating back to the very foundation of the colony.

Aside from the forum, Arles had three grand spaces for public display and entertainment: the theatre, the amphitheatre and the circus. The theatre appears to be the oldest of these monuments, built near the forum shortly after the establishment of the colony. It is huge in conception. A semi-circular structure just over 100 metres in diameter and 20 metres in height, it would have towered over the neighbouring houses, just as those parts of it still standing at their original height do today. Its walls on the circular side, like the amphitheatre, were composed of three levels of arcades, elegantly faced with fine marble and ornamented with pilasters. Like the forum, half of it is built on the side of a hill. In order to build the concentric rows of ascending seats, which did not marry into the topography of the hill, the architects had to construct a complex scheme of foundations and tunnels. This also allowed the public – the theatre's capacity was around 10,000 people – speed of access to their seats.

As with the Cryptoporticus, it is possible to wander through the hidden tunnels and admire the arches and engineering. However, even more to be admired are the suggestions of lost grandeur. After the sixth century AD, the theatre fell into disuse, and was cannibal-ized for its stone. Large portions of it were taken to furnish the new Cathedral of St Stephen, the precursor of the later Cathedral of St Trophimus. Only one bay of the semi-circular outer wall was left at its original height. Facing southwards by the city walls, it was incor-porated into these defences and fortified as the 'Tour de Roland'. Its inner-facing walls are pierced with incongruous Romanesque win-dows. The side facing outwards preserves the features of the original arcade. On the worn surface of the stone, some of the small and deli-cate Roman carvings – *putti* and flowered festoons – can still be seen.

The area of the stage was enclosed and built over, by the eighteenth century becoming a garden for the convent of the Sisters of Mercy. Of the huge curtain wall that stood behind the stage, running the

Remains of the Roman theatre, Arles.

diameter of the semi-circle, decked out to imitate a grand palace, only two columns remained. They still stand today, solitary and majestic, the detritus of the intervening centuries having been cleared away. One is in grey marble, the other is in Troad granite imported from Asia Minor, mottled with pearl, silver and scarlet. They rear above onlookers, perhaps seven or eight times human height; but as evidence of the curtain wall they are still insignificant fragments. The wall of the theatre at Orange, which still stands, gives an idea of its former glory. Although deprived of most of its columns, it looms like a barrel-chested honey-hued cliff, inexplicably wrenched from a

The wall of the Roman theatre, Orange. The remaining columns and the statue of Augustus are vestiges of what would one have been lavish stonework and decoration.

canyon-side or sea front and left to glower at the little tables and para-
sols of the cafés intimidated below. Louis XIV said that the wall of the
theatre of Orange was the finest wall in his kingdom. It still is. Had
Arles been spared, it would have remained a worthy rival.

It is not known for certain what was performed in the theatre of
Arles or the other theatres across Gaul. It is likely that its productions
reflected those that are known from Rome itself. Comedies by authors
such as Plautus and Terence may have featured in the earlier years,
based on stock characters such as the clever slave, the rich but tyrannical father, his scold of a wife, the foolish but romantic son. Later,
these may have developed into mimes and pantomimes: the former a
type of bawdy farce in which actresses may have appeared nude; the
latter a sort of tragic ballet where a single actor mimed a wordless
story, playing all the characters to the accompaniment of an orchestra
and chorus.

Given the desire to convey the power of *Romanitas*, the type of
entertainment mattered less than the mere fact of its existence. The
new imperial ruler could divert and amuse tens of thousands at a
time, far beyond the capacity of any indigenous chieftain to seat at a
Gallic banquet. The medium, essentially, was the message. The theatre, as a gathering place of the masses, was also by its nature a place
to convey messages about the primacy of Rome. Being a theatre, these
came in a suitably thespian guise. Theatres in the ancient world grew
out of mystery cults, and as such were seen ultimately as religious
rites. An altar would therefore be placed in the vicinity of the stage.
Usually, this would have been to Dionysus, the god of drama; but at
the theatre of Arles, the altars discovered are dedicated to his brother
Apollo. As god of the lyre and poetic inspiration, Apollo was not
divorced from the creative process. But he was dearer to the Roman
order. Augustus believed that Apollo had kept him safe through his
personal intervention at the Battle of Actium during the end-game of
the civil war. Dionysus was the god of Mark Antony, his rival, suggestive of the chaos of Egypt and the east 'with its barking gods', as Virgil

wrote, in contrast to the discipline and order of Rome and the west. It is therefore no surprise to find Apollo presiding at the theatre of Arles, built in the time of Augustus.

One small altar is adorned with swans, the bird that flew over Delos, Apollo's birthplace, when the god was born. They hold garlands of laurel, sacred to Apollo, but also symbolize Augustus's victory. Another small altar bears a crown of oak leaves, like the garland at the altar of Lugdunum. A grand altar that would have been set before the stage portrays the god himself, reclining on a couch and propped up on his lyre. There is, however, an empty socket where his head should have gone. This allowed for the head of the emperor to be affixed on the body of the god, changeable whenever a new contender came to the imperial throne. In case any of the spectators should still be in doubt over the association of Augustus, Apollo and the magnificence of the theatre of Arles, a colossal statue of Augustus was placed in a niche above the door in the middle of the stage. Nearby was a statue of Venus, who was in the imperial myth the mother of Aeneas, the ancestor of Caesar and also, by adoption, Augustus. Her statue was discovered at the site of the theatre in 1651, a copy of a Greek original made by Praxiteles in 360 BC. Such was its refined quality that the city authorities offered it to Louis XIV to adorn his new palace of Versailles. It now has its home in the Louvre.

As Arles had three grand places for public display, it also had three grand baths. Two of these are now no more than hidden foundations. One was unearthed in the year 2000 at the southern end of the Rue de l'Hôtel de Ville. It has now been reburied, and lies beneath the site of a weekly farmers' market. Another, however, at the other end of the *cardo*, for the most part still stands. It is one of the best-preserved Roman bathhouses in Europe. It is not part of the original buildings that were erected in Arles straight after the conquest (although it may be on the site of an earlier bathhouse): it likely dates to around the fourth century AD and is known as the 'Baths of Constantine'. However, it still serves to give an impression of the new and elaborate

experience of Roman and Mediterranean culture that Rome introduced to overawe and entice its new northern subjects.

The baths sit by the bank of the Rhône. Without prior knowledge of their function, from the outside their original purpose is not
immediately obvious. They sit in the neighbourhood of a complex
that once belonged to the knights of Malta. Constructed of stone with
bands of rusty terracotta brickwork, the walls bulge towards the river
with a semi-circular domed apse pierced with tall arched windows
to match. However, it is for the most part roofless, and shards of the
walls are missing, allowing one to see inside. In such a place, and with
such a form, it looks at first sight to be a venerable and ancient church,
ruinously neglected. But even scholars from earlier generations were
similarly fooled. In the sixteenth century, the complex was identified
as a palace and attributed to the emperor Constantine. It had indeed
been put to such a use in earlier generations, but not by the Romans:
in the medieval period, the counts of Provence had taken over the
complex of abandoned buildings and converted it into a court. They
named it the Palais de la Trouille, referring to the *trullus* or semi-circular vault that is still preserved behind the apse. It then declined into
a pound for stray animals before being eventually engulfed by adjacent buildings, incorporating the still-strong Roman walls into their
own constructions. It was not until the nineteenth century, when a
civic project was launched to clear away the medieval and Renaissance
accretions from the complex, that its original function as a bathhouse
was uncovered.

The various chambers of the complex can still be traced: the *tep-
idarium*, or warm-room by the entrance; the *caldarium*, or hot-bath
room; and the *laconicum*, or sauna. A grand basilical hall, which may
have been the *frigidarium*, or cold bath, still stands away from the
entrance, but forms part of a later medieval building, the Hôtel d'Ar-
latan. This might be one of the largest buildings from the Roman era
still standing, but the project to free it from the later structures and
investigate it properly was halted by the First World War and never

recommenced. For all this, the technological intricacies of the baths are dissected and laid bare. Ranks of rickety brick piers hold up an interrupted floor; clay tiles transfused with pipes still hold to some of the walls – the hypocaust system, all to circulate heat from the subterranean furnaces. The technology and Roman mastery of the elements did not stop at the walls of the bath. The waters for Arles came from the Alpilles, a range of low limestone peaks several miles north of the city. At the opposite end of the city from the baths, one can see where an aqueduct disgorged these waters into a channel cut into the rock below a remaining stretch of Roman walls. The channel now sits dry, a receptacle for scratchy yellow grass, wilted umbellifers and *bon-bon* wrappers. In the time after the conquest, it is unlikely the Gauls would have passed by such marvels of water technology with so little regard. In one of the last clashes of Caesar's conquest, at Uxellodunum, the fiercest fighting centred on possession of the single well that kept the city supplied. Not long after this, water flowed freely around the country and became, in the marble-lined and centrally heated swimming pools of Roman villas, as much a source of daily pleasure as a necessity for life.

As with the baths, the amphitheatre was a monument of misunderstood magnificence for the post-Roman ages. It may have been used for shows as late as the sixth century AD. Saint Caesarius of Arles, in a sermon at that time, describes human nature as a 'spiritual amphitheatre' with its 'savage forest of vices' so vividly in terms of a real amphitheatre that it is difficult to think he spoke purely from imagination or repeated tradition: 'I see in our character the wild savagery of lions... in our tongues the envy of wild boars, in our consciences the spots of tigers... in our sins the great weight of elephants...' With such a vituperative attack from the Christian hierarchy, not to mention the post-Roman collapse in living standards, it is little wonder that the amphitheatre fell into disuse around this time. Its fate, unlike its neighbour, the theatre, was not to become a quarry, but rather a fortress. Four square towers were added at the cardinal points, the external arches were bricked up, and the stands within were encrusted with houses, workshops, even an open square and a small chapel to hold the relics of a local martyr, St Genesius. The place became a redoubt for the citizens in time of danger, such as when the city was attacked by Saracen invaders or local warlords.

It was not until 1826 that the civic authorities ordered the amphitheatre to be stripped of these barnacle dwellings – 212 in all – and the glory of the ancient monument to be laid bare. By 1844, the structure had been returned, as far as possible, to its first-century AD state. It could seat 21,000 spectators. The floor of the arena was an oval 70 metres by 40 metres, and the whole structure was 136 metres long at its widest axis. It was originally built around AD 70, a contemporary of the Colosseum in Rome, smaller but similar in design. It was not built to fit in with the grid-plan of streets that radiated from the forum and the meeting of the *cardo* and *decumanus*. It broke through the original city wall, spilling over the boundary of the city as first laid out in Caesar's time. Standing outside by one of its gates or pacing around the upper galleries, one can appreciate the shock of its presence. The parchment-coloured blocks of local stone seem hefty, cyclopean, improbably lofted up into the air to create the arcades and pavements that still rest solidly far above the rooftops of the city. They catch the oblique rays of the evening sun, turning the ring of stones into a magnificent coronet of light. They shrug off the irregular smattering of post-holes and rivulets gouged into them to support the shambles of slum housing as just so many irrelevant medieval insults. It matters little that the highest course of the amphitheatre is missing; the sturdiness and the refulgence of Rome still show through.

We do not know precisely who built these monuments. But down on the walkway that encircles the arena itself are a series of large marble panels, damaged and smoke-washed in colour, and only partially covering the coarser stonework beneath. They bear an inscription, mutilated but sufficiently legible to tell us that one Gaius Munius Priscus, a *duumvir* of Arles and priest at the shrine of Augustus, paid for the podium and gates of the amphitheatre to be erected, not to mention a silver statue of Neptune as well as four other bronze statues. He also endowed two days of games in his honour, to be accompanied by public banquets. Given the offices he held, he was probably of Gallic origin.

Such inscriptions are a sign that the decision to display these markers of *Romanitas* in the new settlements of Gaul was not purely the result of central planning or government funding. The propagation of these great monuments of Roman lifestyle – theatres, baths, amphitheatres – was driven as much by the local Gallic elites as by their Roman overlords. Another example lies in the putative original capital of the Aquitanian province, Saintes, where many early post-conquest monuments still survive. A double-gated triumphal arch erected in the early first century AD in honour of the Roman general and imperial claimant Germanicus was erected by Gaius Julius Rufus, the grandson of Caius Julius Gedomo, who had been given Roman citizenship by Caesar. The Gallic nobility, having lost the old means of demonstrating their primacy – raiding, gathering bands of vassal warriors, displaying heads – now used Roman cultural markers to display their wealth and status. Instead of giving banquets in their halls and handing out potlatch, they used the Latin language, assumed Roman civic offices and used their patronage to aid the construction of Roman-style public buildings.

Such were the grand public structures that adorned the new Roman towns. But to see how the Roman presence could transform the home life of the Gauls (or at least that of the more fortunate ones) one must turn away from Arles, where such evidence lies beneath the later city. Following the Rhône northwards to Orange, and then turning north-east to cross to the valley of the Ouvèze, one eventually reaches the town of Vaison-la-Romaine. Here, the sea-change wrought by Rome is clear for all to see.

I come to Vaison on a market day in September. The Provençal lavender season is over by this time, but despite this and the still-intense heat, the place is suffused with colour. The streets are thronged, the stalls bright with shining tomatoes and peppers; grapes, newly cut, are bloody purple and frosted next to the scarlet and red berries of late summer fruits. There are strings of garlic and dried sausages, tawny or smoke-brown, making an understated backdrop for boxes of garish sugared candies and an array of soaps as encyclopedic in hue as a jewel box.

The market stalls give way to shops and the built-up part of the town in the Grand Rue. The street leads to a high, cliff-bound bank looking down over the Ouvèze far below. The river was navigable in Roman times, but is now little more than a playful stream. Beyond the river is a high limestone rock – Castle Hill – on which is perched

View of Vaison-la-Romaine, overlooking a complex called 'The House of the Silver Bust'.

the fortified medieval town, looking down on the flat expanse of the modern streets on the right bank of the river below. The two sides are spanned by a Roman bridge of a single arch, still used by traffic as the main route across. A grey Bugatti sports car, having descended from the heights, noses its way across the bridge, holding a line of vehicles in check as it negotiates the junction.

The Roman bridge is the best spot to begin a survey of the history of Vaison. It was the capital of a Gallic tribe, the Voconti. Before the Roman conquest, the settlement appears to have been confined to the hilltop. But following the imposition of the *Pax Romana** the city came down from the heights. Buildings were put up across the river on the flat and undefended expanse; the hill was neglected. This remained the case until around the sixth century AD, following the collapse of the empire. The town fled back up the hill and – with a few exceptions, such as the cathedral – stayed there until the mid-nineteenth century. At that point, the pendulum swung again, and the town sprawled back down on to land that for centuries had been agricultural, concealing beneath it the secrets of the old Roman *civitas* capital.

There had been a number of archaeological finds around Vaison from the sixteenth century, but aside from a period of work in the mid-nineteenth century there were no organized excavations until the early twentieth. From then until the 1960s, in two large areas on either side of the Avenue General de Gaulle, centuries of topsoil were peeled away to reveal the impress of the submerged town. Although only a district of private houses could be uncovered, such was its extent and preservation that local archaeologists succeeded in a campaign to rename Vaison in a style that reflected its Roman past: in 1929 it became Vaison-la-Romaine, 'Vaison the Roman'.

The stones of the ruins are of the same white limestone as the cliffs nearby. They were locally quarried. They stand companionably – pillars, walls and steps – with the buildings of the modern town that now surround them. The Roman town feels at ease with the modern,

* Literally, 'Roman Peace' – the order which Rome imposed across its imperial territories.

rich in the produce and beauty of its setting, as well as prosperous and well connected. Roman Vaison – Vasio Vocontiorum, Vaison of the Voconti – was described as one of the wealthiest cities in Gaul by Pomponius Mela, a geographer of the first century AD. The area was also praised for its sweet wines in the same century by Pliny the Elder.

Some of its inhabitants were well known and of national renown. A first-century AD inscription discovered at Vaison in 1884 showed that one of the imperial right-hand men, Afranius Burrus, was almost certainly born there, and at any rate the town regarded him as its patron and advocate. Burrus was a military man, and in AD 51 was appointed as the praetorian prefect in Rome. Along with the philosopher Seneca he acted as tutor to the teenage Emperor Nero and hence as one of his de facto regents. His influence is credited with the maintenance of a period of good government throughout the empire in

Vaison-la-Romaine, viewed from 'The House of the Dolphin'.

the AD 50s, while the young Nero was kept distracted from the levers of power with debauchery. It is impossible to think of Burrus's character as anything but unflappable. Nero tried to have him convicted of a scheme to support a usurper, but at another point came running to him in panic when a plot he had hatched to kill his mother, Agrippina (with whom he had previously been having an affair) went disastrously wrong. When Burrus died in AD 62, perhaps of poisoning, the historian Tacitus, a judge of character notoriously difficult to impress, remarked that Rome felt a deep and lasting regret.

Burrus was not the only famous son of Vaison in that era. Lucius Duvius Avitus rose to be consul in Rome in AD 56. A plaque found on the banks of the Ouvèze sets out his career, including a governorship of the province of Aquitaine and military commands on the Germanic frontier. Even in the previous generation, the town was home to the influential scholar Pompeius Trogus, whose Gallic family was given Roman citizenship by Pompey the Great and also served Caesar during the conquest. Trogus's academic work, some of which has been quoted in these pages, spanned the disciplines: it included influential writings on the history of the east and scientific work on animals and plants. He was seen as a more rigorous, scientific historian than his contemporaries, and remains an important source today.

The residences are appropriate to the importance of the inhabitants. In one of the gardens a third-century AD plaque was found with the family name 'Pompeia'. The garden has been much restored. A wall has been rebuilt and replacement Tuscan columns constructed using Roman techniques. Casts of statues have been places in niches. Little care has been taken to allow the new to be distinguished from the old, but nevertheless the scale of the ancient site is clear. Its gracious quadrangle is lined with porticos of such length that some have argued that the garden must have been a public amenity rather than a private space. Yet it seems more likely that it was indeed a garden attached to a private house, whose remnants still lie beneath the neighbouring land.

The sheer size of private spaces at Vaison is striking. Individual houses covered over 2,000 square metres, huge complexes of more than one storey with heated bath complexes, loggia-like dining rooms looking out over colonnaded courtyards cooled and enlivened with ponds and trickling waterways. They had specially fitted kitchens with cooking ranges; stone-carved latrines washed out by rills of running water, with marble slabs on the walls to dignify the activity; frontages carved out facing the paved streets that could be rented out for income as shops and boutiques.

Their inhabitants walked on intricately patterned pavements of marble in rare colours – mottled grey, orange and burgundy – imported from Italy, Greece and Africa. They looked on frescoed walls painted with winged nymphs, bearded grotesques and sea creatures, or huge mosaics, several metres in length, with a bestiary of creatures: a peacock whose tail radiates like a fireball, woodpigeons, ducks, partridges, parrots; geometric confusions of squares, hexagons, diamonds, Solomon's knots, flowers, panthers, deer, eagles, theatre masks, cupids and Tritons riding on dolphins. Some of these artworks bear the stamp of their owners' daily amusements. Into the red

Relief depicting a chariot race, from a tomb of the first century AD,
discovered at Orange.

plaster of one of the frescoes are scratched small images of gladiators at combat: a *retiarius* with his net and trident, pitched against the *secutor* with his short sword, helmet and shield. The pleasures Rome offered were not just commodities, bought and built around the inhabitants of Vaison; they were something seen and remembered, worthy to be engraved on the walls as hero-worshipping graffiti, or else to beguile an idle hour.

But it is not just in Vaison that this way of life can be discerned. In the towns along the Rhône – Nîmes, Orange, Valence, Vienne and Saint-Romain-en-Gal, Lyons, and then beyond – elegant private houses and imposing public buildings, adorned with sculptures, mosaics and inscriptions from soon after the time of the conquest are all to be found. To be sure, the spread of Roman-style towns was not universal. Their density was much higher in the southern region than in the north, closer to the Mediterranean sphere which had given birth to the concept. However, the vision of the Roman town percolated throughout Gaul, affecting how even smaller settlements developed, laying out a template and aspirations even if the ideal was not always copied so perfectly or so opulently. Even on the hill of Alésia itself, the site of the defeat of Vercingétorix where a great shrine to the Gallic god Ucuetis was maintained, the inhabitants seized on the Roman urban template. Although they dispensed with the formal arrangement around the *cardo* and *decumanus*, the place has its theatre, its forum with basilica and temple (which some archaeologists have suggested are modelled in their plan on the forum of Trajan in Rome), its baths and its fine houses, its colonnades with shops and boutiques. Caesar's victory was more complete than Vercingétorix could ever have imagined.

Mosaic discovered at St-Romain-en-Gal, part of a larger ensemble of Orpheus charming the animals, second century AD.

CHAPTER VII

Country Life

locis patentibus, maxime frumentariis
'Unprotected districts, and very rich in corn'
JULIUS CAESAR, *De Bello Gallico*, 1.10

ORANGE

·

CADASTRAL MAPS

·

THE MOSELLE

·

VILLAS

·

CLERMONT-FERRAND

·

LAC D'AYDAT

·

CHIRAGAN

·

GARDENS OF 'VOROCINGUS'

·

AQUEDUC DE BARBEGAL

·

MAS DES TOURELLES

From the fields beyond Vaison, looking back at the town from a distance, the imprint of Rome is always visible: the sprawling remains of the Roman town itself, the Roman bridge, the cathedral built on a foundation of Roman stones, the little Romanesque chapel of St Quentin in whose façade are limestone panels carved with swirling vines dating back to the time of the late empire. But the land itself – the trellised rows of vines, the scattering of pines and Judas trees out of season – does not reveal the traces of Rome so easily. There are no obvious stone walls to divide estates, no drainage ditches nor irrigation channels. The cities can boast their Roman ruins, their theatres, their arches and their baths. But here in the countryside, nothing cries out the presence of Rome.

Paradoxically, the best place to start a search for the Roman countryside is back in the city. In Orange, near Vaison, close to the massive wall of the theatre, a hash of marble fragments was found in the 1920s and 1930s. The fragments are flat, wide and covered with inscriptions. The marble is not the finest, being blotchy and dishwatery in hue, and the furious maze of engraved lettering does not have the monumental grandeur of the plaques and plinths that boast of the careers of provincial officials. This is not to say that the fragments are insignificant in any respect, for they are the remnants of a series of grand and stylized maps, huge in scale (they were originally several metres across) and equally huge in intent. Three can be identified from the rediscovered fragments: one was created at the order of the emperor Vespasian in AD 77, and the other two shortly afterwards as part of a reorganization of the rural territories around Orange. The land was to be surveyed, redistributed as necessary, assessed for taxation, and the results of the exercise recorded on this marble document, which was to be displayed to public view, probably in the forum of the Roman city.

The cadastral maps,* as they are known, are written in a sort of shorthand. Their fragments now hang on the wall of the Orange Museum in the shadow of the theatre. They are crossed with lines, in the manner of a grid. Particular abbreviations can be made out – DD, SD, CK, VK. These are directions for interpreting the map – *dextra decumanum* and *sinistra decumanum* – right and left of the *decumanus*; and *citra cardinem* and *ultra cardinem*, on this side and beyond the *cardo*. The recurrence of the terms *cardo* and *decumanus* is a sign of how the countryside around Orange was treated like a new city. The surveyors would choose a central point from which to work. There they placed an instrument called a *groma*, a pole with a flat cross on top from which hung strings kept taut with lead weights. From the four points of the *groma*, aligned with geographical north by reference to the passage of the sun, they traced an extended *cardo* and a *decumanus*, and from these lines they could then proceed to divide the land in the form of a chequerboard. By describing the location of a plot with reference to the *cardo* and *decumanus* on the cadastral map, it was possible to pinpoint it on the ground itself.

The maps are the subject of persistent research. Not only do they describe the divisions of landholdings, but also geographical features such as rivers. With the benefit of this evidence and references to features that can still be discerned, geographers have attempted to trace out where the original Roman field boundaries lay in the landscape. This is not easy for the walker at ground level; to discover the Roman vestiges, one really needs aerial photography, supplemented with satellite data and computer analysis. The boundaries of the agricultural lots around Orange were frequently drawn at intervals of 710 metres. This was the rough equivalent of 20 *actus*, one *actus* being – on the same principle as an English furlong – the distance a plough led by

---

* Cadastral maps show the divisions, ownership and value of land, particularly for taxation purposes.

Passage inside the theatre of Orange.

two oxen would be drawn before being turned around. With the assistance of the cadastral data, it is therefore possible to look from the air for the recurrence of features at these intervals. Some can be found, in isolated spots. However, they are frequently not what the Romans themselves left behind, but the ghostly negatives of their one-time presence.

The Romans favoured square fields. They were the most appropriate shape for the earth-working technology then available, the scratch plough. The fact that the plough did not properly turn over the earth, but could only cut a furrow, required the land to be ploughed twice, each time at right-angles. Square fields thus made the most sense. The field might be bordered with drainage or irrigation ditches, and in some instances marked by small paths or tracks. The maintenance of these features of rural infrastructure demanded constant attention. However, after the decline of the empire in the fifth and sixth centuries AD, the countryside was depopulated. Ditches silted up as a result of flooding and lack of maintenance. Paths were untrodden and disappeared in the undergrowth. The shapes of fields were lost, and whole areas reverted to woodland.

When the countryside revived later in the eighth century AD and beyond, square fields were no longer needed. The mouldboard plough, which allowed the earth to be properly turned over with a single pass, became popular, and hence long rectangular fields predominated. Yet, when clearing and recovering old lands that once were cultivated in Roman times, the prospecting farmer might find a narrow strip of earth that tended to become waterlogged, while another might seem more densely covered in trees and foliage, as if the spot attracted them. These were the locations of forgotten Roman ditches, which continued to accumulate water more readily because of the disturbance to the earth. Where an area had evidently once been a drainage ditch, it was often easier to redig than create a new one in virgin soil; or a line of well-grown trees on top of an old ditch might well be reused as part of a new boundary, attract a path to run alongside it, or divert the way of another. Thus, as new medieval boundaries came into being, they were not created in knowing imitation of the Roman past, but they were still unconsciously influenced by the old Roman footprint. Such a footprint can still be seen, but only traced with the greatest of subtlety – a row of trees that grows more luxuriantly than those around, or a road turning abruptly through a right-angle for no discernible reason.

In its own age, the impact of the Orange cadastral map was anything other than ghostly. It classified the land around the colony into different categories: land given to army veterans; land given to the Roman colony that it could rent out as it chose; public land that was not let out but under colonial administration; land that had not been divided up by the survey and that remained under public control; and land that was returned to members of the local Gallic tribe, the Tricastini. This last category appears to have been the most marginal and least productive. Such an exercise seems to suggest the indigenous Gallic farmers had been in decline, or else that they had to submit to forcible repossession of their farmland. The poet Virgil in his *Ninth Eclogue* paints a picture of Italian peasants forced off their land to make way for military colonists during the civil war around 40 BC: 'O Lycidas, we have lived to see the day – something we never even dreamed of – when a stranger took hold of our farm and said "This is mine; old tenants, get you gone."' The lament is one that the Gauls too are likely to have spoken as the Roman colonists arrived.

Although the maps narrate a redistribution of land that took place over a century after the Roman conquest, a comparison between the maps and the evidence of aerial photography and other archaeological investigations suggests that the land around Orange had been subject to a previous scheme of division shortly after the conquest itself. Such work also points to similar surveying and allotment of land around many other centres in Gaul – Arles, Narbonne, Valence, Vienne, Béziers. So the tribes around Orange were not the only ones to suffer upheaval. In many places, the Roman presence changed not only the appearance of the land, but also those who were able to possess it.

The landscape of Gaul was transformed not only in its boundaries, but also in its buildings. It is no exaggeration to say that it was covered in villas. Properly speaking, the Latin word *villa* – often the first word to be learnt in Latin as an example of a first declension noun* – means an entire rural estate, not just the complex of residential dwellings at its heart. However, taking the word's modern meaning of a large and luxurious house, villas appear to have been spread profusely across Gaul. Their apparent absence above the surface of the ground led many originally to believe that the culture of villas had not penetrated deeply into Roman Gaul. However, as with the field boundaries indicated by the Orange cadastral map, it has only been with modern technology that many of their sites have been recognized.

Just as the position of an old Roman ditch covered up by later deposits of soil might reveal itself via waterlogging and more vigorous vegetation, in general an old stone wall hidden beneath the earth causes the plants above it to grow more slowly. From the air, when the conditions are right, these variations in plant growth can be seen. The floorplan of entire complexes can be spotted, mapped and precisely surveyed. Projects carried out after the Second World War showed that villas were widespread not just in the south, but also in the region of Picardy and the Somme. Excavations carried out before the construction of TGV lines and new motorways have revealed that villas were not only more densely distributed than had been expected, but were also present across a far wider range of locations. On occasion, they emerge in the fields on the outskirts of later medieval villages, suggesting that there was some form of continuity between the life of the villa and the foundation of the village. These findings give some

---

* Latin nouns are divided into five basic types, or declensions.

credence to the old belief that the Latin names of villa-estates ending in *-acum* or *-anus* evolved into modern French village names ending in *-ac, -at, -as, -y, -é* or *-ay*, thus preserving the identity of their one-time Roman owners.

So the countryside was covered in villas, and villas of every variety. In the fourth century AD, the poet Ausonius wrote of a journey along the Moselle from Bingen to Neumagen. In one section of the poem, after long descriptions of the fish that can be caught in the bounteous river, he turns to a portrayal of the villas that dot its banks at regular intervals. In the previous century the countryside had suffered upheavals on account of disturbances on the frontier. However, by the time of his journey there had been such a revival that the villas he portrays may have been even more opulent than those of earlier centuries.

Ausonius, like many writers of his age, is not averse to hyperbole. The architects of these villas, he writes, might well have been the very ones who had raised the pyramids in Egypt or the Temple of Artemis at Ephesus. Yet he soon passes from hyperbole to more credible detail. The Roman villas dominate the landscape. One stands high on a mass of natural rock, another on a bank jutting out into the river; one rests further back 'and claims the river for its own, making it prisoner in an enfolding bay'. All take advantage of the river, whether for the sake of practicality or beauty. One has its own weir for catching the fish 'between the sunny grass-grown rocks'. Another, sitting on the crest of a hill, is in just the right place to enjoy the beautiful haze of light that refracts around the base of the river valley.

The luxury and ease that they offer seem at one with the landscape around them. There are courtyards and colonnades that meld into the green meadows at their side. There are bathhouses on the low verge of the banks, the smoke of whose hypocausts roll up along the valley. Ausonius watches as bathers spill out of the hot baths and, scorning the cold plunge-pools in the bathhouses, jump into the river itself; refreshed by the running water they 'buffet the cool stream, threshing it with their strokes'. For Ausonius, this is a better and more whole-some place than the great Italian coastal resort of Baiae, the old and notoriously debauched watering-hole of the emperors and Roman elite: 'So great is the charm of its refinement and distinction, while its pleasures breed no excess.'

The residential buildings of a villa-estate might be of any level of opulence or elaboration. As a general rule, they were divided into two parts. There was the *pars urbana*, which was the dwelling of the owner and his family, luxurious and well appointed. For the slaves or dependents who cultivated the land there was the *pars rustica*, less decorated, more in the order of barrack blocks, which also included barns and other agricultural outhouses. The most frequent shape for the complex would be a courtyard or double courtyard around which the various sections of the villa were arranged. Sometimes, these could be extensive, over 300 metres long in some cases. However, this grandeur was by no means universal. In some areas, for example in Normandy and Brittany, villa complexes tend to be rather smaller. Instead of courtyards, they had long corridors connecting two wings or larger rooms at each end. In Belgic Gaul and the areas facing the Rhine, there are also 'hall villas' where, rather than a series of smaller chambers, a single grand room was the focus of the dwelling. These variations may suggest that the social structures of the indigenous peoples were being preserved alongside Roman customs and material luxuries.

The more opulent villas offer more extensive remains, and there-fore more information about the people who lived in them. This includes their literary endeavours. Some of the best descriptions of villa life come from the letters of an aristocrat and cleric named Sidonius who lived in the century after Ausonius, in the mid-fifth cen-tury AD. As with Ausonius, his writings are likely to be a reasonable reflection of what happened earlier, during imperial times. Sidonius had a villa at Avitacum, which may have been by the shores of the Lac d'Aydat, about twelve miles southwest of Clermont-Ferrand in the rich countryside of the Auvergne. Although business required him to be frequently in town, his heart appears to have been on his estate. It was a possession of pride, a family seat that came to him when he married. It was nevertheless a place he was eager to share, and show off.

Early one summer, Sidonius wrote to a friend of his in town, a teacher named Domitius. The weather was getting hot. 'The land is being scored with irregular curved cracks gaping in the heat, gravel lies untidily in the fords, mud on the banks, dust in the fields; even streams that flow all the year round have languidly slowed down; the water is not merely hot: it boils.' In such heat, where even those lightly clad in silks and linens were sweating, it was madness for Domitius to sit in his gown, squeezed into his teaching chair, and 'yawningly expound' to his pupils – 'whose pale faces are due quite as much to the heat as to the fear of you' – obscure lines from the works of old poets. 'Why not rather, if you have any thought of your health, promptly withdraw from the panting oppression of the town and eagerly join our house-party, and so beguile the fierceness of the dog days by retiring to the coolest of retreats?'

To encourage Domitius to visit, in his letter Sidonius takes him on a virtual tour of his villa. Perhaps on account of the heat, he starts with the bathhouse, a structure of which he was deeply proud. He had even written poems about it, comparing it to the Lucrine Lake in Campania, not to mention the resort at Baiae. It even had a specially designed conical roof, in imitation of one of the grand baths there. Sidonius goes on about it for pages: the bathhouse was on the edge of the woods, so close that the branches almost dropped directly into the heating furnaces; he describes the shapes of its windows, the vaulting of the roofs and the quality of the light; he expatiates on the size of the swimming pool itself, which held about 40,000 gallons of water, and on how it was adorned with porphyry columns and fed by a mountain rill that gushed into the building through six projecting pipes, whose heads were in the shape of lions: they had 'genuine wildness in their eyes, and unmistakable manes on the neck'.

Leaving the pool, there is a maze of corridors and rooms: a dining room for the women of the household, store-rooms and weaving rooms; a dining room for the female dependants of the estate where he happens upon them taking a grand midday meal such as might be laid out at a festival for the tables of the gods. There is a winter dining room, whose vaulted fireplace is black with soot, but more appropriate to the time of the year is the summer dining and living room. Furnished with a grand semi-circular couch and polished sideboard, it is open to the lake, so – provided one's attention is not absorbed by the pleasures of the table – one can sit and enjoy the view. Here, or in one of the adjacent rooms, one can enjoy a drink so exquisitely chilled that the glass is frosted. Thus refreshed, one can watch the fishermen on the lake casting for trout or spreading their nets, or simply listen to the chirp of cicadas, the croaking of frogs, and – towards evening – the honking of swans and geese and cawing of crows. As dusk falls, the song of the nightingale joins the chorus of sounds. If one is feeling more energetic, one can venture into the grounds and play ball

Mosaic from St-Romain-en-Gal, part of the Orpheus ensemble, second century AD.

beneath two lime trees whose branches intertwine, providing a most pleasing shade for exercise. Thereafter, one might recover from one's exertions by sitting down to enjoy a game of dice.

We do not know whether Domitius ever took up this invitation. However, the splendour that Sidonius describes at length in his letters is certainly not imagined. If anything, the grandest villas discovered by archaeologists would have made it appear positively suburban. In 1826 at Chiragan, near Martres-Tolosane in the Haute-Garonne, a set of foundations were discovered in fields after heavy flooding washed away the topsoil. Excavations that took place over the following century and a half revealed a villa which comprised eighty buildings totalling 18,000 square metres, spread out over an area of around 16 hectares. Inscriptions at the villa show that it originally belonged to the family of the Aconii. The name seems to have stuck, and as late as the seventeenth century the spot was called Angonia, a corrupted version of the name. In the first century AD, when this family possessed the villa, it was nothing out of the ordinary. However, sometime later in the second century it changed hands. Not only was it vastly enlarged, so that at its greatest extent it was around a third of the size of Hadrian's imperial villa in Italy, it was also covered in an impressive array of marble reliefs and statuary. Indeed its collection of these items, most of which is now held in Toulouse, is second only to that of the Louvre. One hall was set aside to be lined with busts of the emperors. Another part of the house had grand marble panels, each with life-size depictions of the labours of Hercules. Other rooms and corridors were ornamented with roundels of local marble carved with the heads of Minerva, Vulcan and Cybele. It is more than a cut above the villa of Sidonius, who disapproved of mosaics in his swimming baths as being potentially lascivious.* The grandeur of the site suggests that it might have been used by the governor of the province, or even as an imperial palace during the later empire.

---

* This brings to mind the famous 'Bikini Girls' of the fourth-century Villa Romana del Casale in Sicily, of which Sidonius would no doubt have disapproved!

It was not just the architecture and landscapes that gave pleasure to the inhabitants of the villas. They also rejoiced in their gardens. Traces of gardens and even their planting schemes have been discovered by archaeologists at some villa sites, with areas set aside for vegetables, orchards, animal enclosures and outhouses. Once again, surviving literary sources add colour to a fragmentary picture. One of Sidonius's poems is a *propempticon* or ode of dispatch that he sent with a copy of a book to friends in another villa somewhere in southeastern Gaul. Addressing the book, the poem describes the route it must take to reach its destination, and the people it will encounter on the journey. One of these is Apollinaris, a relative of Sidonius. His estate was at a place called Vorocingus, somewhere in the vicinity of Nîmes. Here, says Sidonius, the book would find a night's rest from its weary travels. When it arrived, it would probably encounter Apollinaris walking in his secluded gardens, 'which are like those that bloom on honey-bearing Hybla'.* He would be surrounded by violets and thyme, privet covered in grape-like clusters of white flowers, February daphne, marigolds, narcissi, and blooms of hyacinth. Such was the beauty of their scent that Apollinaris would turn away the travelling incense salesman at the gate, offering Sabaean frankincense at a great price. And if he were not to be found among the flowers, he would be cooling himself in his imitation grotto on the slope of a neighbouring hill, a 'cavern' formed by the branches of trees arching together to create a natural portico – better even than the ancient orchards of the Indian King Porus, which he decorated with golden vines heavy with clusters of gems.

But the countryside was as much for use as for aristocratic ornament. The Romans recognized from the time of the conquest the fertility of the Gallic provinces. 'None of the country', writes Strabo in the first century AD, 'is left untilled except the parts where tilling is precluded by swamps and woods'. The southern regions were similar

---

* A place in Sicily, probably modern-day Ibla in Ragusa, famed in the ancient world for the quality of its honey.

to Italy in their agriculture, he observed, but 'all the rest of the country produces grain in large quantities, and millet, and nuts, and all kinds of livestock'. Even before the Roman conquest, the country was productive and intensively cultivated. Caesar would never have been able to feed his legions and conquer the country had it not been for the requisitions of locally grown food from allied Gallic chiefs; his worries over whether they will deliver the grain he has demanded are a constant note in his *Commentaries*. Yet, the coming of Rome did have an impact on the crops. Archaeological studies of plant remains and burnt foods found in rural sites have shown that grains that were commonly grown before the conquest, such as emmer and spelt, fell in popularity. Others, including common wheat, durum wheat, rye, barley and oats tended to take their place.

Many estates were large, and there are signs that they ran at a considerable surplus. According to Pliny, Gallic wheat was imported to Rome. Loaves of bread baked using Gallic wheat, he reports, seemed to be lighter in texture than those made of grain from other regions. Such imports are mentioned by another author, Claudian, as late as the early fifth century AD. Even if the harvests were large in scale, the Gallic landowners were not entirely dependent on human labour to gather them in. Following the Roman conquest, on large estates based in flat, low-lying areas, a primitive sort of combine harvester called a *vallus* was developed. This was an open-topped wooden box or hopper mounted on two wheels, at the front of which was a large spiked comb at the height of the ears of wheat, facing forwards. Pushed from behind by a single ox, the contraption pulled the ears from the stalks so that they fell into the hopper. The *vallus* is mentioned by Pliny, writing in the first century AD, and – much later – by Palladius, a Gallo-Roman agricultural writer of the late fourth century. It even appears carved on the Porte de Mars – the triumphal arch of Rheims – and on other fragments of reliefs discovered in Belgium and Germany. Palladius states that the *vallus* was used where the land was flat, and in places where straw was not considered to be of much value and was, accordingly, left standing uncut in the fields. It was nevertheless a very efficient time- and labour-saving device: Palladius states that with a single man to guide the ox, the whole of a farm's harvest could be brought in in just a few hours.

The *vallus* was not the only Roman labour-saving device to change the face of the Gallic countryside. A little way beyond the sprawling ruins of the Abbaye de Montmajour, north of Arles, a country lane runs off along a concealed ridge of high ground. It passes through olive plantations and scratchy wasteland, given over to brittle sandy grasses relieved by yellow clumps of St John's wort. In the adjoining fields, tractors throw up lingering clouds of smoky dust. Beetles and moths, red, grey and cream, bask on the tarmac. After several miles, amid a scattered group of Aleppo pines and olive trees, a series of white stone arches come into view. On the left-hand side they are lower than the canopy of the trees, and it is only on drawing closer that one can see that the arches cross the road, and continue to its right. The land slopes gently from left to right, so that the arches gain in height as they progress rightwards, though still not overtopping the branches of the olives that run alongside them.

This sequence of arches is an aqueduct. It has nothing of the height or grandeur of some other examples of the genre, for example the mighty Pont du Gard outside Nîmes, which stands nearly 50 metres high as it crosses the River Gard on a construction of three-tiered arches – a monument that Lawrence Durrell summed up as being a perfect specimen of the poetry of function, but also conveying the 'splendid insolent eloquence' of the Roman remains of Provence. The aqueduct here, at a spot known as Barbegal, has little splendid insolence about it. It is certainly a structure that speaks of power; but it keeps itself low beneath the treetops, and even where great pieces of it lie broken and covered with succulents and scrappy grasses, it has an arresting beauty. As its low arches run straight and serene in their precise course through the olive groves, one can indeed appreciate the poetry of its form.

But of more interest than the form and beauty of the stones is the ingenuity of their structure. Barbegal is not solely an aqueduct: closer inspection reveals that it had a twofold purpose. Further along its length, the ground rises again and reaches the crest of a ridge, a seemingly impassable mass of rock, perhaps nine metres long and well over human height. However, on climbing up into the aqueduct's mortared channel, which carried the water, one realizes that at the point where the aqueduct reaches the ridge, the structure is in fact two closely adjacent aqueducts carrying parallel channels. Here, the two channels separate. One turns abruptly right around a corner, and runs ultimately towards the city of Arles. The other carves a cutting

The aqueduct of Barbegal. Its parallel structure can be clearly seen in this photograph.

about a metre wide straight through the middle of the limestone ridge. Beyond this chiselled gateway, on the other side of the ridge, the land suddenly falls away. These are the slopes of the hills of La Pêne, over 30 metres high, beyond which the yellow-green fields of the Vallée des Baux stretch away towards Fontvieille. The water carried by the second channel was thrown down the side of this hill. Among the scrub that clings to the hillside, low jagged walls rise up, marking the course that the water, cascading downwards, would have followed.

The low walls on the hillside are the remains of the largest known watermill in the Roman empire. Excavations of the complex in the 1930s unearthed a series of buildings climbing the side of the hill. These housed sixteen separate water-wheels in eight pairs, each over two metres in diameter. As the water flowed down the hill, it turned each wheel in succession. The wheels were attached by a gear to a basalt millstone, and each of these millstones could be reached by a service staircase which ran the length of the gradient. Having set the wheels in motion, the water was used at the bottom of the hill to irrigate the fields in the Vallée des Baux. It has been calculated that the mills of Barbegal would have been able to produce around 4.5 tonnes of flour a day. This would have been sufficient to feed 12,000 people, equivalent to the likely population of Arles during imperial times. Archaeologists used to believe that the mills were built in the late third century AD, when the number of slaves available to carry out the laborious task of milling – either by hand or with the help of animals – was declining. It was argued that the Romans only felt compelled to seek such technological advances when the well of free manpower failed them. Yet more recent research has pushed this date back to as early as the second century AD, before any obvious sign of labour shortages in Gaul. It seems that the mill was not built out of desperation, but from a desire to exploit the resources that the local landscape and fields had to offer more efficiently.

It was also originally thought that the mill of Barbegal was a one-off, and that such large-scale watermills were not to be found elsewhere.

However, in 1990 a similar mill was found, albeit on a smaller scale, at Avenches in Switzerland. Since that discovery, more than a dozen sites have been identified across the Gallic territories, some in open country, with a number of them dating back even to the first century AD. Ausonius, in his travels down the Moselle, describes a water mill he saw used for turning millstones and 'driving shrieking saws through blocks of marble'. The sight of labour-saving mills, it seems, would have been not uncommon in the agricultural landscape of Roman Gaul.

Flour was not the only product of the countryside. A basket of *crudités* culled from a Gallic market garden would be for the most part recognizable to the modern diner. Carrots (usually then white or purple) and cauliflower were grown, not to mention celeriac and apples, garlic and onions, asparagus, cucumbers, lentils and beans. The emperor Tiberius made parsnips fashionable in the first century AD when he agreed to accept part of the tribute owed to him by Germanic tribes in parsnips instead of money. As regards fruit and vegetables, the Gallo-Roman palette was in some respects wider than the modern. Lupin beans were commonly cultivated, along with samphire, Alexanders (a plant whose flavour is halfway between parsley and celery), and the edible young stems of black bryony (poisonous until cooked). Olives had been known since the time of the Greeks, and the lower tear-shaped stone of olive presses, carved with runnels for the juice to flow out, can be seen even in pre-Roman sites.

Uncooked black bryony might pose a risk to a Gallic wayfarer. More dangerous, however, were the pigs. Strabo records that Gauls kept these in abundance for their meat (which they ate both fresh and salted), but that they were allowed to run wild. These Gallo-Roman pigs developed into animals of considerable size, speed and boldness. Indeed, it was risky for anyone unfamiliar with their behaviour to approach them; they were as dangerous as wolves. The Romans made their own contribution to the size of farm animals, bringing over larger species of cattle in particular, which were maintained in Gaul

The reconstructed Roman winepress at Mas des Tourelles.

until they were abandoned with the collapse of empire. Flocks of sheep were raised in the south; it was perhaps in the Roman era that the custom of transhumance arose, in which flocks wintered in the lowlands but were taken to the highlands for summer. The Roman legions on the Rhine certainly became dependent on the flocks for their wool; several factories were set up to process the fleeces for military use. But they were also out to domestic use. Pliny records that the stuffing of mattresses with wool was a Gallo-Roman invention, and that flax grown around Cahors was valued for the same purpose.

And then there was the wine. In the countryside near the Via Domitia outside Beaucaire, the fields are rich with vines. They stand in orderly rows, their clipped tendrils trained along low-hanging parallel wires that run the length of desiccated fields. At the end of summer, when the sunflowers in the neighbouring fields hang their heads, petalless and black, and the wayside foliage is beige with dust, it is the very presence of the vines that offers the hope of relief from a long day's walking in the Provençal heat.

One of the vineyards, on a plain that slopes gently to the south, is somewhat unlike the others. At its heart is a seventeenth-century farmhouse whose elegant courtyard, with green shutters and flowering trees in tubs, offers the welcome prospect of shade for the traveller. So much is not unusual. But the vines nearby are dressed differently from the norm. They do not trail along long wires, but rather hang from high trellises like great veils, their fat stems twisting around the straight wooden pillars of the framework. This cultivation method is not of the present age, but Roman. The whole scene would have been familiar to the ancient writers on agriculture – Columella, Pliny the Elder or Paulinus. It is even possible that they drank a vintage grown at this very spot.

The farmhouse and its domain are called the Mas des Tourelles.*
They stand on the site of an old Roman villa and vineyard. It was
first identified as such early in the twentieth century, with finds of
amphorae, roof tiles and vases near the surface of the fields. Later
excavations revealed a villa complex spreading over about three hectares. The villa was established not long after the conquest in the early
Augustan period, and was in operation until at least the fifth century
AD. It possessed all the normal appurtenances of the villa – housing
for the master's family and its dependants, and agricultural buildings. Notably, on top of this, there was a pottery workshop. It was
a significant affair, containing a huge kiln several metres across that
was capable of firing up to 2,000 amphorae at a time. Some of the
amphorae manufactured here and later rediscovered are still kept in a
storeroom in the modern farmhouse. The large numbers of amphorae suggests that this place was significant for wine production. Such
amphorae were signed or stamped to identify the producer and
the variety of wine, similar to a modern label. Close to the town of
Carpentras on the Rhône, it would have been in a good position to
sell to other cities on the river and even to consumers further afield.

Since the rediscovery of its Roman past, the Mas has been dedicated as a centre of research into Roman techniques of viticulture,
with attempts being made to recreate Roman wines using Roman
methods of production. Of these, some things cannot be known.
Vines were probably first introduced into Gaul by the Greeks, but it
is likely they did not spread far from the Mediterranean shore before
Roman times. It appears, however, that following the conquest, the
culture of the vine began to make deep and lasting inroads into the
Gallic provinces. Archaeological evidence suggests that vine cultivation begin to appear throughout the south from the second half of
the first century BC, with plantation pits, winepresses, amphorae and
pottery workshops becoming widespread. By the first century AD it

---

* The word *mas* denotes a farmstead in the Provençal language. It originates from the Late Latin
  mansum ('dwelling place') and is linked to the words 'manor' and 'mansion'.

had spread across the provinces of Narbonne and Aquitaine, as well as the regions of modern-day Burgundy, the Loire valley and even the Parisian basin.

Imports of wine from Italy went into decline in the late first century AD. The emperor Domitian even tried to put a limit on vine cultivation in Gaul to prevent competition with the Italian vintages, but his edicts were ignored. By the third century, perhaps prompted by the development of Trier as an imperial city, vineyards began to appear towards the northeast, around the Rhine, Alsace and the Moselle. By this stage, the vine had spread to the areas in which it would continue to flourish up to the modern age.

Despite the wide and early extent of vine cultivation across Gaul, we do not have detailed knowledge of the varieties of grape that were grown. Their names were preserved by the ancient authors; one of the best varieties, Amineum, originated from Greece and was widely

Outside the Mas des Tourelles.

popular. There were also local varieties: Biturica, grown predominantly in Aquitaine, and Allobrogica, grown around Vienne. Yet, although these names are known, and traces of Roman vine stocks and even seeds have been discovered, these are not sufficient to reveal the modern equivalents of the ancient varieties. So much has to be down to guesswork.

Nevertheless, we know a great deal about the techniques of vine cultivation used in Roman Gaul. The ripe grapes were cut from the vines with pruning hooks, and thrown into great concrete-sided tanks, such as have been reconstructed at Mas des Tourelles. Ropes were hung from the ceiling above the tanks, and the farm workers would cling tightly to these while pressing out the grapes with their feet. Mosaics even show them doing this in time to the playing of a flute. The grapes were then thrown into a neighbouring winepress – a large square wooden box made of slats to allow the juice to flow out. A huge tree-trunk, weighing several tonnes and hanging horizontally above, forced a board downwards into the box by means of a winch and pulleys (again, these have been reconstructed at Mas des Tourelles). The juice ran from the box along gulleys to be collected in *dolia* – large clay pots that are two-thirds buried in the ground. This could be a long process. Some vineyards were able to fill around 2,000 *dolia* from a single *vendage*, equivalent to 300,000 modern bottles. When the *dolia* were filled, the juice was left to ferment, frequently with the addition of herbs and spices.

It is the inclusion of these ingredients that creates a wine contrary to all my expectations. Three varieties are produced at the Mas. The first wine brought out for tasting is a red wine called Muslum. It is served chilled, and it manages to combine a certain lightness with a richness that tells of the cinnamon, pepper, thyme and honey that have been added to it. Turriculae, a white wine, is a sharp contrast, being dry and astringent. Its extra ingredients, as described by Columella, are fenugreek and seawater. The third, Carenum, follows a recipe by the fourth-century writer Palladius; it is deep amber in colour, its flavour enhanced with quinces and boiled grape juice to create a wine of fine and sweetly glutinous quality.

These are nothing like the smooth vintages one would expect after many years' reading of Horace with his Falernian or Caecubian wines, and certainly far removed from Keats's blushful Hippocrene. Their tastes are complex, intense and exotic, almost as if it were an impossibility that the land in that age could give rise to flavours so strange. But not every Gallic wine was pleasing to the palate. Martial wrote an epigram condemning a character, Munna, for sending wines from Massalia 'by sea and length of road' that were not only 'dire poisons' but also at prices more appropriate to the most expensive labels. 'I think you've been so long in Rome so that you can avoid drinking your own wines,' he observes tartly.

Funerary relief of a coppersmith named Bellicus, second century AD.

CHAPTER VIII

The Dignity of Labour

Nam plebes paene servorum habetur loco
'As for the common folk, they are treated almost as slaves'

JULIUS CAESAR, *De Bello Gallico*, VI.13

LES ALYSCAMPS

·

LA CHAPELLE DE LA GENOUILLADE

·

BUILDERS

·

MARINERS

·

MERCHANTS

·

CRAFTSMEN

·

SHAMPOO-MAKERS

·

GLASS-BLOWERS

·

FLOWER-SELLERS

·

GLADIATORS

·

SOLDIERS

·

SLAVES

T O THE SOUTH OF THE ROMAN WALLS of Arles lie the old burial grounds known as Les Alyscamps. Roman custom forbade the burial of people within the walls of any city, an area that was believed to be a sacred space. Thus the tombs and monuments of the dead accumulated just outside Roman cities. The burial ground of Arles sprang up by the side of the Aurelian Way* which fed via a gate into the city's main street, the *cardo*. Graves were usually positioned along the roadside in the hope that passers-by might pay them some respectful attention. But the Alyscamps later became the grandest and most reputed burial ground in the whole of Gaul.

The name Alyscamps comes from pagan myth. It derives from the phrase *Campi Elysii*, the Elysian Fields where the virtuous dead would serenely disport themselves in the classical afterlife. The Champs-Élysées in Paris owes its name to the same origin, but Arles's Elysian Fields are more aptly named, since – unlike the Parisian version, which is dedicated to the pursuit of life – it is a necropolis populated by the shades of the dead.

However, it was a Christian legend that gave the Alyscamps its grandeur and fame. The body of St Genesius, a lawyer who was martyred at the beginning of the fourth century AD, was buried in the cemetery. Christ himself is said to have miraculously presided at the funeral. Kneeling in prayer, his genuflexion left its imprint in a rock, giving a Christian imprimatur to a pagan burial ground. Soon the body of St Trophimus, the first bishop of Arles, was also interred here. In a case of mistaken identity, Trophimus was confused with one of the early Christian converts mentioned in the Acts of the Apostles,

---

* The Aurelian Way originally linked Rome and Genoa, but after AD 275 was extended as far as Arles via Nice and Aix-en-Provence.

the Trophimus who accompanied St Paul to Jerusalem. As a result, the Alyscamps became one of the most sought-after Christian burial places in western Europe. With the decline of the city after the end of imperial Roman rule, the Alyscamps set the tone for the wider perception of Arles as a city of the dead. Burial was its leading industry. It was said that it was sufficient for a body in a coffin (along with a few coins for the expenses) to be placed anywhere upstream on the Rhône, and it would drift safely down to Arles for burial, coming to rest at the promontory of La Roquette. There, monks from the Church of Saint Honorat* would take it up and see to the funeral rites.

Hence the Alyscamps grew without restraint, both in size and in literary reputation. Dante evokes the vast rows of tombs to portray a scene in the *Inferno*. Ariosto makes it the last resting place in *Orlando Furioso* for the fallen companions of the semi-legendary Carolingian hero Roland, who perished fighting the pagan Saracens at Roncesvalles. Later in the Middle Ages, the tombs became a moveable asset. Visiting potentates and members of the French royal family would be presented with an example of the more finely carved of the Roman tombs. King Charles IX of France helped himself so greedily to the Roman relics on offer that his overloaded ship sank in the Rhône. Precious pieces of the classical heritage of Arles were dispersed in royal collections across France and even in European palaces beyond its borders.

The Arlésiens' heedlessness for their ancient legacy went far beyond the dispersal of their finest examples of Roman funerary sculpture. It touched the land as well. In the 1550s, the burial ground was first disturbed by the construction of a canal, intended to assist in the irrigation of the Crau. Once the precedent for desecration was set, it was impossible to arrest. In the nineteenth century, large tracts of the Alyscamps were sold off to the Paris-Lyons-Méditerranée Compagnie des Chemins de Fer. The burial ground was split asunder by railway lines and occupied by warehouses, workshops and

---

* Named after a fifth-century bishop of Arles, Honoratus.

goods yards. Contemporary observers reported Roman sarcophagi being carted off by farmers for use as drinking troughs for cattle, or cut up for building blocks. The land, honeycombed three levels deep with tombs and interments, was scooped away for railway cuttings or levelled out for development. By the end of the century, all that was left was a small island for La Chapelle de la Genouillade ('Chapel of the Kneeling'), marking the spot where Christ had appeared, and a narrow sliver of the original fields, the Allée des Alyscamps, lined with an avenue of trees and a trail of the plainest of the sarcophagi, by then empty, which terminated in the half-ruined chapel of Saint Honorat. Even in this state of decline, the Alyscamps still had an inextinguishable allure. Vincent Van Gogh and Paul Gauguin both went there frequently to paint, absorbing the sense of the numinous that pervades the place even now, despite the centuries of damage. Van Gogh wrote to his brother Théo describing the avenue of poplars, and in particular his delight in the bluish-lilac colour of the remaining Roman tombs against the carpet of fallen leaves in orange and

View of the Alyscamps by the Church of Saint Honorat, Arles.

yellow, and how the leaves with these vivid colours continued to fall like flurries of snow.

Strangely, the significance of the pagan and Roman Alyscamps and its remains is most fully felt in the Christian Chapelle de la Genouillade. This ancient structure is a quarter of an hour's walk from the Allée des Alyscamps. One crosses back over the canal, past a children's nursery, an old people's home and a line of shops on the main road which passes along the city walls. The route then leads over a railway bridge, around a bend in the road and into a functional landscape of pylons, cranes, goods yards and modern flats. The bridge, lined with a crash-barrier, gives way briefly to an old stone wall and a tiny area of green grass in which the chapel sits.

The chapel seems hardly bigger than a camper van. It is abandoned, locked, forgotten. There is not a hint of care or veneration. Its carved stone doorway flanked with stone piers and Corinthian capitals is so gouged and rutted as to be quite asymmetrical. There is no wooden door, as one would expect, but a metal one like those found in prisons; it is painted in battleship grey, scratched, rusted and slightly marked with listless, faded graffiti. There is no glass in its windows. A metal grille and chicken-wire leave the interior open to the elements. Some of the wire is bent back, allowing a better view of the interior. There is little to see. An altar, partly built into the wall of the apse, a pair of angular unornamented wooden candelabra, and a couple of other shards of unidentifiable debris lie haphazardly on the flagstones. Around, the grass is uncut, and would be waist height if it had it not yellowed in the heat and wilted.

Regardless of the truth of the legend, it is pleasing to think of Christ's appearance here in a back-end dump of the city, surrounded by suburban roads, railway lines and kebab wrappers. Like a poet, his visitation brings an obtuse sanctification to something utterly ordinary. But it did not need a visitation from Christ for the Romans to grasp the significance of the Alyscamps. Since the earliest times of Roman colonization, this and other burial grounds – albeit less favoured by legend – were a sanctification, or better to say, a celebration of the ordinary business of ordinary people. The Roman presence increased the diversity of the lives that people led, and – sometimes even for those as lowly as slaves – celebrated their lives and doings in the monuments they left to dignify their ends.

The much neglected and decayed façade of the Chapelle de la Genouillade on an isolated fragment of the Alyscamps, Arles.

Many of the inscriptions on the sarcophagi and *cippi* (rectangular grave markers) offer no more than a few abbreviated words. However, a number of them are much more informative, offering a clear perspective into the life and work of the departed. Here, for instance, are the words of a memorial to one Quintus Candidus Benignus:

> Master builder of the Arles guild: he had absolute mastery of the craft of building, as well as dedication, knowledge and discretion. Great craftsmen declared him on every occasion to be a master; no-one else was skilful enough to possess such an accolade; nobody could defeat him; he knew how to make machines to direct the flow of the waters; here he was a welcome guest; he knew how to cherish his friends with sensibility and eagerness; he himself was good-natured and kind-spirited. To her sweetest father, this monument has been raised by Candidia Quintina, his daughter, and to her dearest husband, by Valeria Maxima.

The date of this monument is not known, but it probably belongs to the first or second century AD. Regardless of its exact date, it shows from another angle how the Gauls began to accord prestige to different things. As with the nobility, who now had careers in public office and the chance to display their wealth in the creation of public buildings, the lower classes in Gaul could win their own esteem by the pursuit of trade. Quintus Candidus Benignus was worthy of respect not for his skill in battle nor for being the retainer of a chief, but because no one could match him for knowledge of his craft.

It is not that pre-Roman Gaul lacked trades or craftsmen. However, with the advances that Rome brought, it was increasingly the case that the lives and skills of tradesmen and artisans were worthy of memorialization. Caesar commented that Gauls who did not fall into the priestly or warrior classes were considered little better than slaves.

Now, a builder, thanks to his ability to make machines that could direct the flow of water, deserved to be remembered for all time.

The range of trades practised appears to have increased following the conquest. In Arles alone there are records of the men who crewed sea-going vessels, carpenters, the *utricularii* (who carried goods along the Rhône on rafts buoyed up with inflated animal hides), the *lenuncularii* (operators of larger boats equipped with oars), the *centonarii* (rag-traders), and *lapidarii* (jewellers). A previously unknown group called the *partiari* have recently been discovered. The nature of their work is unknown, but they raised a memorial to someone named Hermia bearing the picture of a ship, suggesting that their trade had maritime associations.

Many of the trades listed above arranged themselves into guilds. These were not monopolies, as was the case with their medieval successors, nor was membership of these guilds compulsory for those who wished to practise the trades that they represented. Their main concern appears to have been the welfare of their members. They seem to have operated more as clubs, and remnants of their clubhouses have been found on the sites of Gallic cities. Some of the guilds appear to have worked closely with government officials to pursue their trade or even to carry out government contracts. Such connections brought prestige both to the guild as well as to the officials. For example, at the end of the second century AD the seafarers of Arles raised a monument to one Caius Cominius, an official who was responsible for the *annona*, or grain supply. They declared him to be their patron, a man who was 'excellent and irreproachable'. Thus, the guild was able to share the respect that was owed to their patron as a member of the governing classes.

Beyond Arles, many more guilds and types of trade have been attested. In Lugdunum, there stands a *cippus* (a small inscribed stone) to 'the eternal memory of Septimus Julianus' who was a *saponarius*, a tradesman in cosmetics. Pliny notes that Gaul was responsible for the invention of *sapo*, which is sometimes translated as 'soap' and is the origin of the modern word, but is better interpreted as 'pomade' – a substance, Pliny wrote, used to make hair shinier and blonder. One of Julianus's colleagues from Lugdunum was Pisonius Asclepiodotus, an *ungentarius*, or perfume-seller. The name of his wife Severa Severia, with whom he lived for thirty-five years 'without any injury of the spirit', is equally prominent on his tomb inscription. The perfume trade did well for his family: Pisonius and Severa became respectively a priest and priestess of the cult of Augustus.

The traders of Gaul catered to every delicacy and luxury. For a civilized dinner, one might acquire the foodstuffs handled by Gaius Sentius Regulianus. His epitaph describes him as trading olive oil from southern Spain and Gaul from his office in Lugdunum; he also traded in wine out of Lugdunum, captained a ship on the Saône, was patron of the guild of wine merchants, as well as of the guild of the captains of the ships and a patron of the priests of the imperial cult. On top of this, he accumulated the wealth to become an *eques*, or member of the order of knights.

Julius Alexander – 'African by birth, a citizen of Carthage, the best of men, a master glassmaker' – would have provided drinking vessels in which to pour the wine bought from Regulianus. As well as evincing pride in his origins, Julius's memorial is particularly precise about his dates – he lived 'seventy-five years, five months and thirteen days', was married to his wife ('a virgin when they married') for forty-eight years, and had four children. His Carthaginian background is telling, since glassmaking technology is known to have been more advanced in North Africa than elsewhere in the empire.

The imposition of the *Pax Romana* allowed tradesmen to move freely and relatively easily around the Roman world, taking their knowledge and skills with them. Inscriptions across Gaul, and in Lugdunum in particular, record the movement and resettlement of people, some of them tradesmen, both to and from Gaul and across the empire. In Arles, a Greek doctor named Dionysius was given a fitting burial by a grateful local student, Julius Hermes; Constantius

Aequalis, 'decorator of parade armour and cloth of gold' and a priest of Augustus at the shrine of Lugdunum, was originally a citizen of the Syrian town of Germanicia. In other cases, Gallic officials travelled to the Syrian and Palestinian provinces to fill positions in the magistracy; moving in the other direction, demobilized soldiers who had served in Pannonia and elsewhere on the Danube settled in Gaul. Alexander the glassmaker might well have been a pioneer, bringing new techniques or seizing the opportunity to set up a new atelier where a gap presented itself in the market. Six glass bottles, four glass bowls, two glass cups and a glass hair-pin, in perfect condition, were found buried with him. They were almost certainly his own work, and thus constitute the only glassware surviving from the ancient world that can be attributed to a specific maker.

There were also sellers of tableware to go with the glasses. Vitalinus Felix was a veteran of the 1st Legion, which was nicknamed 'Minervia' and spent most of its time on active service on the frontier in Lower Germania. Following his demobilization, Felix went into business. He lived fifty-nine years, says his epitaph; he was born on a Tuesday, enlisted in the army on a Tuesday, was honourably discharged from his legion on a Tuesday, and died on a Tuesday.

For the finishing touch to a feast or else as a token of affection, it was possible to enlist the services of a flower-seller. One woman engaged in the trade at Nîmes is recorded in a carving, sitting behind the counter of her shop and holding one of her garlands. Above her is a motto which acted as much as a mark of distinction to her customers as to herself – *non vendo nisi amantibus coronas* – 'I do not sell garlands, except to lovers.'

Not only the more delicate or refined trades merited a memorial for their workers. Trades involving hard manual labour are also mentioned in inscriptions, both on tombstones and in other dedications. By the marble quarry of Saint Béat in Haute-Garonne, four master stonecutters from the works made a sacrifice to the god Silvanus on behalf of themselves and their colleagues. The event warranted the record of their names: Serverus, Natalis, Martialis and Sintus. Likewise, in the gallery of a lead mine below ground at Bastide-l'Évêque in the Aveyron, the miners – perhaps slaves – placed a short inscription in memory of their 'overseer and master' Zmaragdus. In Sens, a grave marker is carved with the portrait of Bellicus, a blacksmith. He stands in his forge, surrounded by the tools of his trade – curved rods and pincers – clutching an ingot, which he is hammering into a knife blade on an anvil. Here, it is not just the trade itself that is memorialized and dignified, but the physical activity associated with it.

Soldiers likewise had individual memorials. It was perhaps only some two thousand years later, in the era of the First World War, that similar regard was paid to commemorating the lives of soldiers, whether they fell in active service or otherwise. Sometimes grand careers would be recorded – centurion, military tribune, legate. But

Mosaic depicting the pleasures of the table, from St-Romain-en-Gal,
second century AD.

equally worthy of remembrance was the non-Roman from outside Gaul who had gained citizenship and settled as a veteran in Gaul. At Arles, Titus Carsius Certinus was laid to rest sometime in the second century AD: 'Veteran of the 20th Legion (Valeria Victrix) – Carsia, his daughter, to her most virtuous father.'

Even the very lowest in society might leave their names and a trace of their lives behind. Many of the gladiators who fought in the amphitheatres at Arles and Nîmes are known from more than the admiring graffiti of their supporters. If they had the bad luck to perish in the arena, they could be buried with dignity and a memorial. At Nîmes, a small stone for Beryllus: 'Fought twenty times, Greek by nationality, lived twenty-five years. Nomas, his wife, made this for her well-deserving husband.' At Arles, one Marcus Julius Olympus, leader of a troupe of gladiators, set up an inscription to one of the favourite members of his team, Lucius Granius from Rome 'on account of the great merit of his victorious grandfather'. Olympus himself, who, socially speaking, would have been regarded as little better than a pimp, attempted to dignify himself with the title *negotiator familiae gladiatoriae* – 'business manager' of the gladiatorial group. Actors also, though as a social class beneath contempt, might advertise their profession: 'Primigenus, actor from the company of Eudoxus' was buried on the Alyscamps, a short walk from the theatre of Arles where he would have performed his unknown roles.

Even the identities of humble agricultural workers are recorded. The name of Publius Brittius Saturninus, a sheep-shearer, is crudely chiselled into a stone, the letters picked out in red paint, with a picture of his shears laid down in disuse beneath. Likewise the vine-dresser Vallonus, 'excellent brother to Quartina', remembered only in those words and in a picture of his pruning hook. Even an ex-slave and cattle breeder was dear enough to his former master to merit a long metrical inscription above a chiselled bucolic scene of a shepherd with his sheep beneath a tree, its quiet mood curiously at odds with the grim story of murder that it records:

Iucundus, freedman of Marcus Terentius. All you travellers who pass by, stop and read how I, snatched away
unjustly, complain indignantly that I was not able to
live for more than thirty years. For a slave took away my
life from me and then threw himself headlong into the
River Main. The river took from him what he took from
his master. Terentius erected this memorial at his own
expense.

It was not necessary, to have a craft or a particular story to boast of
on one's gravestone. Simple affection deserved to be recorded in a
few simple words: *'Zosimus Matri Pientissumae'* – Zosimus to his
most affectionate mother; 'Lucius Aponius Severianus, died aged four
months nine days'; *'Symmacho Alexandria Victoria Tatae'* – Alexandria
Victoria for her papa, Symmachus.

Those who could not afford to make themselves known to the
wider world with fine inscriptions in marble or limestone sometimes
had other ways of entrusting their names to posterity. In workshops,
particularly near the River Allier, small clay figurines of animals – for
example dogs and monkeys – were signed with the names of their
makers: 'Ritogeno', 'Priscus', or 'Rextugenos'. Pots and drinking vessels
might in some instances be stamped with the name of a workshop –
for example 'OFBASI', short for *Officinum Bassi*, 'workshop of Bassus'
– but in others with the name of the individual potter: 'PATERNIF'
records the work of Paternus ('Paternus fecit') while 'ATTICIM' is
short for 'from the hand of Atticus' (*Attici manus*).

The humblest of trades might also be memorialized via representation in the artistic commissions of the better-off. Thus, in a mosaic
of St-Romain-en-Gal opposite Vienne, the hard rustic labour of every
season is recorded in a pictorial agricultural calendar: grafting of
the trees at springtime; the collection of wood in the summer; the
harvesting of apples, grapes and olives in the autumn; the sowing of
beans, the milling of grain and the weaving of baskets in the winter.

Tombstone of a vine dresser, Nîmes. The tombstone, dedicated by 'Vallona to the soul of her excellent brother Vallonus', is decorated with the vine-pruning hook, the tool of his trade.

In reliefs for funereal and other monuments the shoemaker hammers at his last, carpenters saw logs and toil with the axe and the plane, the carter rolls barrels (a Gallic invention) onto his cart, and even the fuller wearily treads his bolts of raw material in his tanks full of urine and watery clay. These Gallo-Romans may have remained mute, but they did not remain inglorious.

These traces of Gallo-Roman working lives are testament not only to the rise of the artisanal life under Roman rule, but also to the increased *quality* of life that these developments brought – not just for the artisans themselves, but for the poorer members of society. The oak-bottomed barges that plied the great trading route of the Rhône, for example, were more than 30 metres long. The sailors who guided them along the river did not live on hard tack or freeze to death in the winter; boats recovered from the depths of the Rhône have revealed specialized galleys built for their comfort. They were equipped not only with cauldrons and mortars, plates and bowls, but also with ingenious lead stoves for cooking and warmth, which were themselves water-cooled to prevent overheating and to stop the lead from melting. The cargoes that they carried, which have also been recovered, show the boon that their labour and that of other artisans brought. There were amphorae of *garum* (fermented fish sauce), salted fish, meats, wine and olive oil; limestone and marble for building and lead ingots for water-pipes; bars of iron, copper and tin. From the giant ceramic works at La Graufesenque in the Aveyron, which covered many hectares, as well as other workshops, the beautiful red glossy pottery known as Samian ware was exported over the whole of Gaul and further afield into Britain and around the Mediterranean; the rise of Gallic production after the conquest even forced the Italian producers into decline. Samian ware had once been regarded as a luxury item – as fit to grace a Roman table as dishes made of metal. With the Roman conquest, however, Samian pottery was produced in Gaul in vast quantities and became available to even the humblest home.

Simple material trinketry became far more widely available with the presence of Rome: not just crockery and plates, glass vases and vials of perfume, kitchen equipment, weighing scales, but also tools, stone and clay figurines, charms, ex-votos, keys, hinges for doors and chests, jewellery, finely crafted hairpins, medical equipment such as lances and tweezers (which might, as inscriptions show, have been administered by professional female doctors and not just male ones). The very bread that people ate could be of extraordinarily high quality. Pliny remarks that in Gaul the bakers used sieves made of horsehair to ensure a bread that rose easily, and that they used yeast gathered from the froth of beer to make the bread light and with an

Bas-relief from a tomb of two men packing merchandise for shipment by boat, dating to the third century AD, displayed in the Arles Museum.

agreeable flavour. The discovery of a well-preserved Gallo-Roman bakery attached to a house in Amiens dating to the end of the second century AD proves Pliny's point: the level of skill and knowledge of such Gallo-Roman artisans was great, and the product they made was particularly fine. The bakery was kitted out with sieves and traces of linen baskets in which the bread was placed to leaven. Bread from every stage of the process had been preserved: wheat and barley ready to be ground, flour, bread in the midst of rising, as well as fragments of baked bread still sitting in the oven. Analysis of the remnants of the bread showed it to be finely milled rye mixed with ordinary wheat flour, enhanced with fat or oil: a sophisticated concoction that might nowadays be bought in an artisanal bakery.

The growing wealth and prosperity brought by the Roman empire was by no means evenly spread. This was a thoroughly unequal society: the descendants of Gallic nobles, now in Roman guise, might luxuriate in grand town houses or elegant villas at the head of great estates, but many still lived close to subsistence level on rural plots, as bondmen or slaves, in lives untouched by the development of Roman towns and Roman amusements. The Roman presence, as we have seen, had been bought at vast human cost: death, violence and social dislocation on an epic scale; the usurpation of identities; and the disruption and extinction of ancient cultures. Nevertheless, the conquest led to an age of comparative peace, which, it appears, had not been known before in the discernible history of Gaul. To those who had much, much was given; but even the less well-off would benefit from this long period of stability, enjoying work, freedom of movement, and access to a quality of life that before had only been open to the highest. There was wine for the masses, fine bread and elegant crockery, all to be enjoyed if not in sprawling villas, at least in an environment of order and tranquillity. There was also the notion that there was dignity in the everyday doings of people; it is from this age that numbers of ordinary people in Gaul began to leave their mark. In the ancient world, this was an extraordinary and rare achievement.

For even the lowly of Gaul, there is still much to be said for the judgement of Edward Gibbon on the second century AD:

> If a man were called to fix the period in the history of the world during which the condition of the human race was most happy and prosperous, he would, without hesitation, name that which elapsed from the death of Domitian to the accession of Commodus. The vast extent of the Roman empire was governed by absolute power, under the guidance of virtue and wisdom.

The Porte d'Arroux, a Roman gateway at the northern end of the cardo
maximus *in Autun, dating to the end of the third century* AD. *Its arches
inspired architects building the Benedictine Abbey of Cluny in the
twelfth century.*

CHAPTER IX

In Their Own Words

summae genus sollertiae
'A nation possessed of remarkable ingenuity'
JULIUS CAESAR, *De Bello Gallico*, VII.22

JEAN, DUC DES ESSEINTES

·

LATE LATIN: THE 'ROTTED CORPSE'

·

SCHOOLS OF MARSEILLES

·

AUTUN

·

THE MAENIANAE

·

GREEK WISDOM

·

AUSONIUS

·

BORDEAUX

·

A TEACHER'S LIFE

·

'THE DOINGS OF A WHOLE DAY'

·

POEMS OF LOVE AND LOSS

·

THE REPUBLIC OF LETTERS

T HE MOST DANGEROUS BOOK in French literature – or at any rate dangerous to impressionable and sensitive young minds – is *A Rebours*, or *Against Nature*, by Joris-Karl Huysmans. Published in 1884, it stood against the tide of naturalism in contemporary prose fiction, becoming in itself a manifesto for fin-de-siècle aesthetes and the Decadent Movement.

The hero is Jean, duc des Esseintes. He is the last in the line of an ancient and noble family, worn out by generations of inbreeding and the demands of aristocratic life. An only child, he is brought up in the gloomy ancestral seat in the vicinity of Paris, the Chateau des Lourps. His distant parents send him to a Jesuit school, but he refuses to engage in any education that would fit him for employment and ordinary life, and his teachers leave him to indulge his own recondite tastes in French and Latin literature. When he leaves school, he grows weary with Parisian society, finding no companions who share his intellectual tastes. Those he encounters are either 'submissive believers' or 'rapacious and insolent puritans whose breeding he considered inferior to the neighbourhood bootmaker'. He tries to restrain his growing contempt for all humanity by engaging in a passion for debauchery, as one who is 'beset by pangs of desire yet whose palate rapidly grows dull and surfeited'. But this is without success, and after indulging in every possible coupling from the aristocratic to the 'dregs of society', he holds a funeral feast to mark his final collapse into impotence.

To mollify his ever-increasing hypersensitivity, des Esseintes finally decides to go into a permanent retreat where he can devote himself to the untrammelled pursuit of aesthetic pleasures and a life of 'studious ineffectiveness'. He sells the remains of his family estate, buys a house on the far outskirts of Paris, and decorates it to suit 'the requirements of his future solitude'. His walls are covered, like bound books, in morocco leather; the domed ceiling is painted in febrile orange and royal blue. His furniture includes ancient reliquaries with copies of Baudelaire's poems hand-copied on vellum and illuminated like a medieval prayer book. His bedroom is decorated like a monastic cell, but with the most expensive possible materials: saffron-coloured silk to imitate stucco, and white silk on the floor to counterfeit bare plaster. There are instruments with which he can generate new scents for perfumes and liquors, and, best of all, a tortoise whose shell he had had gilded and set with rare gemstones: chrysoberyls, azurite and sapphirines.

It is not only des Esseintes's taste in décor or notions of animal welfare that are so arresting. His preferences in Latin literature are equally revolutionary. For him, there is no merit or pleasure to be had in the classic authors of the 'Golden Age' such as were propounded at the Sorbonne, not to mention in the traditional curricula of other universities and schools of Europe. Virgil's *Aeneid* is an 'indescribable inanity'; his Latin hexameter verses have a 'tinny hollow ring'. Horace is loathsome, the 'prattlings of an insufferable bungler as he archly tells off-colour stories worthy of a senescent, white-plastered clown'. Cicero is 'ponderous density'. Caesar himself has 'a martinet's aridity, a sterile log-book style, an incredible, uncalled-for costiveness'. Livy is 'sentimental and pompous', Seneca 'turgid and lack-lustre'.*

It is only in the period of so-called Silver Latin, after the first century AD – an age held by common consent to herald the Latin literary decline – that des Esseintes begins to take pleasure in the corpus of Latin literature. The novelists Petronius and Apuleius delight him. However, it is not until the fourth century, when the Latin language begins to acquire a 'gamey redolence' that his interest becomes deeper. It is a redolence that 'the odour of Christianity imparted to

* Des Esseintes's words are translated here by Margaret Mauldon in the Oxford World's Classics edition.

the language of pagan Rome, which decomposed like venison, falling apart' as 'the Ancient World crumbled into dust'.

Many of the poets to which des Esseintes keeps returning are products of, or associated with, late Roman Gaul. There is Claudian, in whom paganism 'lived again, sounding its final fanfare, raising up its last great poet high above Christianity'; Ausonius and Rutilius, writing of their journeys across the late empire, describing the quality of landscapes reflected in water, the mirages of mists and the swirling of fog around the mountain tops. Into the fifth century – with Paulinus of Nola, Ausonius' pupil, the letter-writing Sidonius, and the Christian poet (and grandson of Ausonius), Paulinus of Pella – des Esseintes's 'interest in the Latin language remained undiminished, now that it hung like a completely rotted corpse, its limbs falling off, dripping with pus, barely a few firm parts, which the Christians took away to steep in the brine of their new idiom'.

A number of these authors, particularly Ausonius and Sidonius, would have been horrified to learn of des Esseintes's reasons for enjoying their works, not to mention his judgements on Virgil, Cicero and Horace. They would have seen themselves not as decadent, but as the careful yet vigorous defenders of a tradition of Roman education and Latin literature that reached back in Gaul to the time of the conquest. One may choose to like these authors for the reasons given by des Esseintes – if indeed, his judgement of the decayed state of their Latinity is sound – but regardless of this, his preference for these authors over the classical staples of Virgil and Cicero, and indeed the fact that he gives them such limelight at all, deserves to be celebrated. In some ways, the lives of a number of these authors, withdrawing into a hypersensitive aristocratic gloom in the face of a decline in central Roman power and order, simply mirrors des Esseintes's escape from the vulgarity of modern life. Yet they deserve more attention than they customarily receive, in that they are a reflection of wider life in Roman Gaul, not only of their own time but also of the eras that preceded them. They embody not only one of the great reasons for the long-standing success of Rome, but also stand as a waypoint towards literary traditions that would come after them. So they deserve their space on the bookshelves of des Esseintes, not to mention our own, even if we do not possess the morocco-leather-bound walls and the gilded tortoise to go with them.

The Romano-Gallic authors on des Esseintes's shelves were born out of a tradition of education. It was in Massalia – a Greek city – that this Gallic tradition of Roman education and letters, along with many other things, began. Strabo suggests that following its submission to Caesar in 49 BC the city's energies, which were previously engaged in navigation and commerce, were turned towards erudition. In all likelihood, however, Massalia possessed good education facilities long before this point. It was a melting pot of Gallic, Greek and Latin culture, in which ideas from all three traditions were present, but Greek appeared to predominate. Various writers give accounts of the higher branches of study that could be pursued there – astronomy and mathematics, rhetoric and natural philosophy. An edition of Homer was collated in the city in the third century BC, and the natural philosopher Euthymenes speculates on the causes of the flooding of the Nile. Ammianus Marcellinus, a historian of the fourth century AD, claims that these higher studies at Massalia did not derive their impetus merely from the Greek presence, but also drew on native Druidic traditions. The availability of these high-level studies in the city was more than enough to bring in an audience for the many teachers who had set up there in business. Many local Gauls were attracted simply by the prospect of learning the Greek language, which they mastered to the extent that they began to use it for their legal contracts.

Massalia was a draw not only for Gauls, but for Romans from Italy. Upper-class Romans, for whom a knowledge of Greek was a vital part of their higher education, began to send their university-age children to Massalia rather than Athens to acquire proficiency in the language. For many, it was seen as a better choice, since it was closer to Rome than Athens, the climate was healthier and its morals were more vehemently guarded. The first-century AD writer Valerius Maximus calls Massalia the 'fiercest guardian of strictness', for the city authorities banned the famously licentious performances of pantomime from their theatres, put limits on the wearing of expensive clothes and prohibited women from drinking wine. According to Tacitus, Massalia was a place where 'refinement and provincial frugality were blended and happily combined'. Its reputation was such that at the end of the first century BC and the beginning of the following century, even the emperor Augustus himself, well known for his strait-laced credentials, sent his sister's grandson there, at least ostensibly for study; though Tacitus, who reports it, says that this was to cover the imperial princeling's exile.

But with the conquest of Gallia Comata, the scholarly resources available in Massalia were nowhere near sufficient to satisfy the sudden and urgent requirements for education in the new province. A Latin education, at least for the aristocratic classes of newly conquered territories, was the handmaiden of Roman government policy. It was necessary not just to inculcate in the noble classes a habit of loyalty towards Rome, but also to equip them for the administrative and military posts that they, and no one else, were in a position to take. Tacitus describes this process explicitly in his biography of his father-in-law Julius Agricola, a Gallo-Roman general who was himself an alumnus of the schools of Massalia. Agricola was responsible for securing the conquest of much of Britain, and Tacitus gloomily describes how a Roman education, as part of a wider acculturation in contemporary Roman ways (which he himself saw as decadent), was one of the weapons he used to bind the indigenous upper classes to the order of Roman rule. Agricola, in the midst of his campaigns, provided 'a liberal education for the sons of the chiefs... that they who lately disdained the tongue of Rome now coveted its eloquence'. As a result 'a liking sprang up for our style of dress, and the toga became fashionable. Step by step the British were led to things which dispose to vice, the lounge, the bath, the elegant banquet. All this in their ignorance they called civilization, when it was but part of their servitude.' These opportunities for education and civilization, visited on the British by Agricola in the latter part of the first century AD, had been brought by the Romans to Gallia Comata in the years following the conquest. The leading seat of Gallo-Roman education in these times appears to have been the new city of Augustodunum, now Autun in Burgundy.

Present-day Autun seems well suited to academic life and the pursuit of otherworldly meditations. Its streets, with their medieval timber-framed houses, pinnacles and statue-niches, enjoy an atmosphere of antique quietness, though its surviving Roman gates and circuit walls have a striking – even ostentatious – air to them. The town was built shortly after the conquest. Although on a small hill, it was located in the flatter land about fifteen miles east of the Aedui *oppidum* of Bibracte. Situated here, its role was clear: to draw away the life from the established Gallic town and into a closely controlled Roman centre. In this, it was successful. Without application of force, the high stronghold of Bibracte was left to be rapidly devoured by the forest. However, to achieve this mastery over the rival settlement, Autun had to display boldly to the Aedui the extent of Roman wealth, and the opportunities available for those who co-operated with the Roman project. Although it was not one of the settlements formally endowed with colonial status like Arles or Nîmes, it was still given the right to be surrounded by walls, the privilege of a colony. Extensive remnants of these still stand today – ivy-speckled and louring over the green verges of an empty peripheral road – some of the longest stretches of Roman city wall anywhere in western Europe. In their prime, the walls were 6 kilometres (nearly 4 miles) in circumference, tracing out a lozenge-shaped area of around 200 hectares, which the city itself struggled to fill. Nevertheless, the sight of the walls, at that time 12 metres high, almost 2 metres thick and relieved at regular intervals by around fifty semi-circular projecting bastions, would have made their point to the local Aedui.

The ingredients listed by Tacitus for the cultural subversion of a conquered indigenous group were soon in place. There was a theatre – at 150 metres in diameter the largest Roman theatre yet known – as well as an amphitheatre and baths. However, for Autun, the pinnacle of these constructions was a school. Such a feature was, certainly in the western part of the empire, unusual and notable. Education was usually a parasite activity, taking place in a borrowed location – a

The Roman walls of Autun, dating to the first century BC. *Their main purpose was to display Rome's power to the region's influential Aedui tribe and to overawe the nearby* oppidum *of Bibracte.*

public portico, or sometimes within a private dwelling. This was not so at Autun. The school appears to have been located at the centre of the town, probably beneath the modern post office. It was opposite the temple of Apollo, a god who, as mentioned, played a special role in the doctrine of Augustus. That education had a place of its own, next to a temple that flaunted and proclaimed the Roman imperial ideology, shows not only the importance placed on it here, but also its importance in the context of the development of Roman power.

It is perhaps less surprising that such privileged access to education, and hence an entrée into the systems of Roman power, was made available in Autun rather than elsewhere. It was not just that the city was close to the geographical centre of Gallia Comata, making it easy for young nobles from all three provinces to reach; but its location looks like a particular reward for the Aedui. The Aedui were allies of the Roman people even before the conquest and for nearly the whole period of Caesar's campaign remained loyal to Rome. It was not long before they developed a tribal mythology that made them brothers to the Roman people: a mythology that claimed that they too, like the Romans, were descendants of the refugees who had fled the fall of Troy.

The school at Autun rapidly gained a reputation. It was known as the Maenianae, after an architectural feature of a balcony raised on columns, which the school presumably possessed. Tacitus states that by AD 20 it was where the noblest youth of Gaul went for their education. It was very likely the fact that they were gathered together in Autun that made it the target for starting a failed uprising among the Aedui by Julius Sacrovir in that same year; indeed, it may have been the congregation of a large student body that made it vulnerable to unrest. Nevertheless, as with any ancient and established school, it attracted a deep sense of loyalty. In around 270, the school was seriously damaged during a period of civil war. A teacher named Eumenius, appointed to oversee the school by the emperor Constantius Chlorus, made a public appeal to have his entire salary – an enormous 600,000 sesterces

– dedicated to the school's rebuilding. He made this appeal as a formality during a public address to the provincial governor, delivered either in Autun or in Lugdunum. His pride in the institution and its work was unbounded. He states that its work in developing the intellects and oratorical abilities of young Gallo-Roman males should not be hidden away but it should be 'in public display, in the very eyes of this city'. It was fitting that the Maenianae was built in the heart of the city, close to the temples of Apollo and Minerva, since visiting emperors and other high dignitaries would pass it as they arrived. Such was the importance and challenge of the school's work, it was only right for it to be near the shrines of the gods who were friends not only of Rome, but of learning.

Eumenius's speech also tells us a great deal about the relationship between education and power in the Roman empire. He praises the importance of the school in creating alumni destined for high

The Porte Saint-André, Autun, third century AD.

office. Its rigorous standards, overseen by the emperor's personal care, ensured that anyone advanced to 'any tribunal or to the service of the sacred judiciary or perhaps the very offices of the palace, should not follow uncertain oratorical standards as if caught unexpectedly amid the surging seas of youth'. We also learn from Eumenius that the school possessed a large selection of maps painted on the school walls beneath its porticoes. The students, said Eumenius, should 'see and contemplate daily every land and all the seas and whatever cities, peoples, nations' over which the Roman empire ruled. These locations were marked with their sizes, locations, extent, and the distances between them, together with rivers, shores and bays. Contemplating these maps, students could imagine the emperors 'hurling lightning on the smitten Moors' or 'trampling upon Persian bows and quivers'. Thus did Roman education, among the conquered Gauls, create a class that sensed itself destined to hold a wider power.

The education offered by this school and others like it was not just about acclimatizing the Gallo-Roman elite to holding and wielding political power. It also brought to Gaul an international and aristocratic culture of poetry, philosophy and pleasure, Greek in tone but wholeheartedly adopted by Rome, which would be recognizable as far east as the Levant and Asia Minor. Such a culture became a defining mark of the aristocratic life in Gaul, but it probable that those brought up in such a culture valued it for itself rather than just as a marker of class. The physical footprints of this culture have been found in Autun. At a site not far from the city's *cardo*, a large room was discovered during construction work that was decorated with mosaics dating to around the second century AD. These mosaics do not feature the animals, fruit, or agreeable scenes from the rustic year that we have encountered hitherto, but Greek philosophers and poets. They sit on their couches, bearded, clad in sandals and heavy togas, slightly hunched, their faces (where they are still visible) intent in calm but profound meditation. In their hands they hold scrolls, presumably of their work, which they offer to us. Although mute, they are not silent.

Written on the panels behind them are quotations from their writings in Greek. Epicurus himself reminds us (if the text of the mosaic
has been properly restored): 'It is not possible to live with pleasure
without living with prudence, honesty and justice; nor can one live
with prudence, honesty and justice without living with pleasure.' His
follower Metrodorus makes the point more insistently: 'We have been
born just once. It is impossible to be born twice, and we cannot live
out eternity. But you, although you are not master of tomorrow, waste
your chances for enjoyment. Life is worn out by procrastination and
each of us dies with no time on our hands.'

The Epicurean message of seizing the opportunity for pleasure
and putting away disturbances of the spirit may have been expressed
sternly by these philosophers, but poets voiced it more pleasantly.
Anacreon sings on the panels: 'Bring water, boy, bring wine, and bring
the garlands of flowers – come now, bring them, for I shall not struggle against Love (Eros)! Anyone who wishes to fight when the chance
presents itself, let them fight! But as for myself, let me drink to the
health of my friends, boy, with honeyed wine.'

The purpose of the room with the mosaics is still debated by
archaeologists. Some have suggested it was a lecture theatre, but
others, warming to the Epicurean theme, believe it was part of the
town-house of a learned aristocrat, intended for use in Greek-style
symposiums, or dinner parties, where the display of such knowledge
was a prerequisite for attendance. But the most attractive idea is that
such a house belonged not to a conventional aristocrat, but a rich
teacher such as Eumenius, devoted to wine and friendship, erudition
and song.

The culture of the symposium was self-consciously aristocratic,
but other finds from Autun suggest that literacy and even echoes of
the symposium culture were to be found across the classes. Bobbin
weights are inscribed with what might be pub chat: *'Ave Vale, Tu Bella'*
– 'Hello dear, you're beautiful'; *'Ave Domina, Sitiio'* – 'Hello lady, I'm
thirsty.'

Despite the prominence of Autun in the Gallic educational fir-
mament, it was certainly not the case that learning and literacy were
found nowhere else. The Gauls had a reputation among the Romans
for cleverness. Caesar himself commented that they were a people of
great ingenuity. Massalia aside, the transalpine province produced a
number of noted teachers before the conquest. One of them, Antonius
Gnipho, is reported to have tutored in Caesar's own household, and
Cicero was also one of his pupils. Another, Valerius Cato, a freed slave,
is recorded as having taught a number of poets, and as having written
two books of verse himself before falling into debt, losing his villa
and dying in poverty and extreme old age. Preserved scraps of Latin
doggerel ask how 'The great grammarian, chief among our poets,
could solve all questions, but solvent could not be.' Perhaps as a result

*The 'Temple of Janus', Autun, first century AD. Dedicated to an unknown
Gallic divinity, the temple combines Roman building techniques with a Gallic
temple design.*

of Transalpine Gaul's reputation, the newly conquered provinces were a draw for the most famous teachers. The imperial biographer Suetonius records a number who went to teach in Gaul after the conquest, including one, Oppius Chares, who taught to the very end of his life '...when he could no longer walk, or even see'. Teachers, either from outside or trained within Gaul, set themselves up in the major towns across the Gallic provinces. Memorial inscriptions to them survive in Limoges, Trier, Vienne, Strasbourg and Narbonne. In Nîmes, there are also inscriptions to two *paedagogoi*, or slaves owned by rich households who were responsible for the good conduct of the children and assisting them with their learning. One was a woman named Porcia Lada. A good education became highly desirable; an inscription in Nîmes set up by a mother to her dead foster-son recounts her misery at the waste of his education: 'A most wretched mother, who educated this boy in the place of a son, and endowed him with the study of liberal arts – but, O unjust stars, he did not get to enjoy adulthood, and it was not fated for him...'

The migration of teachers into Gaul and the consequent widespread availability of education there had a notable and beneficial cultural impact. In the years after the conquest, the Gallic reputation for education and literacy grew exponentially. Tacitus, in a dialogue on the art of oratory, makes all but one of the learned participants Gauls. Juvenal portrays Gaul as excelling in rhetoric, particularly that of the courtroom, even training the lawyers who went on to plead in the British courts. The poet Martial, in a number of epigrams, depicts Gaul as a place of literary culture. He suggests that his poems are read in Vienne, and describes volumes of his verse being sent to acquaintances in Narbonne and Toulouse. Books were easy to acquire in Gaul. Pliny the Younger expresses surprise that some of his works are available at a bookseller in Lugdunum, and later on he mentions a bookseller at Reims.

Gaul was soon producing its own authors of note. Pompeius Trogus has already been mentioned in connection with Vaison-la-

Romaine. Tacitus himself was probably of Gallic origin. But it is from the later period – the fourth and fifth centuries AD, which spanned the final flowering of the Roman empire in Gaul, its eventual collapse and the rise of Christianity – that there is a large body of surviving Latin literature from Gaul. This may be a result of the establishment of an imperial court on the frontier at Trier in the fourth century. The proximity of this court seems to have acted as a stimulus to the Gallo-Roman aristocracy, not only to throw themselves more wholeheartedly into imperial service, but also to greater literary production. The fact that a number of the surviving works are panegyrics addressed to emperors and high dignitaries may be a matter of chance, but could also be evidence of a reaction by the literate classes to the ending of Roman rule in Gaul. I will explore the possible reasons for the appearance of these encomia from writers of the late Gallo-Roman period in due course; but what is not in doubt is that their writings give us a picture of the lives of at least a handful of Roman Gauls that is more intimate, more revelatory than anything offered by an artefact, inscription or ruin.

> Dear wife, let us always live the way we have lived, and keep the names which we took when first we were wed. Let no day have it that we should be changed with time, but that I should always be 'my boy' to you, and you to me 'my girl'. Even if I should live to be as old as Nestor, and you also older than Deiphobe, the priestess of Apollo, let us refuse to know the meaning of ripe old age: let's not count down the years; all we should do is know their worth.

This short love poem, eight lines long in the original Latin, was written around AD 340, and is addressed by Ausonius to his new wife,

Attusia. Ausonius was in his late twenties or early thirties at the time, and was working as a teacher. His poem, although short, breathes a heady optimism. The love it expresses is genuine, and the poet is looking forward with hope and confidence to sharing his life with Attusia. However, his optimism is undoubtedly bolstered by an expectation of impending professional success. It was not just that he had gained a fairly prestigious job in his home town of Bordeaux, which was then overtaking Autun as the premier seat of learning in Gaul. Nor was it that in marrying Attusia, even if he was doing so for love, he was entering into an alliance that would be hugely advantageous to him: she was of an old and noble lineage, and the match brought lustre to Ausonius and his family, which only two generations before had been in domestic service. No; on top of all of this, a connection even more promising had come about. Ausonius's maternal uncle, Magnus Arborius, also a teacher, had been summoned to the new imperial capital of Constantinople to work as a tutor in the household of the emperor Constantine himself. The sense of proximity to the throne was upon Ausonius, heightening his cheerfulness and increasing his expectations for what was to come. All pointed to a bright future with his new wife and young family. Fate, however, was not going to gratify all his hopes.

Ausonius was born around AD 310. His father Julius was originally a native of Bazas in what is now the department of Gironde, but he moved before his son's birth to the nearby centre of Bordeaux. Although the family was of lowly origin, Julius – as his son would do later – married well, taking a wife named Aemelia from a distinguished family of mixed Aedui and Aquitanian background. Julius had trained as a doctor, and was able to give his son an excellent education in Bordeaux. Ausonius was appointed to a teaching position in the city in 334, and around this time married Attusia. They had three children together. However, the hopes expressed in his short love poem were dashed. Attusia died in 343 after nine years of marriage, at the age of twenty-eight. He never remarried.

Ausonius spent some time practising at the Bar in Bordeaux, but his heart was more in teaching. He ended up devoting himself fully to the profession and was promoted to a professorship in rhetoric. After nearly twenty years working in this fashion, he managed to repeat the feat of his uncle: in 364, he was summoned to the imperial court to be a tutor to the young prince Gratian. He remained in this position for around ten years. His life was not without incident; in 368 he accompanied the imperial entourage as it went to fight a campaign on the German frontier. In 370, he was given the title of *comes* ('count'), and in 375 he entered more fully into the imperial civil service, gaining the position of quaestor of the sacred palace. In the same year Ausonius's protégé Gratian succeeded to the emperorship. It was the start of a golden age for Ausonius. Having started life as a teacher, he was now showered with honours and became a person of great influence. In 378 he was appointed prefect of Gaul; Ausonius's father, who was then still alive, was given the honorific title of prefect of Illyricum, and other of his relatives were awarded similar distinctions. Some scholars have even seen traces of Ausonius's influence in the development of the law at this time, particularly in statutes relating to education. In the following year, 379, Ausonius achieved what was, even in this late imperial age, the much-desired capstone of a Roman career: the consulship. It was a huge achievement for one who had started life as a teacher.

However, his good fortune was not to persist. In 383, a revolt broke out in Britain, and a usurper, Maximus, made a bid for the throne. Fighting broke out in Gaul, Gratian was killed in Lugdunum and his old favourites such as Ausonius fell out of favour, if not under threat. Maximus lasted in power for only five years, and was killed by the eastern Roman emperor, Theodosius I, in 388. However, by this time, Ausonius would probably have thought himself too old, and was perhaps too shocked by the turn of events, to return to public life. He spent his last years on his estates near Bordeaux, occasionally visiting the city on business, but he preferred life in the countryside away from the bustle of urban life. He died either in 393 or 394, having lived well into his eighties.

Around 300 pages of Ausonius's literary work have survived from the fourth century AD. It is, for the time and the place, a rare survival. His work is a collection of letters, some written in verse, exchanged between him and the emperor, other aristocrats, his son or his local friends. There are long, creative poems; short verses addressed to his family and to his teaching colleagues around Bordeaux; poems that are little more than academic jests; a welter of epigrams on a range of subjects; poems on divinity – he appears to have been a Christian of sorts – and poems that describe his ordinary experience of life. Ausonius is one of the most complete characters to survive from any period of Roman Gaul, and it is through him that we can see the lives of those of his ilk and those who surrounded him in the provincial aristocracy and its dependents.

Many details of Ausonius's career and background can be gleaned from his writings: he recorded not just the notable events of his life, but also the daily round. The first cycle of poems to be preserved in the collection is called *Ephemeris*, meaning 'day-book' or 'diary', and subtitled 'The Doings of a Whole Day'. It does not, however, present a perfect record. A number of the poems are missing, with the result that the afternoon is mostly a blank. Moreover, part of the object of the cycle is to showcase the poet's metrical skill. Each stage of the day is recounted in a different Latin metre, and the reader inevitably wonders how much the poems are meant to reflect Ausonius's experience, and how much they are a literary construct. The fact that he refers to his retainers by the names of the characters of slaves from early Roman comedy adds to this suspicion. However, literary allusion is an adjunct to the writing of such learned verse, and its presence does not mean that Ausonius is merely regurgitating the substance of other writers. His work may be decorated with literary jokes, but it rings true as an account of his life, and enough of it survives to give us a clear view of the pattern of his days.

On the day he writes, his first job is to wake one of his slaves:

> Already bright morn is opening her windows, already
> the watchful sparrow twitters from her nest; but you,
> Parmeno, sleep on as if it were the first or middle watch
> of the night. Dormice sleep the winter round, but they
> leave food alone; while you slumber on because you
> drink deep, and swell out your paunch with too great a
> mass of food… Up with you, you waster! What a thrash-
> ing you deserve!… Out with you, Parmeno, from your
> downy bed.

Ausonius is at least able to rely on other retainers and slaves:

> Hey, boy, get up! Bring me my slippers and my fine-
> cotton cloak. Get all the clothes you have just got ready
> for me to go out. Get me spring water to wash my hands
> and mouth and eyes. Get me the chapel opened… I must
> pray to God and the Son of God most high… Now I have
> prayed enough to God, boy, put out my formal wear. I
> must exchange my greetings with my friends… And now
> the time for inviting my friends to lunch draws on…
> So that no fault of mine may make them late for lunch,
> hurry at your best pace, boy, hurry to the neighbours'
> houses – you know without my telling who they are. I
> have invited five to lunch; six persons, including the host,
> make the right number for a meal. If there be more, it is
> no meal but a *mêlée*… Off he goes…

He is similarly full of instructions for his cook:

> Sosias, I must have lunch. The warm sun is already passed
> well into his fourth hour, and on the dial the shadow is

moving on towards the fifth stroke. Taste and make sure – for they often play you false – that the seasoned dishes are well soused and taste appetising. Turn your bubbling pots in your hands, and taste the hot gravy with your tongue…

Then the time comes for Ausonius to turn to matters of business. His secretary is a person whom he apparently held in higher regard than his other retainers:

> Boy, skilled in dashing shorthand, make haste and come! Open your folding tables… I have grand books in my mind… thick and fast like hail the words tumble off my tongue. And yet your ears are not at fault nor your page crowded… you have the thoughts of my heart already set fast in wax before they are uttered…

With these frequent admonitions to his retainers, his cook, his secretary, Ausonius gives the impression of being, among other things, a particular and precise person. This certainly applies when it comes to enumerating his achievements. In a prefatory poem he lists carefully the honours he has received – *comes*, quaestor, consul – but adds the detail that he was the senior of the two consuls of the year, 'and was given precedence on assuming the insignia and the *curule* chair, so that my colleague's name stood after mine'.

Ausonius is similarly meticulous when he comes to the achievements of his family. One of the cycles in the collection is entitled *Parentalia*, a collection of elegies in memory not only of his parents, but also of his extended family. His maternal grandfather, Arborius, is first remembered for 'uniting the blood of many a noble house, both of the province of Lyons and of that land where the Aedui held sway, and in the country of Vienne bordered by Alpine heights'. His son-in-law, Valerius, who died an untimely death, surpassed even his

ancestors in that he held 'the prefect's seat, the Illyrian shore as governor, and the Treasury itself was one of [his] clients at law'.

Ausonius's care over the recital of such honours has led some
classical scholars to dismiss his writings as being stilted and without
feeling. The formal enumeration of dignities, they argue, has expunged
any element of personal experience and recollection from his writing.
Such criticism, however, misses the mark on two grounds. First, the
use of literature to mark social position and that of one's family was
a fundamental aspect of the intellectual world of late Roman Gaul.
Thanks to the way Gaul had evolved, there was an essential connection between high education, culture and social class. The possession
of literary culture was in itself proof of belonging to the aristocracy,
and to display that culture was to confirm one's membership of the
elite stratum of Gallo-Roman society. To refuse to acknowledge the
connection between literature and class would have been a rebellious

Modern sculpture of Ausonius in Bordeaux, by Bertrand Piéchaud.

act, and Ausonius was no rebel. However, there is a second reason for decrying such criticism of Ausonius. It is simply untrue to say that his writing is devoid of personal feeling.

Ausonius wrote the elegy for his wife Attusia, which forms part of the *Parentalia*, around the time of his consulship, the pinnacle of his career. He is clear about the number of years that have elapsed since her passing – thirty-six. By then, he would have been nearly seventy. When he speaks of her, he does not omit to mention that she was noble in birth, and sprang from a line of senators; indeed, this is one of the first things he says. But he also has rather more to say. The poem is an expression of his grief for her, still undimmed by the passing of time or by his professional successes:

> In youth I wept for you, robbed of my hopes in early years, and through these thirty-six years, unwedded, I have mourned and mourned you still. Age has crept over me, but yet I cannot lull my pain; for ever it keeps raw and well-nigh new to me… My wounds become heavier with the length of days. I tear my grey hairs mocked by the widowed life, and the more I live in loneliness, the more I live in heaviness.

His verse does not eschew self-analysis and introspection. He does not hesitate to lay out the complexities and contradictions of his continuing grief for his wife: 'I grieve if one man has a good wife; and yet again I grieve if another has a bad. For you are always with me to throw everything else into relief: however it be, you come to torture me: if one be bad, because you were not like her, or if one be good, because you were like her.' The continuing pain of losing the sensuality of Attusia's presence belies the apparent parlour politeness of his verse: 'That my house is still and silent, and that my bed is cold, that I share not my ills with any, my good with any, these things feed my wound.'

The emotional honesty of Ausonius's confessions – direct, never overstated, and always overlaid with the requisite social veneer – make his work unexpectedly poignant. He remembers his first-born son, named after him, who died 'Just as you were practising to transform your babbling into the first words of childhood'. The one consolation is that he lies on his 'great-grandfather's bosom sharing one common grave, so that you do not suffer the reproach of being alone in your tomb'. His grandson, named Pastor, also died in infancy, killed when a workman carelessly threw a tile down from a roof, hitting the boy on the head. 'That tile, carelessly flung, hit my own head too.'

Ausonius's *Parentalia* commemorates thirty of his late relatives. They are a varied group, including his uncle Clemens, a merchant who died and was buried on a trading mission to Britain; his aunt Aemelia who, 'hating her own sex', appears to have lived as a man and practised as a doctor; and his maternal grandfather Arborius who was skilled in astrology and who, says Ausonius, had predicted the outline of Ausonius' own life. Some members of the family, such as Arborius, were long-lived; Arborius himself reached his nineties. Many, however, died unexpectedly or before their time. Just because such early deaths were common in this age does not mean that they were felt any less keenly by those left behind. Ausonius does not dissemble: the ubiquity of early death could never lessen the intensity of human affection, or diminish the misery of loss.

But it did not take the spectre of death to turn Ausonius to intro-spection and anxiety. A letter to his surviving son, Hesperius, describes the moment when the news of Maximus's uprising reached them both at Trier, and Hesperius decided to flee for safety to Bordeaux. The letter is written in verse, but unfinished. Ausonius recalls the sight of his son (by this time grown up) borne away on a boat down the Moselle as he stood on the riverbank with his companions:

Alone! Though compassed round with a throng of friends,
I was alone, and offered prayers for that fleeting craft:

alone, though I still saw you, my child, and grudged the speed of the oars plying against the stream... Forlorn I pace the empty, lonely shores. Now I strike down the sprouting willow shoots, now I crush beds of turf, and over green sedge I poise my slippery footsteps on the pebbles strewn beneath... So the first day passed away, and the second, and the two nights which wheeled, revolving after each, so others: and the whole year for me will so pass by until your destiny gives back me, your father, to you.

In other circumstances, his writing is similarly self-revelatory. During his time on the German campaign, he was given a slave captured during a Roman action – a girl named Bissula. He wrote a collection of poems about her, which is unfortunately incomplete. They were sent to a friend as an intimate poetic gift. One wonders if a later transmitter, eager to preserve Ausonius's reputation, did away with a part of the manuscript. Despite his persistent grief for his wife, he appears to have been quite infatuated with Bissula:

> Born and bred beyond the chilly Danube, Bissula... a captive maid but made free, she queens it as the pet of him whose spoil of war she was... not so changed by Roman blessings but that she remains German in features, blue of eyes and fair of hair. A girl of either race, now speech, now looks present her: the last declare her a daughter of the Rhine, the first a child of Rome.

It appears he had her portrait painted, but the painter's skill, says Ausonius, was not up to capturing the fullness of her complexion. 'Darling, delight, my pet, my love, my joy! Barbarian and adopted you may be, but you surpass the Roman girls. Bissula – a clumsy name for so delicate a girl, an uncouth little name to strangers: but to your master, charming.'

When Ausonius chooses, he can be fresh, original, with a clarity of sight and a sensibility for landscape and immediate experiences that can be arresting and unexpected. Brief mention has been made in an earlier chapter of his long poem on the Moselle (see page 207), which was almost certainly written in 368 when he accompanied the imperial court to the campaign on the Germanic frontier, while he was still engaged as Gratian's tutor. His poem is a record of this journey, and has some antecedents in classical literature. The poet Horace, for example, wrote a satire describing a journey through Italy in the company of Augustus's inner circle to attend a peace conference during the civil war. Yet where Horace's poem is self-deprecatory and bawdy, describing his bowel movements and other nocturnal accidents, Ausonius is more interested in describing the sights and sounds of his voyage, and the beauties of the landscapes through which he passes. His vision is rare for the corpus of Latin literature. He observes the way that the light scatters on the water and changes its colour; how the sand beneath the river is rippled and furrowed by the current, how the water grasses dance sinuously as the force of the stream presses against them. He describes the fish that could be caught in the river, the fishermen with their nets, the villas and vineyards and the expanse of the countryside, the bawdy banter of vine-dressers shouting at the bargemen as they float cheerfully by. His descriptions, at times direct, at other times interwoven with erudite allusions and references to earlier literature, are – at their best – as fresh as the day on which he made his journey, an almost-forgotten antecedent to the canon of travel literature.

Such forays into evocative description of the natural world do not, however, reflect Ausonius's primary concerns as a writer. His central focus was literature and literary culture itself. His writing, for the most part, was intended to confirm, preserve and exalt the literary canon of Rome and the assumptions it brought in its wake – the civilizing influence of Roman laws and Roman government, its ideas of *humanitas*, its notions of order and conduct. Access to this high level of culture was open only to a privileged few. Part of the function of the literature was to mark a fellowship among the cultural, and hence political, elite. Ausonius's writing is a constant play on the canon of earlier authors: Virgil, Horace, Cicero, Terence. The endless exchange of letters and of poems alluding to the older Latin canon marks out the qualification of the writers and recipients as members of a virtual confraternity of learning. Such learned exchanges are the behaviour of the aristocratic and civilized. With such a note of superiority and withdrawal, one can perhaps see why this stratum of Latin literature had a particular appeal for the duc des Esseintes.

Ausonius is one of the first great proponents of the 'old school tie'. Although earlier writers in the classical canon praise their teachers and the fellowship brought about by their schooling – one of Plato's intentions in his dialogues is to praise his teacher Socrates, and Horace is always grateful to his schoolmaster, 'thrasher' Orbilius – none quite give their education the prominence that Ausonius gives his in his writing. He devotes an entire cycle to commemorating the teachers of Bordeaux, both those who taught him and those who were educated with him and who later became his colleagues. The cycle appears to have been written late in life, but even sixty years after his schooling he is still in awe of his own teachers. Victor Minervius, he says, 'gave a thousand pupils to the bar, and twice a thousand to the Senate's rank and purple robes'. Minervius was a master in speaking and oratory, but Ausonius still remembers him for his prodigious memory: he could recall entire board games and every throw of the dice. Attius Patera, teacher of rhetoric, who had a gift for rolling eloquence, is revered for reputedly being the descendent of a family of Druids from Bayeux.

Ausonius feels that his colleagues always deserve to be commemorated in his verse, but to win his unalloyed praise is more difficult. He does not hold back from recording failure or from recalling old scandals, even if he feigns unwillingness to go into details. Delphidius, for example, had a reputation for being a genius. In his youth, he wrote an epic poem, and was soon appearing in great court cases. However, palace intrigues drove him from the Bar to the classroom, and he ended up as a teacher of rhetoric, 'but a lack of diligence in teaching disappointed the hopes of your pupils' fathers'. His early death, says Ausonius, at least spared him the sight of his wife's execution as a heretic by the usurper Maximus.

It could have been worse, however. Marcellus, the son of Marcellus, went to teach at Narbonne, where he found fame in his position. His classes were thronged with students, he soon became wealthy and married a noble wife. However, comments Ausonius, 'Fortune never favours a career of unvarying success, especially when she finds a man of crooked nature. Nevertheless, it is not for me to make heavier your destiny: my task is to recall it. It is enough to say that you lost all at one stroke. I do not rob you of your title as teacher, but give you a place among grammarians of very scant deserving.' To be embroiled in a scandal – even an unidentified one – is bad enough in Ausonius's estimation, but to be unlearned is even worse. 'I will sing of Ammonius also – for indeed it is a solemn duty to commemorate a teacher of my own native place – who used to teach raw lads their alphabet: he had scant learning and was of an ungentle nature, and therefore – as was his due – was held in slight repute.' The fact that someone such as Ammonius possessed a little learning brought him into the outer orbit of Ausonius's regard as a civilized person, but only just.

When Ausonius writes about recreation, the leisure activities he describes seem little removed from the schoolroom. Early one summer, Ausonius writes a letter – in verse – to his friend, Axius Paulus, who teaches rhetoric in Bordeaux. Ausonius longs to get away from the city, he says. He is weary of the throngs of people, the 'vulgar brawls at the crossroads', the narrow lanes swarming with people, the rabble that blocks the city's broadways. 'Here is a muddy sow in flight, there a mad dog rushing around, there oxen too weak for the waggon.' It may be a true portrayal of Bordeaux, but it is also a literary joke. Ausonius's description of the chaos of the city is drawn from a letter of the poet Horace, and the reference is a knowing nod on his part to the culture he shares with Paulus. Paulus, urges Ausonius, must keep the promise he made to visit him. He will have hours of leisure with the right to do whatever he wants. However, Ausonius urges him to bring with him all the 'wares of his muses: dactyls, elegiacs, choriambics, lyrics, comedy and tragedy – pack them all in your carriage, for the devout poet's baggage is all paper'. He will have a holiday of literary creativity: Ausonius promises to match him poem for poem, no matter how much verse he brings with him.

Letters to Ausonius from friends and colleagues, praising his published verse, alternate with letters from Ausonius himself in which he rates his outpourings as but feeble scratchings and doggerel. This is the constant quadrille of politeness, whether he is corresponding with an emperor or with a fellow poet. When the emperor Theodosius writes to Ausonius demanding that he 'consent to favour me with those treasures stored away in your desk...', Ausonius replies, 'I have no skill to write, but Caesar has ordered it... and what book would not be Caesar's own in the hope to escape thereby the countless erasures of a wretched bard, always emending and emending for the worse?' The greatest offence is to be slow in responding to a letter received, to fail to match one's correspondent quickly, verse for verse and *bon mot* for *bon mot*. The punishment that results is gentle mockery. Theon, a poet, is tardy in responding to Ausonius, and the latter demands to know what is keeping him: 'What busy life are you leading on the coasts of Médoc? Are you busy trafficking, snapping up for a clipped coinage goods presently to be sold in dear salerooms at outrageous prices – balls of sickly tallow, greasy lumps of wax, pitch, torn paper and rank-smoking torches, your country lights?'

The verses of thanks that Ausonius writes to Theon for a gift of thirty oysters are threaded with allusions to Virgil and include an evocation of the books of the Sibylline Oracles kept in Rome; they also complain that the oysters, although large, were few in number. Another element of Ausonius's literary output was a vast stream of epigrams with such pungent titles as 'Written under the portrait of a lewd woman'; 'What sort of mistress he would have'; 'On mangy Polygiton, sitting with ulcerated legs in the baths'; 'On Castor the fellator who performed an act of cunnilingus on his wife'. If many of them are bawdy and filthy, it was not because this was in Ausonius's essential nature, but because he was following the proper literary model for Latin epigrams, Martial. Ausonius also produced macaronic verses combining Greek and Latin; musings on ancient philosophers, on the twelve Caesars, on the gods, on types of food and 'on things that have no connection'. There are attempts to play with the verse forms: to write hexameters whose every line started and finished with a monosyllable; verses on the shapes of Greek letters; an entire nuptial ode constructed out of lines of Virgil, taken out of context, and rewoven to give them an unexpected and risqué air.

For all the pleasures of his evocation of the River Moselle and the earthiness of his epigrams, it has to be said that the extant works of Ausonius are not at all easy to read. They are self-consciously exclusive. Their prime concern is social display and the confirmation of status. To enjoy them to the full and to realize their ingenuity demands a thorough knowledge of earlier Latin literature. Such originality as Ausonius's works possess resides principally in their obsessive, fugue-like manipulation of the earlier canon, rather than in their freshness of observation. For many modern critics, this is enough to condemn Ausonius and other writers of late Roman Gaul to remain untouched on the bookshelves. After the Renaissance the notion took root that Ausonius and his ilk were representatives of a twilight age of decadence, and not of the best Latinity. This perceived shortcoming – which was, of course, the very quality that attracted des Esseintes – was sufficient to keep Ausonius off the school and university syllabus. But these criticisms miss the point. It is not just that he provides a precious and direct insight into the aristocratic world of late Roman Gaul, nor that some of his writing does in fact comprise fresh observations of his surroundings – which makes him even more valuable as a witness of the age; what is perhaps most striking about Ausonius is that he cherishes a foreign culture that was a calculated import from Rome into Gaul. His writing and the life that it reflects offer remarkable evidence of how the Gallic elite embraced and made that imported culture its own. And they reveal its power to bind them together in a community of shared social values and a common literary heritage.

*Modern wooden stele in Gallic style depicting the local goddess,
Sequana, at the Source of the Seine.*

CHAPTER X

Blood of the Martyrs

Natio est omnis Gallorum admodum dedita religionibus
'The whole of the nation of the Gauls is greatly devoted
to its religious duties'

JULIUS CAESAR, *De Bello Gallico*, VI.16

SOURCE OF THE SEINE

·

THE GLANIC MOTHERS

·

NÎMES

·

VIENNE

·

CULT OF CYBELE

·

BOURG-SAINT-ANDÉOL

·

AMPHITHEATRE OF LYONS

·

FIRST CHRISTIAN MARTYRS

·

HERESY

·

ST PIERRE'S CATHEDRAL

·

BISHOPS: THE NEW ARISTOCRATS

·

SAINT-SEINE-L'ABBAYE

NOT A COLD, BUT A WET COMING I have of it: the worst possible weather for a pilgrimage. Chaucer and his companions to Canterbury merely had the sweet showers of April to contend with. I, going from Alésia to the Source of the Seine, have continuous, steady rain from dawn until dusk. Perhaps it is a divine warning against making pilgrimage to an old pagan site. I am being visited, as retribution, with the essential nature of the place – an all-pervading wetness – as retributive justice. Perhaps it is a warning that all pilgrimage is folly: an injunction not to strive ahead, but to stop and consider that sanctity is not confined to the terminus of my walk, but that the rich green land of Burgundy is imbued with the divine at every step: the land, blessed in perpetual generation, rolling in the valleys, robed with a plush of thick grass, fat cattle such as would have pleased a heroic chieftain, gemmed with the scattered wealth of corn poppies and yellow cockscomb.

Perhaps the baptismal dampness that has reached into every part of my clothing and rucksack, warping my maps, my clothes and my notebook, is in fact a benediction. The source of the Seine is a shrine of healing. In many ancient cultures, water, wells and springs were revered as a giver of life. Maybe this drenching is a form of welcome to the initiate, drawing close to a sacred place that represents a gateway to the dark and primitive divine. Certainly, the waters are healing, after a fashion. I am too numb to ache, too overcome by the waters to think of changing my course. And although the countryside wears a face of beauty, it is not one of hospitality. The little stone villages on the way, perhaps lulled into a dream by their own loveliness, are far too deep in sleep to think of opening an *auberge* to shelter the wet passer-by. There is no choice, no other thought, but to tread the narrow paths and roads, before plunging down into a wooded valley, where the bright Seine rushes, a sprightly and muddy trickle over a web of protruding tree roots, and follow the little rill all the way to the clearing at its very source.

The source of the Seine, as it appears now, owes its form to the nineteenth century. The plot on which it rises was bought by the city of Paris in 1864. The interest in the site had its roots in the antiquarian project of Napoleon III. Before long, the spring from which the head of the Seine wells up was turned into a romantic grotto, presided over by a statue of a scantily clad nymph, reclining on a couch and bearing aloft in her right hand a festoon of ripe fruit – an ensemble that seems

Statue of a water nymph symbolizing the Seine, in the grotto built above the river's source in 1866.

to owe more to the Parisian imagination than the real genius of the place. This is perhaps better captured by a small statue erected in 2014. It is a copy of one found in earlier excavations at the site in the nineteenth century. A represents a female figure, stiffly seated and stiffly dressed in a tunic that hints at the Roman but is rigid, geometric and stylized, not suggesting the elegant and cosmopolitan, but the heavy, numinous and local. This is Sequana, goddess of the place and of the river.

Some other visitors before me were more reverent, and came to pay honour to the shrine. A corn dolly is placed at her feet, and at the square base of the statue sits a wicker basket, and a wooden tub with lily bulbs, waiting to sprout. A wooden stake with an elongated head, roughly carved, peers from the overgrown grass and wild flowers on the gentle slope behind it. A small blue hand-painted sign, perched by the bottom of the spring, reads *votum solvit libens merito – 2015, Année de la Renaissance*. The Latin is the traditional formula for one who repays a vow to a god, and would have been seen on many a statue base in the time of the Roman occupation.[*]

The elegant clearing, with its grotto and its little bridge over the infant stream of the Seine, is redolent of the bucolic; a peaceful, untroubled and contemplative haven. But this quietness and ease belies the site's Gallo-Roman past. A stretch of the stream beyond the grotto is fenced off and overgrown. This is the place where the sanctuary of the source stood in Gallo-Roman times. Two temples and a colonnaded precinct were built here sometime in the first century AD. However, such buildings were only an official acknowledgement of a shrine and religious practices that had been in place at the source of the Seine for at least two centuries beforehand, if not more. It was a meeting place for the sick and the suffering. Pilgrims would come to bathe in the spring and seek cures for myriad ailments. Excavations at

---

[*] The Latin formula, meaning one has 'willingly fulfilled one's vow as is merited', is frequently found in ex-voto inscriptions offered to the gods in thanks for their prayers for health or some other benefit being answered.

the site before it was fenced off in the 1960s brought to light over 300 wooden ex-votos that had been preserved in the damp conditions. These were models, made in oak or beech, of the parts of the body that had been afflicted with illness, which had been presented to the goddess Sequana at the shrine. Their purpose was either to take the illness miraculously from the real limb or organ unto themselves, or else to remind the goddess of what was wrong. There were arms and legs, adult or child-sized, heads, torsos or whole bodies in Gallic capes showing signs of goitre, hernias or blindness. Breasts and genitals were also discovered, perhaps suggesting milk deficiency and malnutrition on the one hand, or infertility on the other. The figures are crudely carved, but with a powerful presence. They are almost certainly the product of the indigenous Gallic populations, for whom Sequana was a local and powerful goddess of healing.

However, it was not only the indigenous population that paid honour to the shrine, or sought the assistance of the goddess. There are inscriptions from Romans, or wealthier Gauls who were now part of the Romanized culture, expressing their thanks in a proper Latin form. One inscription found at the site reads 'Flavius Flavinus, for the health of his nephew Flavius Lunaris, has willingly repaid his vow as is proper to the Goddess Sequana', ending with the correct Latin formula – *votum solvit libens merito*.

The shrine had Roman devotees as well as local Gauls. It was given a Roman appearance in the form of a colonnade and temples. On top of this, the goddess Sequana herself was kitted out in Roman dress. She was shown in a Roman-style tunic and cloak not only in the stone statue reproduced at the site, but in a representation of her in bronze also discovered there, crowned with a diadem and standing proud on a boat adorned with a duck's head and tail. But she owed the Romans not only for her costume, but also her body. The Mediterranean habit of giving anthropomorphic form to gods, goddesses and local spirits who were for the most part not endowed with physical form was brought to Gaul by the Roman presence.

The Romans had effectively suppressed the order of the Druids, but the indigenous gods were treated much in the same way as the local Gallic aristocracy. The Romans were happy to leave them in place, respect them, work with them, and even add to their lustre by providing them with new clothing, new dwellings or even new names to enhance their standing among their devotees. The polytheism of the Romans was never exclusive, and they saw in the gods of Gaul manifestations and reflections of their own. Thus it was that the Romans not only brought the worship of their conventional deities in their conventional appearances with their conventional Roman rites – Jupiter, Minerva, Apollo, not to mention the recent cults of the imperial family; the Gallic gods were blended with those of Rome, many of the local gods taking on a Roman veneer and dual identity.

Caesar himself was an early witness to this process. He writes in his *Commentaries* that the Gauls worshipped Mercury ahead of all the other gods – the inventor, in Gallic eyes, he states, 'of all arts, the guide for every road and journey and the greatest influence for all money-making and trade'. After him, says Caesar, they revered Apollo, Mars, Jupiter and Minerva. Seeing these gods as common to Gaul and Rome, he does not trouble to record the Gallic names in his writings. By Mercury he was likely referring to Lugus, a god after whom many places, not least Lugdunum, were named, and who was conventionally described as 'possessed of all the talents'. His characteristics as described by Caesar are similar to those of the Roman Mercury, god of travellers and financial gain, not to mention eloquence. Apollo was probably seen as the equivalent of the Gallic Belenos, who like Apollo had powers of healing. Jupiter was taken as parallel to Taranis, a god of thunder who bore a lightning bolt in one hand and a six-spoked wheel, the sign of the sun, in the other.

But this process of drawing equivalents between gods at the national level also went on locally. Indeed, many gods and goddesses like Sequana were not national but local, honoured only by particular tribes or in particular locations. Nevertheless, they were still seen as being manifestations of the Roman deities. Lenus, a god of the Treveri tribe of the lower Moselle, was equated with Mars on account of his warlike role in protecting the tribe. At Trier, a temple stood to him where he was revered with the combined name of Lenus Mars. In other instances, a Roman god in a certain district was portrayed as being married to one of the indigenous Gallic divinities – usually a Roman male god married a Gallic female deity. In eastern Gaul, Rosmerta, a local goddess of fertility and abundance, was frequently shown as a consort to the Roman Mercury. In Autun, they are depicted on a stone relief sitting side by side, while Rosmerta clutches a cornucopia of flowers and fruit – a Gallic goddess in Roman dress with a Roman husband depicted in the Roman form of a stone relief, holding an imported Roman symbol of plenty.

The Romans, when they were not destroying the woodland groves sacred to the Druids, were respecters of the sacred places of the Gauls. Such places would be incorporated into Roman religious structures. The source of the Seine and the goddess Sequana was a rural example. But sacred places prominent in the heart of cities, fully Roman in appearance and character, would be protected and given the sort of adornment and veneration that seems surprising for the deities of a defeated and subject people. At Glanum, near the centre of the settlement, a set of steps leads down into a sacred pool, still fed with fresh water from a spring. This is the well sacred to Glanis and the Glanic mothers, local Gallic healing deities that gave their names to the place. They were there for at least 200 years before the Roman presence. Now the incoming Romans vied to pay their tributes to the indigenous Gallic spirits. Clustered around the well, as if attracted to the numinous power exuded by the spot, are temples to gods and goddess brought by the Romans – Hercules and Valetudo, the Roman goddess of health. The latter temple appears to have been erected by Augustus's right-hand man Agrippa as early as 39 BC, when memories of the brutality of the conquest would still have been fresh in Gallic minds. Even ordinary Roman soldiers rushed to seek the blessings and pay honours to the gods of the defeated nation. By the steps down to the pool a large stone altar, set up as an ex-voto, records that 'Marcus Licinius Verecundus… veteran of the 21st Legion (Rapax)… fulfilled his vow willingly' to Glanis, the Glanic mothers, as well as the Roman goddess Fortuna Redux, probably in thanks for the safe completion of a journey.

A still-living example of this veneration for sacred spots is to be found in the city of Nîmes. Fed by waters rising several miles away to the northwest, a spring emerges near the green peak of the Mont Cavalier, which rises high above the elegant city. It comes to light below the Tour Magne, a hulking octagonal turret built by the Romans on a Gallic base to watch over this spot, before splashing down through tree-shaded rivulets and basins where lily pads float, and finally debouching into a series of wide stone-lined pools set in a serene terrace at the base of the hill. The spot is now a pleasure garden. The curving pools are fringed with finely carved balustrades. At their corners languishing *putti* swirled with drapery and a spiral of cornucopia bear up unfeasibly large classical urns. Goldfish turn with pleasing brightness through the narrow water above the careful pattern of limestone slabs that line the pools, echoing the tremulous reflection of the sunlight on the carvings above.

Although the area was relandscaped in the eighteenth century, it always had such a character. The Gauls venerated this spot before the Roman presence as the haunt of the god of the spring, Nemausus, and its other spirits, the Matres Nemausicae. In 25 BC, shortly after Nîmes was founded as a Roman colony by Agrippa, taking its name from the god of its holy spring, this area was developed into a sacred precinct, an Augusteum. It was an enclosure for veneration of the local deities of the waters combined with that of the genius of the emperor Augustus, an altar to whom appears to have stood at the centre of the arrangement. To one side there was a theatre, and to the other a building named by later antiquarians as the 'Temple of Diana' which in reality was most likely a library. The theatre was covered over in

the eighteenth century, but the remains of the temple were left standing, and the original pattern of the pools around the Augusteum was
used as a template for the relandscaping. With a theatre and library
(the ruins of which were being used for a summer's afternoon of
pot-smoking by students when I went to visit), the place was as much

*The Tour Magne, Nîmes. A ruined Roman tower, built on a third century BC
Gallic rampart, the Tour Magne rises thirty metres on the hill above
the Augusteum.*

then as now a pleasant resort for sunshine and contemplation, with the mixture of Gaul and Rome at the heart of it.

The Romans did not worship only their own gods and goddesses in conjunction with those they found locally in Gaul. The symbol of Nîmes is a reminder of how the coming of Rome tied Gaul into a wider geographical commonwealth. This symbol, introduced by Agrippa in 27 BC and still in use, is of a crocodile chained to a palm tree. It represents the legion settled in Nîmes that had earlier triumphed over Cleopatra in Egypt during the civil war. Gaul was interlinked via Rome with Africa, the Levant and Asia Minor. We have already seen how the empire allowed migrants to come from these parts, bringing their trades with them. New religions also, which seemed exotic to the Romans, and which were themselves not a part of the traditional Roman pantheon, were able to follow these wide movements of people engendered by empire; and they introduced themselves into the tapestries of belief followed by the Roman Gauls.

Much further along the Rhône, a short journey away from Lyons, is the city of Vienne. It was a trading station when the Romans first took control of Transalpine Gaul after 124 BC, and one of the centres of the Allobroges tribe. It was one of the first wave of settlements to be made a colony in the 30s BC, even before Nîmes, and was soon established as a Roman centre. The town seems unassuming in the present age. It is small compared to Lyons and Nîmes, and only the busy *autoroute* by the Rhône disturbs its quiet. A medieval square tower on the opposite bank of the river gives the place an aura of forgotten chivalry, and modern villas pinned among the green wooded slopes above the city lend an air of weary leisure.

However, Lawrence Durrell, in the person of one of his characters in *Caesar's Vast Ghost*, calls it a 'malefic town... a centre of the Black arts in the alchemical sense'. It certainly has a striking pedigree in the darker realms of Christian religious history, some of which is quoted by Durrell's character. Pontius Pilate, according to the early church historian Eusebius, was exiled to Vienne for an unspecified

The 'Temple of Diana', in Nîmes, was most likely a library attached to the sacred precinct known as the Augusteum.

misdemeanour and committed suicide there around AD 37. His body, according to legend, lies below a pyramid-like Roman structure raised on four arches – which in fact marks the turning point on the chariot course of an otherwise disappeared circus arena. Herod Archelaus, ruler of Judea, son and successor of King Herod the Great (responsible, according to scripture, for the Massacre of the Innocents) was also exiled to Vienne in AD 6 by Augustus, followed repeated complaints about his cruelty. In 1312, Vienne was also the site of the Church Council that ordered the suppression of the Knights Templar – an order so powerful and yet so popularly associated with the occult that, in the mind of Durrell's character at least, the ease of its suppression smacked of 'sulphur and the black arts'.

Vienne certainly adhered to the norms of Roman and Gallic religion. In its centre, at the site of the old forum, a perfectly proportioned temple is preserved, built at the beginning of the first century AD and dedicated to the worship of the emperor Augustus and the empress Livia. However, close by are the confusing remains of a complex of buildings, some of which have remained above ground since antiquity and others that were only brought to light in a series of excavations after the Second World War. Two tall arches stand proud over the site, which now provides a green space for recreation in the midst of the town. However, running through the grass beside them are the unexpected traces of a small enclosed theatre: unexpected because Vienne appears, at first sight, to have been perfectly well furnished with theatres. Nearby, on the hillside above the city, is one of the biggest Roman theatres in Gaul, second only to Autun in size with a capacity of 13,500; next to it, for good measure, lies an odeon with room for 3,000. The enclosed theatre, by contrast, could probably not seat more than a few hundred. Nearby are small pools and subterranean chambers, linked to a large building in the centre that appears to have been a temple.

On their own, such ruins seem difficult to interpret and at the mercy of conjecture. However, two finds there seem to explain the

purpose of the complex. On a marble plaque in the theatre was found
the inscription 'DEND…' This can only be an abbreviation for *dendrophori*, a type of priest who were characterized by carrying trees.
The plaque signalled that certain seats in the theatre were reserved
for these curious tree-carrying clergy. Also discovered at the site was
a fragment of a relief showing three people, one bearing a basket of
fruit, another a lighted torch, making an offering before an altar and
a goddess. By them are symbols that help to identify the scene: a cap
with a point at the back and long ear-flaps (usually called a Phrygian
cap and believed to have come from the east); a tree, apparently a
pine, with a bird in its branches; a shepherd's crook, and a flute. The
goddess, these symbols suggest, is Cybele, the Great Mother Goddess
– to whom the *dendrophori* usually owed their devotion – and the site,
although some still dispute it, is a cult complex for the celebration of
the mysteries of Cybele and Attis, imported from Asia Minor.

Cybele found her origins as an ancient near-eastern earth goddess,
a spirit who ruled over the death, rebirth and regeneration of crops
and vegetation. Legend links her with another mortal or god as her
lover and devotee, a shepherd named Attis, who is reputed to have
castrated himself against a pine tree when she drove him into a frenzy.
He perished, but his body was preserved and later resurrected by the
goddess. Cybele was worshipped by a transgendered priesthood that
imitated the self-castration of Attis, and also wore women's clothes.
One name for the priesthood, by a strange coincidence, was 'Galli',
leading to an easy play on words for Roman poets and satirists whenever they wished to make disparaging remarks about the Gauls.

Although, by this measure, such a goddess and form of worship
should seem quite unRoman and inimical to Roman ideals of strength
and hostility to barbarian ideas, the worship of Cybele was admitted to Rome during the late third century BC. This was when Rome
was fighting the Second Punic War with Carthage. It faced a crip-
pling famine and hence a likely defeat. Following the oracles of the
gods and an ancient prophecy, the cult was given official sanction in

Rome and was said to have been instrumental in the salvation of the city. The famine abated and the Carthaginians were defeated. From Rome, the worship of Cybele was carried further out into the empire. Cult complexes, such as those at Vienne, were required for the rites and mystery initiations that formed part of the worship. The religious calendar of Cybele, as it appears during Roman times, bears strange echoes of the Christian holy week and Easter. Three days before the spring equinox, a pine tree would be cut down by the *dendrophori*, hung with an image of Attis, and carried in procession to the temple. The devotees would lash themselves with whips to sprinkle the tree with their blood, before laying it to rest in a ritual tomb in the heart of the temple. There were three days of mourning before nightfall on the spring equinox, at which point the tomb would be reopened by torchlight, and Attis would be reborn with great joy. Around this time,

Ruins of the Cybele sanctuary, Vienne, first or second century AD.

initiations into the cult would take place. Devotees, according to some accounts, would be led into an underground chamber whose ceiling was a latticework or grille. Above this, a bull would be slaughtered so that the initiate below would be baptized in its blood; its genitalia, cut off, could also be seen as a substitute for the devotee castrating himself. After initiates had washed away the blood, they might view a re-enactment of the myth of Cybele and Attis. Such rites required the sort of enclosed theatre and subterranean pits around a central temple building that are all to be found in Vienne.

Other finds in Vienne seem to attest that the Cybele cult was by no means unpopular. There are inscriptions recording individual *dendrophori* and charitable distributions of food made in connection with the company of these priests as a whole. There are also sculptures and reliefs of Cybele, sometimes shown riding on a lion (a sign of her exotic, still dangerous and eastern nature) and her lover Attis, wearing the Phrygian cap and playing his shepherd's flute. It is notable that the two names of the clergy attached to the temple, datable to the first or second century AD – Attia Priscilla and Tiberius Julius Diadochus – both suggest (despite the Greek overtone of the last name) that the foreign cult appealed to an affluent stratum of Romanized Gauls.

Cybele was not the only exotic deity to be imported by the Romans into Gaul. On the sheer but low valley wall of the river Tourne at Bourg-Saint-Andéol is carved in the open air a relief of the Iranian deity, Mithras, carrying out the sacramental act of slaying the bull. This carving, cut between two springs, marks the site of a Mithraeum, devoted to the worship and initiatory rites of Mithras. Like Cybele, Mithras was an eastern import, but newer to the Roman empire. Given that the rites were secret, little is known for sure about the meaning of the cult. It may again, like Cybele, have been a fertility rite. Others have argued that depiction of the struggle between the god and the bull was a symbol of a cosmic battle between good and evil (similar to ideas in Persian Zoroastrianism) or else an astronomical allegory whose significance is now lost. His worship was confined to men and became highly popular among Roman soldiers, though some have conjectured that this particular shrine was put here by Greek or Eastern merchants with trading interests along the nearby Rhône.

Such imports of the divine came not only from the eastern parts of the Roman empire, but also North Africa and Egypt. In Arles, not only did Cybele and Mithras find devotees who left behind evidence of their devotion in statues and tombstones of their priestesses or priests; the Egyptian goddess Isis was also worshipped. Like Cybele, Isis was a mother goddess connected in her essence with the fertility of the crops, and the death and resurrection of vegetation. Found in the Alyscamps at Arles was a small tombstone, crudely inscribed with the lettering picked out in red paint, to Maximius Festus, a *pausarius* of the cult of Isis, one of the priests who was likely responsible for the processions made by the statue of the goddess as part of the cult's devotions. There was also a statue of Harpocrates, the Greek version of Horus, the son of Isis, who represented not only the rising sun and resurrection, but also the keeping of secrets that were to be held within the cult, away from the impious and uninitiated profane multitudes.

The foreign religions tended to be most visibly popular where the requirements of empire provoked the greatest movements of people. Mithras flourished especially on the Rhine frontier among the legions. Cybele and Isis were most commonly worshipped in the great trading towns of the Rhône – Arles, Vienne and Lyons. It is in the latter two that the most successful foreign religion of those imported under the Romans – Christianity – first appears in the light of history.

Close by the great altar raised to Augustus and the Roman emperors in Lyons an amphitheatre had also been built. Some of it can still be seen today at the western end of the Rue Burdeau. There are no grand arcaded walls still standing as at Arles or at Nîmes, but most of the floor of the arena is still open to the air, and some of the lower levels of seating and steps have been restored on the northern side, which was built, like the Arles amphitheatre, on the slope of a hill.

Around the arena are the plodding skeletal traces of thick stone walls and stairways which would have led to the *vomitoria*, or network of tunnels that traversed the structure of the amphitheatre to lead the spectators to their seats. A necklace of lime-green ivy and scratchy grass hangs upon the old stone. Beige blank-fronted buildings and a tangle of power cables look down from the top of the hill. Broken columns are laid on their side in one corner of the arena, near a single square-wooden stake that has been set upright in the ground.

It is a spot that betrays a diversity of historical suffering. A tablet hangs on the wall of a nearby apartment building commemorating one Lucien Sportisse, a member of the Resistance, shot in that place by French agents of the Gestapo in March 1944. Auguste-Laurent Burdeau, after whom the street was named, suffered a slower end around fifty years earlier: a brilliant civil servant, he is said to have worked himself to death. However, the wooden stake in the arena itself bears witness to an earlier and more brutal stratum of violence: the first Christian martyrdoms in Gaul.

The deaths of these first martyrs, drawn from Lyons and Vienne, are recorded extensively in a letter quoted by the fourth-century church historian Eusebius. The letter purports to be an eye-witness account of the deaths which took place in AD 177. The second century was not an easy age for the adherents of the new religion. Early Christianity was frequently met with hostility by the Roman authorities. Many of those who adhered to Christian ways did so not because they were an eastern import or ostensibly foreign, but because they demanded an exclusive devotion. Unlike Cybele, or Isis, or Mithras, the Christian God looked for the whole of the Christian's allegiance. There was no room for worship of the divine genius of Rome or the emperors. This was more than a matter of metaphysics. To deny worship was seen as a denial of authority. To refuse the worship of Rome and the emperors was seen as a species of subversion, suggesting that powers other than the emperor and the official establishment had the prerogative to rule and make laws.

Such suspicions, generally held during this period, were exacerbated by the circumstances of the time. Some historians have suggested that tensions in Lyons may have been heightened by difficulties on the Rhine frontier. The Christians might have been used as scapegoats for these external difficulties. It also appears that the killing of the Christians was ordered at the time of the annual festival at the altar of Augustus, a moment in the year when the show of and even genuine feelings of devotion to Rome would have been at their greatest. At any rate, the letter preserved by Eusebius describes a febrile atmosphere in Lyons. There were 'cat-calls, hootings and blows, draggings, plunderings, stonings, and confinements, and everything that an infuriated mob is accustomed to do to those whom they deem bitter enemies'. As many members of the community as possible were rounded up and imprisoned before they could be tried in front of the governor. About half of them were migrants from Greece and Asia Minor, and the others indigenous Gallo-Romans. An aged Gallo-Roman of high social standing, Vettius Epagathus, offered to represent the Christians, but when the governor discovered that he too was a Christian, he was prevented from defending them and also imprisoned.

According to the letter, the group were accused of 'Thyestean banquets* and Oedipodean connections' – in other words cannibalism and incest – before being put to excruciating tortures. Some were whipped and had their flesh torn; others were hung up by their feet in the stocks. Sanctus, a deacon from Vienne, had burning-hot metal plates placed against his genitals on consecutive days. A handful recanted in the face of such torments. A woman named Biblias denied her faith, but then, as if waking from a trance, says the letter, renewed her confession as a Christian despite the continuation of the torture.

Following this, the executions and killings began. Pothnius, the ninety-year-old bishop of Lyons, was brought before the governor and asked 'who was the god of the Christians' to which he replied 'if

---

* Thyestes was a character from Greek myth who was served the flesh of his sons at a banquet as revenge for his adultery; hence, Thyestean banquets are those at which human flesh is eaten.

you were worthy, you would know'. As a result, he was dragged around in front of a furious crowd who kicked and punched him and pelted him with whatever missiles came to hand, 'all of them believing that they would sin greatly and act impiously if they in any respect fell short in their insulting treatment of him'. Two days after this, confined in prison, says the letter, he died. Pothnius at least avoided a public end. Other Christians were not so fortunate. Those who were Roman citizens were sentenced to beheading. Those who were not were condemned to die before the crowds in the amphitheatre. The usual course was for them to be tortured and whipped, and in their weakened state thrown into the arena to be mauled by wild beasts. Some, after being mauled but not killed, were placed in a scalding hot iron chair 'in which their bodies were roasted, and they themselves were filled with the fumes of their own flesh'. The remains of the dead were then burnt and thrown into the Rhône.

The most courageous of the martyrs in the face of this treatment, says the letter, was a young woman called Blandina. During the preliminary tortures, her body was 'virtually torn up' but 'like a noble athlete' she did not give in to any of the pain inflicted on her. She was tied to a wooden stake in the amphitheatre on the first day that the Christians were brought in, but the wild beasts refused to harm her. Her preservation, says the letter, was down to the power of her faith and prayer. The Roman authorities, foiled in their attempt to kill her, brought her back every day to witness the deaths of her fellow Christians in the hope that she would crack under the pressure and betray her faith. This did not happen. As a result, she was one of the last to be killed. She was brought into the amphitheatre with a boy named Ponticus, aged around fifteen, whom she encouraged to remain steadfast despite the ordeal. Ponticus was the first to die, being tortured in front of the crowds. She herself was again whipped, thrown to the wild beasts, then placed in the iron chair. Still alive, she was wound up in a net and thrown in front of a bull, to be gored, tossed about and trampled until finally she was dead.

The account of the death of the martyrs in the Lyons amphitheatre is one of the few to cast light on the early history of Christian worship in Gaul, which for the most part is dark and obscure. Another brief moment of clarity is found in the life of Pothnius's successor as bishop of Lyons, Irenaeus. Like many of the other early Christians in Lyons, he was also a migrant from the east, in his case Smyrna (now Izmir) in Asia Minor. He was lucky to be absent from Lyons during the persecution of 177; at the time he was in Rome to warn the church authorities over the danger of various types of heresy among the young Christian communities. Returning to Gaul and being elected the new bishop, he made the extirpation of heretical doctrine one of his chief concerns.

One of Irenaeus' works, *Adversus Haereses* ('Against Heresies') is still preserved. In it, he claims that there was a heretic named Marcus who was active in the towns of the Rhône valley, working false miracles and prophesying by means of a demon. One of Marcus's particular interests, says Irenaeus, was in seeking out female followers, 'and those such as are well-bred, and elegantly attired, and of great wealth...' whom he would convince he could also endow with the gift of prophesy. Having done so, they would each make 'the effort to reward him, not only by the gift of her possessions (in which way he has collected a very large fortune), but also by yielding up to him her person, desiring in every way to be united to him, that she may become altogether one with him'. Marcus would also use love potions to achieve this end, says Irenaeus. He laments that even one of his own deacons, a man from Asia Minor, had lost his wife for a time to Marcus by these means. She followed him around the country for some time until the real Christians managed to convert her back to the true faith, after which 'she spent her whole time in the exercise of public confession, weeping over and lamenting the defilement which she had received from this magician'. The consciences of such women were 'seared, as with a hot iron'.

Irenaeus' greater concern is not with Marcus's sexual appetite, however, but with his intellectual and spiritual pretensions. Marcus's disciples, when they themselves were not attempting to deceive 'silly women' in emulation of their master, would describe themselves as 'perfect' as regards their spiritual knowledge. They had imbibed, so they claimed, a complete and unspeakable knowledge of the divine from a direct experience of the godhead. This knowledge gave them a supernatural protection such that they were immune from harm and free to act as they pleased. In this, they were superior to St Peter and St Paul or any of the saints and apostles: they had consumed and knew beyond words the real nature of God himself.

Tomb of a Gallo-Roman Christian boy named Ursus, who died aged sixteen on 6 March, 493; displayed in the Gallo-Roman Museum of Lyons.

This belief, that a Christian devotee might win a personal and direct knowledge and experience of God – an idea condemned as the 'gnostic heresy' – was held by a number of early Christians across the Roman empire. It likely owed much of its vigour to ideas from Greek philosophy, but also to the initiatory cults of deities such as Cybele and Isis, which offered to their adherents a personal and direct engagement with their deities. Irenaeus's fears mark the diverse religious background in Gaul at the time, and show that the other imported religions would have been contributing their ideas to the developing Christian faith in a way that was unwelcome to its higher clerical authorities. The persecution by Rome also told on the attitudes of Irenaeus. It is revealing that he took up the rhetoric used by the Romans against the Christians, for example accusations of a vain higher knowledge and sexual deviancy, and used them against those Christians who did not conform to his idea of the faith; and those who had fallen had been seared by a metaphorical 'hot iron', just as the martyrs had suffered for real.

But aside from the accounts of Eusebius and Irenaeus, there is little to go on regarding the earliest years of the Christian presence in Roman Gaul. Legend and anachronism take the place of verifiable history. Bishops of the third and fourth centuries, such as St Trophimus of Arles or Daphnus of Vaison are attributed to the generation after Christ by sixth-century Gallic writers and were declared to have been followers of the twelve apostles. Later, the belief crystallized that it was not followers of the apostles, but the close intimates of Christ himself who brought the faith to Gaul. The story was retold as late as the nineteenth century by Frédéric Mistral that after the death of Christ the Virgin Mary, her sister Mary and Mary Magdalen were hounded out of Jerusalem and thrown onto a boat without sails or a rudder. They were joined by Lazarus and Joseph of Arimathea. The ship was cast adrift at sea but was drawn by divine guidance to the coast of Gaul, to put ashore in the Camargue near Arles at the town later to bear their name, Saintes-Maries-de-la-Mer. Some say that they were miraculously borne further inland to the strange mountain fastness of Les Baux-de-Provence just south of Glanum and Saint-Rémy-de-Provence, and from there began the evangelization of the Gallic provinces. Carved in a rock face at Les Baux is a relief of three figures side by side which are said to commemorate *les trois Maries* ('the three Marys'), though the motif of goddesses appearing in threes belongs to earlier Gallic religion; it may be the case that *les trois Maries* are the Christian reincarnation of an earlier stratum of belief.

The Christian faith became quickly more visible over the course of the fourth century. When the emperor Constantine, who had declared Christian worship legal in 313, called a council of bishops at Arles the following year – a meeting that is seen as marking the foundation of canon law in the west and is notable, among other acts, for ordering the excommunication of Christian clergy who took part in chariot races, gladiator fights and theatrical performances – only a small handful of Gallic bishops appear to have attended, including those from the cities of Massalia, Vaison, Orange, Apt, Nice and Arles itself. However, over the course of the century dozens of new bishoprics were founded across the Gallic provinces. Christianity became a notable presence in the cities of Gaul with the foundation of cathedrals for the service of the developing Christian communities. These sites have for the most part remained in use since this period, the early Christian buildings covered over by newer and larger cathedrals during the Middle Ages. However, in a few instances, excavations have made it possible to recover a physical sense of this pristine age of Christian Gaul.

By a strange irony, one of the best places to visit for this is Geneva, a city that – thanks to John Calvin and the Reformation – was devoted to iconoclasm and the obliteration of its ecclesiastical links with Rome. But below the floor of St Pierre's Cathedral, where Calvin's wooden chair is still preserved as a relic, the unspoiled foundations and lower walls of the first Roman Christian buildings dating back to the fourth century remained safely forgotten and untouched though the chaos of the Reformation and the Wars of Religion. Excavations at the end of the twentieth century brought them to light; and rather than the space being filled in afterwards, a false floor was fitted, allowing visitors to descend to the original level of the Roman city below the modern cathedral and inspect the remains.

The modern cathedral is for the most part a gothic building with a grand classical façade that was slapped on in the eighteenth century: a temple frontage with steps, six massive columns with well-carved Corinthian capitals and an ugly iron-hued coat of arms on an otherwise blank pediment. It overlooks an unruffled brick-cobbled square shaded by lime trees and overlooked by prosperous but restrained Haussmann-style stone-fronted apartment buildings and offices. But in the dimly-lit narrow passages below ground, elegance gives way to antique zeal and the original footprint of Rome. It is possible to see the low walls of the first episcopal group of buildings, dating about to around 350. There is the threshold of the first cathedral, its walls built with rows of rough cobbles placed between stern and irregular tall stone uprights – a building technique called *opus Africanum*, which, unsurprisingly, came from North Africa. The first cathedral reaches into a choir and apse that can now only be seen narrowly like a cave, thanks to the remaining stonework that supports the present cathedral above. However, the trace of the apse in parchment-coloured stone at the eastern end behind a sanctuary, which would have been screened off with columns and contained the tomb of a holy person to sanctify it, can still be made out in the low light.

Strange to relate, the first traces of building on the side, just south of this sanctuary, take the form of the grave of a person of importance dating back to pre-Christian times, around 100 BC. This may well have been a chieftain of the local Gallic tribe, the Allobroges. The strata of soil have been peeled away to reveal the lower half of his skeleton, while his torso remains sealed within the earth. The ground reveals an attempt in early history to burrow down and remove his skull – a reminder of the Gallic interest in the possession and display of heads for their prestige and magical properties. It is impossible to know whether some sense of sanctity accrued to the site from this original pre-Christian tomb, leading to its choice for the siting of the Christian monument; but it is feasible.

Clinging to the first cathedral's northern walls and accessed through a courtyard is a series of individual rooms, side by side, each having the area of a large tablecloth. These were set aside as dwellings for monks or clergy attached to the cathedral. The rooms were small and bare, of two storeys in height with a simple low wooden ceiling creating the upper storey, but not entirely devoid of comfort. Below their plain grey tiled floor, little hollow runnels cut across the diagonals, a restrained form of hypocaust heating to take the chill off the mountainous climate.

South from the monastic cells came the water supply for a baptistery. Again, Roman technology was harnessed to meet the needs of the new religion. A conduit drew water from a nearby well over 30 metres away. Originally, this filled the pool in the apse of the baptistery, allowing the new converts to be completely immersed in water, as was the custom in the fourth century. The change of this custom can be traced in the alterations to the font, which was shrunk and remodelled in successive centuries so that instead of immersion, the neophyte was drenched with a jet of water from above as the bishop looked on from one side.

Near the source of the water lie the bishop's quarters. The floor of his reception hall stands out colourfully among the beige labyrinth of stonework and differing archaeological strata. From this chamber, it is possible to surmise his increasing importance as a civil official as the Roman administration declined in the fifth century. It is an intimate hall, a square with sides of about 5 metres in length; its lavish mosaic floor, now undulating and pockmarked, has a series of panel designs that included Christian motifs – crosses with grapes and vines. From here, as Geneva passed from Roman to Burgundian control over the course of the fifth century, the bishop would not only see to church business, but also to decisions over the government of the city, as well

as relations between the city and the new panoply of rulers who succeeded to the mandate of Rome.

In the whole ensemble of remains at Geneva – the monastic cells,
the baptistery, the cathedral (and its two successors, which can also be
traced out on the site), and the bishop's quarters – it is the bishop's
quarters and his reception hall that leave the strongest impression.
Here, one feels, was the seat not only of temporal power, but perhaps
also the spiritual motor of the whole complex. Christianity may have
been a religion that gave precedence to the humble and the outcast;
yet in these formative centuries of the church's presence in Gaul, with
Christianity's legalization and later adoption as the official religion
of empire at the end of the fourth century, the deeds of the bishops
had real primacy. They not only played an ever-increasing role in the
administration of the cities, but it was by the force of their character
that the cultural and religious tone of Gaul were for the most part
to be set in the later years of Roman rule and beyond. And although
the office of bishop can be traced back to the non-Roman origin of
scripture and Christ's apostles, the way it was manifested in some of
its earliest holders in Gaul was to be dictated by ideals drawn from the
Roman presence.

Despite the professed reluctance of early Christians to involve
themselves in fighting, the Roman army provided one of the patterns
for its early churchmen to follow. The most outstanding example of
this is St Martin, bishop of Tours. Despite later becoming one of the
great patron saints of France, he was not of Gallic origin. He was probably born in 316 at Savaria in Pannonia (modern-day Szombathely
in Hungary). Thus he came from the frontier territories, a barbarian
fringe with a reputation for revolt that Rome had to work hard to
keep within the fold of the empire. Martin was born into a military
family. His father started as an ordinary soldier, but, like many Roman
emperors at this time, he was able to rise through the ranks to gain a
high status; he in fact reached the grand position of military tribune.
His dedication to the traditions of Rome is perhaps evident in the

name he gave his son. 'Martin' was drawn from Mars, the Roman god of war, and perhaps signified not only a devotion to the practice of arms, but also, shortly after a time of the persecution of Christians, to the old Roman gods themselves.

The name, however, did not deter Martin from taking an interest in Christianity. When he was a young child, his father was posted to the garrison town of Ticinum (modern-day Pavia) in northern Italy. His family followed. There, Martin discovered the church, which would have been a large town house converted for Christian use. Drawn to the faith, although probably not yet in his teens, he sought baptism and enrolled there as a *catechumen*, or one preparing for full and formal admission to the Christian community. According to Martin's biographer, Sulpicius Severus, Martin intended even at this age to become a hermit and desert contemplative. However, his father strongly disapproved of his son's vocation and sought to put an end to it. In the 320s, the emperor Constantine made a law that sons of veteran soldiers were liable for conscription into the army. Martin's father, hoping to dissociate his son from the church, submitted him for a term of twenty-five years' military service.

Martin's time behind the colours is treated as somewhat of an embarrassment by his biographer Severus. To spare Martin's blushes at the idea he would have borne arms, Severus relates a story in which he refused to fight a barbarian column at Borbetomagus (modern-day Worms) but told the then emperor, Julian the Apostate – a non-Christian – that he would stand before the Roman lines unarmed and still be able, under the protection of Christ, to penetrate the enemy ranks. Severus says that Martin was thrown into prison for this demand the day before the battle, but that on the day itself, the barbarian column surrendered and Martin's boast was never put to the test.

However, it is almost certain that Martin saw active service, and that he had to serve out the normal term of twenty-five years. His time in the army came to an end in 356, at which time he took up residence for a while with the Christian community in Poitiers, before journeying across the empire in an attempt to convert his parents and also to spend some time in solitary contemplation. On returning to Poitiers in 361, he founded a community of hermits in the ruins of an old villa about 16 kilometres (10 miles) outside the city, at a place that became known as Locociacum, 'The Place of the Little Cells', in modern French Ligugé. Ten years later, he was elected to be bishop of Tours, an office which he held until his death in 397.

Even as bishop, Martin retained a reputation for extreme asceticism, spurning all comforts, and even founded a new hermit community at Marmoutier outside Tours, from where he carried out many of his episcopal duties. He gained a reputation as a miracle-worker, and Marmoutier was to become a place of pilgrimage. Yet, aside from the developing tradition of the hermetic life in the Christian west, the Roman army was undoubtedly one of the sources of his approach to a Christian way of living. He frequented couched his ascetic tendencies, and his encouragement of his followers, in the language of military service.

On one occasion, a former Roman soldier came to Marmoutier and asked to be able to join Martin's community. The soldier was married, but professed absolute devotion to the Christian hermitic life. Martin admitted the soldier, who built his cell some way apart from the others to show his absolute commitment to the hermit's path. As for his wife, St Martin placed her in a house for religious virgins that he had founded in Tours itself. After some time, however, the soldier sought him out and begged for permission to spend some time with her. He said that he was a soldier of Christ, and that Martin should allow people who were 'saints' to serve as soldiers together even if of different sexes, since their profession of faith meant that they no longer had any thoughts of carnal union.

Martin's response came straight from the parade ground. 'Tell me,' he asked the soldier, 'Have you ever stood in the line of battle and been present in war?' 'Frequently,' said the soldier, 'I have often stood in the line of battle and been present in war.' 'Did you ever see any woman standing there, or fighting?' The old soldier was unable to reply. Martin continued, 'This would render an army ridiculous, if a female crowd were mixed with the regiments of men.' Thus, Martin was dependent on principles of Roman military discipline and order, ahead of any drawn from the gospels, to organize his new Christian community.

The same martial spirit informed Martin's approach to the pagan temples and shrines that were still in use throughout the district of Tours and beyond. They, and the people who still worshipped there, were an enemy to which no quarter could be given. The shrines had to be destroyed, and the worshippers forced to surrender. Martin set about smashing statues, pulling down temples and burning ancient images with all the dedication, brutality and singlemindedness that Caesar showed when he came to conquer the country four centuries previously. Passing one day through the settlement of Leprosum (modern-day Levroux in the Indre), he saw a well-maintained temple, which he immediately sought to destroy. When the local population learnt of his plan, they gathered in an angry crowd, beat him, and drove him out of the village. Martin then spent three days nearby praying for God to assist him. He fasted, and in the words of most translations of Sulpicius put on 'sackcloth' as a sign of penitence, though the original Latin has him wearing a *cilicium*, a rough cloak of goats' hair sometimes worn by soldiers. In answer to his prayers, two angels appeared, armed with swords and spears, and commanded Martin to return to the village. They would protect him from the villagers, they said, while he completed the destruction of the pagan shrine. Martin returned and carried out their orders. The villagers, who before had been so hostile, did not dare to fight the bishop this time; they merely stood mute and astonished thanks to the power of the two warrior angels.

Indeed, Martin's attacks on the ancient shrines often cast him as a soldier on the front line of warfare. His behaviour was redolent of an ancient Roman tradition in which a commanding officer would consecrate himself and the opposing army to death before launching himself in a suicidal attack against the enemy, which would doom them together but guarantee Roman success. However, in Martin's case his offer of self-sacrifice, being to the Christian God, was a guarantee of self-preservation and true divine protection. Near Autun, he earmarked another ancient temple for destruction, and a sacred pine tree that was growing nearby. The fact that it was a pine suggests it might have been dedicated to Cybele and Attis, though this cannot be known for certain. The local people accepted the destruction of the temple, but their attachment to the tree was far greater. Martin told them that 'there was nothing sacred in the trunk of a tree' and that it must be cut down, 'since it had been dedicated to a demon'. The people told Martin that they would cut it down themselves if he stood in the place where it should fall and 'receive it' as it came down. Martin consented to do so. When the trunk had been cut through and the whole tree began to topple towards him, it seemed that he was certain to be crushed. However, just before it struck him he made the sign of the cross, at which the tree stopped, spun like a top, turned round, and landed elsewhere. Martin himself was unscathed. Like a good general securing a territory newly conquered, Martin built a Christian church on the site as a stronghold against paganism. Indeed, Sulpicius remarks at this point that this was Martin's normal practice after destroying a pagan shrine.

The ascetic tendencies of so many followers of the new faith flummoxed the traditional Gallo-Roman aristocracy. In the latter part of the fourth century, those who promoted the ascetic life were sometimes seen as so subversive that they were viewed as a threat to public order. One ascetic Christian, Priscillian, who was originally from Spain but who attracted followers in Gaul on account of his teachings, was accused of sorcery at the prompting of the Emperor Maximus and executed in 385. His teachings, dubbed 'Priscillianism', were likewise banned. Among other things, they encouraged private worship in villas away from the developing hierarchy of the established church, thus emancipating educated and wealthy single women: a development that was seen as particularly unhealthy and unwelcome.

At worst, such behaviour was seen as dangerous; but the mildest and most frequent reaction to it was perplexity and dismay. The ascetic life was seen as a perversity: something that without proper cause or benefit could break down traditional social ties and destroy the very bedrock of Roman culture. The fears of the old aristocracy are summed up in an exchange of letters between Ausonius and one of his former students, Paulinus of Nola.

Paulinus had been one of Ausonius's star pupils. He was born in 352 in Bordeaux to a noble family, and had studied at the schools there before embarking on a glittering career in the imperial service. It probably did him no harm that he was of the circle of Ausonius and therefore of Gratian, the heir to the throne. After Gratian became emperor, Paulinus was made one of the consuls in 377 and then governor of the south Italian province of Campania. He kept in close touch with his old and beloved teacher. One on occasion Paulinus writes for Ausonius a poem on kings, based on the writing of the historian Suetonius. Ausonius's rapturous reply survives. He addresses Paulinus as his son, and calls himself his father: 'It was early in the night... when your wonderfully worded letter was delivered to me... along with your brilliant poem.' Preserving the aristocratic niceties of correspondence along with a careful interest in the maintenance of correct Latin, Ausonius is as unrestrained as he could be in his praise: 'How skilfully and neatly, how harmoniously and sweetly you have written, conforming at once to the character of our Roman accent... and then what shall I say of your gift for expression? I can swear that for fluency in verse none of our Roman youths is your equal.'

But soon this intimacy turned to bitterness. After the assassination of Gratian in 383, Paulinus's political career, like that of Ausonius, came to an end, and he returned to his native Bordeaux. Not unlike other talented poets from future ages when the chance of political glory was shut down for good – John Donne and George

S. PAVLINVS, *ex diuite, Senatore, Consule, pauper,*
Monachus, Presbyter, Episcopus Nolanus, mundi contemptu,
eleemosynarum Largitate, feruore fidei, caritatis ardore
Scripturarum studio & Scientiâ, cordis humilitate, man
suetudine spiritûs, bonis omnibus egregiè carus, obiit
Anno Christi 431. ætatis 78.

St Paulinus of Nola, as portrayed in a seventeenth-century engraving.

Herbert spring to mind – he was seized by religious fervour. He married a Christian woman from Spain named Therasia, converted to Christianity and was baptized, perhaps by 389. They moved to Spain, but after the birth of their first child, a son who died when only a few days old, they decided to embrace the secluded and ascetic religious life.

Ausonius was, at least nominally, a Christian. He said his prayers every morning in his private chapel, knew his scripture well and could give a long and detailed exposition of Christian theology and doctrine. However, this never for one moment dimmed his love for the traditions of Roman literature and education, both for the pursuit of intellectual pleasure but also as markers of what it meant to be civilized and a part of the governing class of the empire. The muses were never far behind the angels in Ausonius's writing.

So when Paulinus moved to Spain and stopped replying to his letters, it seemed to Ausonius to be something between obstinate unreasonableness and a barbaric insult. To refuse to engage in the literary discourse and the learned discussion of classical literature that was not only a correct pursuit for people of their class, but also a sign of their intimacy, left him confused and upset. Ausonius continues to write, accusing Paulinus of being impious, not to God but to their *amicitia* (friendship). He claims to know what was at the root of it: his wife, Therasia – 'that Tanaquil', he calls her, likening her to a notoriously domineering and scheming wife of one of the early kings of Rome. The brand of Christianity with which she has infected Paulinus is laying waste to everything that is civilized and dear. 'Why have you not answered my letters? Even enemies say '*salve*' ('greetings') to each other in battle. Rocks and caves are not so rude as to refuse to echo the human voice.'

The unanswered letters pile up. Ausonius keeps writing. He seeks to make Paulinus understand the true nature of his silence. 'Let this impious one turn no sound to advantage; let no joys bring him pleasure, no sweet odes of the poets... nor Echo, who hidden in the woody groves of the shepherds, consoles us, returning our words.' His silence, says Ausonius, is akin to savagery or madness: 'Sad, needy, let him dwell in deserted wastes and in silence let him roam around the peaks of Alpine mountains, as it is said Bellerophon, out of his mind, avoiding the company and traces of men, vagrant, wandered through the trackless places.'

Eventually, stung enough by Ausonius's words, Paulinus engages, blaming the slowness of the post for his failure to reply earlier. However, he defends his new and ascetic life. 'Mine is not the crazed mind of a Bellerophon, nor is my wife a Tanaquil...' He has chosen a new and a better path. 'Why do you ask the deposed Muses, my father, to return again to my affection? Hearts which have been consecrated to Christ give refusal to the Muses, and are closed to Apollo... God forbids us to spend time on empty things... and on literature full of idle tales... For these things steep our hearts in false and vain ideas, and train our tongues to say nothing worthwhile, nothing that could bring the truth...' Ausonius loves the old Roman idea of *otium*, aristocratic retirement and leisure; Paulinus himself loves *otium*, but as a means of devoting himself to the worship of Christ.

But, Paulinus assures Ausonius in the last letter that he will send him (dated to 393, shortly before the latter's death), he takes all that Ausonius has said without acrimony, and declares his old teacher to be still as dear to him as life itself. But it is in faith that they will find their final union, rather than in a visit from Paulinus on earth: 'And when, released from the prison of the body, I shall have flown forth from the earth, in whatever place our common Father shall place me, there also shall I keep you in my heart; nor shall that end which severs me from my body unloose me from the love of you.'

Characters such as St Martin and Paulinus – who after Ausonius's death departed Spain for Italy and, like Martin, became a bishop against his will – battled for the ascetic way to become the predominant mode of Christian life in Gaul towards the end of the Roman period. However, even with the military fervour of St Martin, they were unable to claim the victory of dictating the ultimate character of the church and its bishops; another archetype was to be imported from the late Roman world.

The name of Sidonius has already been mentioned in earlier chapters, describing his villa in the countryside near Clermont-Ferrand. Born in 430, he was from a noble family of the region. His father-in-law, Avitus, rose to be emperor in 455, and even after he was deposed and possibly assassinated two years later by a rival claimant, Majorian, Sidonius was still treated with respect on account of his great ability and his unbending support for the imperial government. He addressed panegyrics to Majorian (despite the treatment he meted out to Avitus) and also to one of his later successors, Anthemius. His eloquence secured him a statue in Rome, the titles of count, senator and patrician, as well as in 469 the office of urban prefect of Rome. However, after around three years he moved to the ecclesiastical sphere, and was enthroned as bishop of his native Clermont-Ferrand.

A huge quantity of letters survive from Sidonius's pen, not to mention a short collection of poems. No other writer's works from the fifth-century Roman empire in the west have been preserved in such abundance. A reason for this great profusion can be found in one of the letters of the collection, written after Sidonius became bishop and addressed to one of his fellow clergymen, Bishop Lupus of Troyes, an eminent cleric who had held his position since 429 and had even managed to prevail on Attila the Hun to spare Troyes from being sacked in 451. It is a long and convoluted letter. Sidonius passes through self-deprecatory excuses about his 'slipshod style of writing'; he praises Bishop Lupus for having maintained their mutual affection for so many years. However, its main substance is a discussion of a book that Sidonius had sent Lupus a little while before: a book that Sidonius himself had composed 'crammed and loaded with a motley assemblage of topics, times and places': in fact, it was a compilation of some of Sidonius's own earlier letters. The current letter to Lupus is an elaborate and learned piece of politesse concerning how this book had been received by him and other readers: 'I knew that you knew how modesty better becomes an author than self-assurance on the occasion of publishing his works and that from austere critics favourable notices are less readily drawn by brashness on the part of an author than by nervousness.' Though Lupus is hardly one of these austere critics, suggests Sidonius. In fact, he is a great patron of the arts and encourager of literature: 'Never to mention myself, you bring to light the talents of all men of letters however much they seek obscurity – just as the sunbeam is wont, by means of its thirsty particles, to draw out the water hidden in the bowls of the earth... Thus when you, my saintly friend, find any men of literary tastes inactive or shy or hidden in some obscure retreat where their fame languishes, your brilliant eloquence with its skilful admonition urges them on and thereby brings them to public notice.'

So the survival of Sidonius's letters stems not just from the fact that he wrote so many – nine volumes' worth in the end – but that he saw to their publication and their wide dissemination among his fellow Gallic literati, who would approve of his work and give it their protection. Lupus, a fellow bishop, was one such person. But everything inscribed in Sidonius's letter to him – the elaborate courtesies, learned allusions to classical literature and the law, the obsession with preserving one's name by a literary endeavour focused on anything but Christian piety – would have been hateful to ascetics of Martin's and Paulinus's stamp. These features represented the typical behaviour of the Roman aristocracy, and this letter is an example of how that aristocracy, towards the end of the imperial period, had been able to move in to the institution of the episcopacy, and make it for the most part its own.

It is little wonder the role of bishop became a draw to the aristocratic classes towards the end of the imperial period. The role was one of authority within the city. It offered an outlet for the energetic and public-spirited who wished to make their mark, or else to work for the general good. As such, it was a perfect substitute in the late empire for the jobs in the imperial administration that were beginning to disappear as the barbarian armies took over responsibility for Gaul from the Roman government. The office of bishop might require diplomatic talent in negotiating with other cities, barbarian leaders or the retreating apparatus of the Roman state. It gave scope for patronage and display via the building of churches and other public works. The bishop became a considerable landowner, holding large estates for each diocese, able to command great wealth and power within the city, and often effectively taking over the decaying institution of the city council. Besides, the role was also tax free. It is little surprise that the aristocratic classes were tempted to become churchmen, bringing with them their habits and assumptions, their ease at possessing wealth and their devotion to the traditions of classical education. Even if they inhabited a new spiritual world, the old literature and the old philosophies that were intrinsic to the identity of their class were to be maintained and not condemned. The pagan writers with their eloquence and ideas were instead to be preserved to enhance the Christian message. Thus, through the institution of the Catholic Church, the preferences of class helped maintain the accumulated wisdom of the classical world for posterity – especially in Gaul.

It was not only high literary culture and the ideals of the aristocratic classes that managed to survive by taking refuge in the church. The traditional religious customs of the Gallo-Roman peoples also managed to do so for the most part, albeit frequently in altered or hidden form, despite the best efforts of some in the church hierarchy. One of the most conspicuous bishops who attempted to maintain the fight of Martin and Paulinus for the ascetic life and against pagan customs was Caesarius of Arles. Caesarius, like Paulinus, was of an aristocratic background, born to a high-class Roman family in Chalon-sur-Saône in around 470. He was drawn to the ascetic life, and spent some time on the island of Lérins off the southern coast of Gaul, where austere ideals about monasticism had been established by St John Cassian, an ascetic and mystic who, like St Martin, had come to Gaul from the Danubian frontier. Caesarius was noted for his extreme levels of abstinence, not only fasting so much that he made himself ill, but also getting into a fight with a monastic cellarer for, in his view, allowing other monks to have too much food.

Caesarius withdrew from Lérins, but by around 502 he was enthroned as bishop of Arles. He built up a strong reputation for good works, in particular ransoming prisoners taken by the Burgundian, Visigothic and other factions who were competing for primacy in southern Gaul at the time. He assisted in the development of the parish system, something which St Martin had helped to pioneer, and which was to remain a deep-seated part of local administration in France up to the Revolution. However, many of his fulminations from the pulpit were directed against the pagan practices which, despite the work and preaching of people like St Martin, remained strong throughout Gaul.

Caesarius's use of the word 'pagan' to describe practices he considered to have no basis in Christianity, or indeed to be anti-Christian, reflects an aristocratic hauteur. *Paganus*, meaning country-dweller, did not suggest that Christianity had a hold in the town but was slow to penetrate the countryside; it was rather that reverence for the old gods or maintaining aspects of their worship and taboos smacked of the uneducated rustic, whether pursued in the town or in the country.

There were many instances of this rustic behaviour of which Bishop Caesarius disapproved. The people sang bawdy songs 'inimical to chastity and honour'. They blew horns and rang bells to help the moon recover whenever there was an eclipse. They used charms and spells to overcome illnesses, or to ensure that their crops flourished for a bumper harvest. They delayed their journeys so that they would start or finish on 'auspicious' days. They bathed in rivers, lakes and springs at midsummer (such as the source of the Seine) for the sake of their healing power. Worst of all, they celebrated the Roman festival of the Kalends of January, or New Year's Day: there was feasting and drinking, the exchange of presents, as well as 'carnal and luxurious celebrations' in which the people enjoyed masquerades, dressing up as heifers or stags (redolent of the Gallic stag-god Cernunnos) or, if one were a 'soldier', as a prostitute.

Caesarius used every means at his disposal to get rid of these pagan practices. Sometimes, he appealed to rational argument. The moon, he intoned from his pulpit, was a 'sphere set afire by a natural physical cause, which was hidden at fixed times or overcome by the nearby glow of the setting sun'. How could, he asked, 'sacrilegious noise-making' make it propitious? Days of the week should no longer be named after the pagan gods; there should be no more days dedicated to Jupiter or Mercury.* He cajoled landowners to get rid of any pagan 'trees, altars or shrines' that might be on their property 'where wretched people customarily offer prayers', otherwise the landowners would be 'accessory to what was done there'. And if such persuasions should fail, then full coercion should follow. Those who were social equals should be ostracized. 'If they belong to you, however, beat them even with whips, so that they might fear a blow to their bodies who do not think about the salvation of their souls.' Like St Martin, the Roman laws on desertion for soldiers furnished the mindset of Caesarius: 'The man who deserts the church of Christ... must therefore... be judged the same as a man who deserts the army of a terrestrial king.'

However, the old Gallic and Roman ways fought back against the battle waged by Caesarius. The practice of divination and foretelling the future by casting lots, watching the flight of birds, or, as Caesarius relates, the interpretation of birdsong or sneezes, was prohibited. Yet foretelling the future by the *sortes biblicae* – letting the Bible fall open at random to seek a prediction of what was to come – made up for the suppression of these earlier practices. Written spells to cure diseases

---

*   Only Portuguese of the western European languages has obeyed Caesarius' injunction. Except for Saturday (*sábado*) and Sunday (*domingo*), the days of the week in Portuguese are numbered: *segunda-feira* (second day, i.e. Monday), *terca-feira* (third day, i.e. Tuesday). This contrasts with other European languages, in which the days of the week are still named after pagan deities, e.g. English *Wednesday* after Woden, or French *mercredi*, named after Mercury.

were also condemned, but amulets containing biblical verses and Christian prayers filled the gap. Charms, such as shepherd's crooks, to avert hailstorms from the crops were disallowed, but a cross planted in the fields or on the hills would now fulfil the same function. The New Year parties would not go away, but at least Caesarius could appeal for exchanges of gifts to be turned into alms-giving. 'Drunken' and 'lewd' dancing was performed as a back-handed honour before the shrines of Christian saints. And bathing in rivers, lakes and springs was tied to the feast of St John the Baptist, and still carried out – under the cover of commemorating Christian baptism – at midsummer on 23 June, as the earlier tradition demanded.

Bishops such as Martin of Tours and Caesarius desired to live humbly, but they were buried lavishly. Gregory of Tours, one of Martin's successors as bishop of Tours in the late sixth century, described how a shrine had developed around his tomb, and proudly outlines the opulence and grandeur of the building that had been put up to house it: 'It is 48 metres (160 feet) long and 18 metres (60 feet) wide and 13 metres (45 feet) high to the vault; it has thirty-two windows in the part around the altar, twenty in the nave; forty-one columns; in the whole building fifty-two windows, 120 columns; eight doors, three in the part around the altar and five in the nave.' It is a scale of building one would hardly expect from the so-called 'Dark Ages', and seems more appropriate to the classical Roman era. But Martin, even in death, was now fulfilling another Roman archetype. In the reported piety of his life, he was seen as being closer to God than the ordinary run of mankind. Thus, it was imagined, he had special access to the divine mind; in other words, he had God's ear. In the Roman order, people would always seek the protection of the well connected. If one were in trouble but had access to a well-placed imperial official, someone in the court who could speak to the emperor, for example, then this was the most reliable way to solve a problem. Such a well-placed person was a *patronus*, 'patron'. The patron was a secular and usually aristocratic figure. St Martin, thanks to the special position in heaven he was perceived to possess, was co-opted into being a spiritual patron: a patron saint. It is for this that the tributes paid to his remains and his shrine were similar to those that would be paid to any emperor visiting the town. To have Martin's body was the same as having an emperor, in person, present; it was a sign of his continuing presence and his intention of helping both the city of Tours and those who visited his shrine. His access to God would allow the resolution of any number of problems that were seen to have at their root a spiritual cause. Hence at the end of the Roman imperial period, and for centuries beyond, Tours became one of the leading sites in Gaul for healing. Instead of the old springs and pools where the rivers rose, the lepers, the halt, the lame and the infertile made their way there to seek wholeness at the new Christian shrines, and to adorn them with gifts and ex-votos in the event of the patron fulfilling a promise.

Devotions at the source of the Seine came to an end around the fifth century. Certainly by the time that Caesarius was calling for the destruction of shrines and an end to the practice of bathing in holy wells and springs, the precincts and temple by the source appear to have been pulled down and abandoned. However, a busy road leads from the source to the nearest town, Saint-Seine-l'Abbaye, in the heart of which stands an abbey and old Benedictine monastery dedicated to its own patron, St Seine. Seine was not the original name; the first saint was Sigo, the son of a local nobleman, the count of Mesmont. He lived during the sixth century, a little after the shrine at the source would have been abandoned. He came to this spot to pursue the life of a hermit, and the monastery was founded after him, but his name was changed by posterity from 'Sigo' to 'Seine', after the nearby river. Even the source of the Seine was accounted for in later Christian legend as one of his works: his mule knelt to allow him to dismount easily, and from the animal's knee print the source of the river rose.

The Abbey itself possesses a medieval fresco on the south wall of the choir. It was much damaged during the Revolution, but the visitor can still make out episodes from the now mythical life of Saint Seine. In one of the panels close to the end, he sits surrounded by the unfortunate: a lame man perches, showing him his knee; a blind man, however, draws the first blessing of the saint, who is making the sign of the cross above his eyes. The other men, says the text beneath, are waiting for him to cast out demons. In the final panel, the saint's body, now translated to the Abbey and surrounded by blue-robed bishops, continues for many years to perform 'glorious miracles'.

Once again, there was a holy place by the source of the Seine where people could seek healing. The Roman irruption into Gaul with all the religions and ideas it had brought had changed everything; but, curiously, it had also changed nothing.

A dolium (large earthenware storage jar) at the Puymin site in Vaison-la-Romaine.

From an Empire to a Dream

Unum consilium totius Galliae effecturum, cuius consensui ne
orbis quidem terrarum possit obsistere
'…establish one policy for the whole of Gaul, whose unanimity
not even the world could resist'

JULIUS CAESAR, *De Bello Gallico*, VII.29

LE MANS

·

THE NORTH-EASTERN FRONTIER PROVINCE

·

BARBARIANS AND ROMANS

·

IMPERIUM GALLIARUM

·

TRIER

·

ADRIANOPLE

·

CHÂLONS

·

CLERMONT-FERRAND

·

HOW TO SAVE AN EMPIRE

ONE CITY THAT CAN COMPETE with Autun for the complete-ness and grandeur of its remaining Roman walls is Le Mans. Its great ramparts run facing the east bank of the River Sarthe. They hang over a grassy margin of land that is now traversed by a busy dual carriageway, but which is still beautiful with gardens and grassed walkways, and lightened by sprays of purple lilac flowers with the onset of summer.

In many ways, the ramparts of Le Mans echo the walls of Autun. They rise several metres, magnificent and imposing, their flatness broken up by mighty semi-circular bastions. Their higher levels and crenellated tops are now missing, but are crowned instead by a vista of Renaissance and later rooftops, with the towers and tracery of a Gothic cathedral in their midst.

However, their dissimilarities are also striking, and significant. Autun's walls were built at the time of the city's foundation, shortly after the conquest. The walls of Le Mans (called Vindunum in Roman times) date to around the third century AD. Autun's walls, while grand and stout, are not as sturdily built or as thick as those of Le Mans. It is a sign that the walls of Autun, although they served to keep the city safe during a long siege in the mid-third century, were built not necessarily for actual defence, but as a mark of honour. They were designed to showcase Roman power and wealth to the leaders of the local Aedui tribe, and demonstrated the advantages of co-operating with the new Roman regime. The walls of Le Mans, however, in spite of the lattice patterns picked out in them with white stone, look as if they were destined for real use against possible attackers.

There is also an arresting difference between the extent of the walls of these two Gallo-Roman towns. A walk around the course of the Roman walls of Autun takes a good hour at the very least. The walls of Le Mans, by contrast, although stronger in character, are less ambitious: a walk round them is no more than a short stroll. Autun's walls were far longer than they ever needed to be, taking in the whole of the original town apart from the theatre. As such, they appear to have contained a good deal of undeveloped space. The walls of Le Mans, however, encircled only a small part of the original Roman city. Indeed, a vast swathe of the city, a band of about 90 metres in width, was destroyed to make way for the walls: not only the land over which the walls themselves ran, but also what is now the pleasant grassy margin by the river. The forum and the areas of the city beyond the river were excluded from the walls' protection, and the city's baths were also pulled down. This destruction served a twofold purpose: it removed any cover that attackers might be able to gain from the surrounding buildings; and the rubble from their demolition could be reused in the construction of the new walls. However, it was not

The Roman walls of Le Mans, with the cathedral of St Julien in the background.

just the ordinary bricks and stone that were to be recycled in this way. Fine statues, elegant columns, the boastful inscriptions of the earlier generations of Gallic aristocrats proud to have taken their Romanized offices as councillors, priests and public benefactors – all were used to fill up rough cores of the new bastions.

Such a pattern is repeated widely across Gaul. The first cities to be granted walls after the conquest received them as a sign of honour or official favour, signalling their status as official Roman colonies (as at Autun or Vienne), or else as a demonstration of Roman power, as at Autun. Otherwise, cities rarely had walls; they only became common throughout Gaul late in the third or early fourth centuries AD. The walls of the later period were generally sturdier, more practical, and smaller in extent, defending only small parts of the cities and happy to devour the great buildings and honorific inscriptions that were once an expression of Gallo-Roman identity. Given that the early architecture and the original displays of adherence by the Gallic aristocracy to the Roman vision were such a vital part of the incorporation of Gaul into the empire, one has to ask what had changed by the end of the third century that these monuments, so cherished originally, could be thrown away so lightly.

The literature on the end of the western Roman empire is so vast and complex that at times confronting it seems as daunting as facing the Burgundian and Visigothic chieftains, who are supposed to have brought the western empire to ruin in the fifth century. I do not propose to follow the facts and dates of this decline in detail, with its spiral of rebellions, incursions, coups, counter-coups and palace intrigue. However, as I approach the end of this account of Roman Gaul, it is appropriate to consider the wider circumstances that overwhelmed the Roman project. It still seems startling, given the hugely positive changes that Rome wrought in western Europe, that things could pass from the prosperity of the Flavians and the Antonines – celebrated by Gibbon as one of the most contented eras in human history – to an age, at the end of the fifth century, when the unity of empire was shattered, long-distance trade went into decline, the fine houses and buildings of town and country were abandoned and the standard of living collapsed. The views of contemporary scholarship have advanced much in recent years thanks to developments in archaeology and the reappraisal of source material, and what follows is an attempt to bring some of these recent notions to bear on the salient themes of the Roman presence in Gaul as discussed in earlier chapters.

Caesar's conquest of Gaul was not undertaken for any noble purpose. He did not have in mind any ideals of spreading civilization or extending the benefits of Roman rule to outsiders. It was a pragmatic and political act, designed to win him military glory, freedom from debt and access to manpower; it was an escape route from the dangers of prosecution before the courts, and a move towards the attainment of absolute power. However, as frequently happened in later history with other empires – and not infrequently in apparent imitation of the Roman example – the acquisition of large tracts of new territory prompted ideological soul-searching. First, a practical means had to be found to ensure the lasting and profitable obedience of the people now under Roman rule. Second, an active justification had to be identified for Rome's possession of the new territory, especially since its area was so large. It might be difficult to believe, but certainly since the second century BC there had been some unease about the possession of overseas territories. The conquest of Greece, completed by 146 BC, made many fear the corruption of the old Roman virtues of simplicity and frugality by the flow of wealth from the captive territory and the close contact with dubious foreign cultures. The same notions could only have loomed yet larger in Roman minds following Caesar's conquest, especially given that the peoples of 'Long-Haired Gaul' were seen as Rome's oldest and most dangerous enemy.

The approach taken in the decades that followed the conquest was to engage with these difficulties en bloc – and the route chosen was via culture. The Gauls were to be offered a way to become Roman. The upper classes were offered access to a Roman education; others were given the opportunity to fight in the Roman armies. The former, by taking up official positions in government, and the latter, by fighting for Rome, acquired the legal benefits and prestige of Roman citizenship, access to wealth and a deeper acquaintance with the wider empire and its customs. For those Gauls lower down the social scale, the sight of new Roman colonies, and the presence of temples, theatres, amphitheatres, baths, roads, villas and forums would encourage them not merely to accept the dominion of Rome without demur, but actively to embrace it. The Roman presence, although initially imposed with egregious brutality, killing hundreds of thousands, devastating the land and shattering an ancient culture, offered a break with the endemic tradition of Gallic tribal feuding, protection from external enemies, access to new ways of displaying prestige and new sources of trade and wealth.

The propagation of Roman culture and identity in Gaul, so those in Rome must have felt, was a triumph of Roman policy. Pragmatically, it allowed Rome to govern and garrison the new territories cheaply and with little demand for new manpower from elsewhere. It promoted the swift development of a governing and military class that was loyal and likeminded – to an extent, it must have taken the edge off the ancient fear of the Gauls that was so deep rooted in the Roman psyche. It must have felt like a policy that was both apt, and culturally sensitive. The Gauls were renowned in Rome for their eloquence, cleverness and bravery: what better way of harnessing their talents than to give them access to a system of education that revered rhetorical excellence as the apogee of its attainment, before paving the path for Gauls to enter the Roman system of government and the Roman courts? Moreover, like Roman gods and Roman religion, the Roman identity was not exclusive. Just as long as the reverence due to Caesar and Rome was paid, Roman citizenship, or else presence as a resident in the empire, allowed other loyalties and other identities. Ausonius himself, the most Roman of Gauls, wrote that 'I love Bordeaux, Rome I venerate; in this, I am a citizen, in both a consul; here was my cradle, there my *curule* chair.' Becoming consul was his proudest achievement, yet he could happily move between that Roman identity and his inheritance as an inhabitant of Bordeaux and Aquitaine, descended as he was from both the Arverni and the Aedui. The genius of Rome was to allow both identities to coexist, and to show that acquiescence to Rome not only benefitted an individual in a material sense or in the Roman scheme of things, but also allowed that individual to succeed better within the framework of his original cultural identity: to be a more committed Roman gave a Gallic aristocrat the chance to be better and more successful within the old hierarchy of Gallic society as well.

Caesar's manipulation of the identity and intentions of the dangerous northerners for his own political ends needs to be viewed in the context of the development of the empire in Gaul over the following centuries: the northerners were not as dangerous as demagogic Roman politicians presented them. The Gauls could become Roman in the blink of a generation or two, while still fulfilling many of the cultural ambitions they had absorbed from their 'barbarian' past.

The idea of the 'barbarian', therefore, did not leave the Roman political vocabulary or mindset: it was merely pushed back across Gaul. The Gauls passed from being barbarians to being Romans. However, those parts of Caesar's conquest that lay close to the Rhine were hived off into the militarized frontier provinces of Upper and Lower Germania, and here the perpetual war against the 'barbarians' continued. Emperors made their name and established their reputations by campaigning on this new frontier. Indeed, its presence acted as a justification for the empire's very existence – the barbarian threat had never gone away, and the newly embraced territories of Gaul were safe under the umbrella of Roman military might and order. There was also an economic benefit: the presence of huge armies and encampments were a spur to trade on a vast scale. Taxes paid from across the empire to the frontier armies financed the large-scale import of goods from the south and the Mediterranean throughout Gaul, and formed, it is most likely, the lion's share of economic activity in the region. Rome encouraged and hugely expanded commerce, but it is probable that the needs of the army, more than private initiative, were the real motor of Gallic trade.

Roman emperors made great play of their military prowess when fighting the barbarian threat. Fighting, however, was only a part of life on the frontier. Much more of it was diplomacy and engagement. There were other means of heading off the threat of incursions, which did not involve military engagement between Roman and barbarian: facilitating trade between the empire and the regions outside it; giving gifts to, or withholding them from, barbarian chiefs; encouraging dissent and civil war among the barbarians themselves whenever they appeared to be forming wider coalitions against Roman interests. Divide and rule was an old, tested and successful policy. However, despite this manipulation of the barbarian world and the constant talk of its threat to Rome, the two sides were intertwined and interdependent. The barbarians needed Rome. Roman trade changed society beyond the frontier over the course of time. In particular, barbarian chiefs became dependent on Roman patronage to shore up their power bases. As with the Gallic chiefs before the Roman conquest, the possession of Mediterranean goods became a sign of prestige for the barbarian warlords beyond the Rhine and allowed them to secure their positions. To punish barbarian leaders and bring them to heel, Rome might cut off trading opportunities or subsidies. Mismanagement of this policy, however, may be one of the reasons why barbarian groupings ended up launching attacks against the frontier. The frontier was not a drawbridge that could be raised and the world beyond it ignored; it was a region that demanded constant engagement in order to maintain its security and stability.

The Romans, likewise, were dependent on the barbarians. It was not only that the danger of barbarian incursion was a justification for the imperial presence and imperial order. The barbarians themselves became crucial to the maintenance of that order. As Gaul prospered economically in the second and third centuries, recruitment to the colours from the Gauls themselves and the wider empire appears to have become more difficult. Another factor was that Roman citizenship had been made universal throughout the empire at the beginning of the third century. Service in the army, which was one way for inhabitants of Gaul to obtain this benefit, now became unnecessary. Besides, a military life was no longer the guaranteed passport to social advancement and financial security for lower-class citizens that it had been in the earlier centuries. However, the barbarian tribes beyond the frontiers, well acquainted with fighting and the Roman army by long proximity, made excellent and cheap recruits to the Roman standards. Large numbers of Germanic-speaking migrants from beyond the frontiers settled in Gaul, who quickly became Romanized and who were as loyal to the Roman army and empire as those within the empire itself. The allure of becoming Roman seduced them just as it had the Gauls.

In this way, Roman Gaul became part of a newly internationalized world. It was a land that looked outwards, dependent for its security on the management of its frontiers and the peoples beyond. It also looked inwards, dependent on trade with the other provinces, the circulation of taxes through the army, as well as good governance and attention from the Roman centre. Gaul, by the conquest and the acquisition of Roman culture, had the opportunity to engage in the wider empire. In the great address that Claudius gave in Lugdunum, granting the suitably qualified nobles of the Three Gauls membership of the Senate, he made a tacit acknowledgement that if Rome were to rule profitably and effectively over Gaul, then the Gauls must also have a role to play in the wider government of the empire. If Rome wished to possess Gaul, then the Gauls should have their own portions of Rome.

These were the ingredients needed for Gaul to remain a successful and close-knit part of the Roman empire. It appears, by their actions, that the emperors understood these needs and, when governing well, tried to fulfil them. However, given the wider circumstances of the empire or the carelessness of those in central government, these needs were not always observed. One of the first problems to occur was a betrayal of Claudius's vision for the integration of Gauls into the Senate. Following the civil wars of AD 68–70, which arose when Gaius Julius Vindex (as mentioned above, a Gallic nobleman who was also a Roman senator and governor of the province of Lugdunum) rebelled against Nero both for his high taxes and his behaviour which, in his view, did not befit a Roman emperor, it can be conjectured that the old fears about Gaul were resurgent in Rome. Although the rebellion against Nero was triggered by a Gaul claiming to protect traditional Roman values, it appears to have harmed the integration of Gauls from the Three Gauls into the government of the wider empire. The number of Gauls from these regions who joined the Senate in the decades after the fall of Nero appears to have been very low indeed; instead of taking opportunities to play a role in the wider imperial government, they tended to remain in Gaul and pursue personal glory within their native territories.

Hand in hand with this disengagement of Gaul from the centre was a disengagement of the centre from Gaul. It will be remembered that the new Gallic provinces were closely associated with the Julio-Claudian house from the time of Caesar himself. Caesar had close associations with many Gallic chiefs from the time of the conquest and made individual deals with them and their tribes to ensure their loyalty. Augustus visited the provinces a number of times, including a three-year-long visit in 16–13 BC. Tiberius knew the provinces well, Caligula grew up on the frontiers and took a great interest in the imperial shrine at Lugdunum, and Claudius himself was born there. Although the imperial presence in the provinces was not always propitious – Caligula's riotous behaviour at Lugdunum springs to mind – there was almost always a benefit associated with the emperor visiting and being on the spot. The long-standing Roman institution of the patron showed the importance of personal contacts for getting things done and problems solved. All the better if the source of power himself were present, able not only to solve problems but bringing with him the access to wealth and patronage that belonged to the imperial office. However, with Nero, the close association between Gaul and the imperial house began to wane. The complaints of Vindex over central tax policy may have been partly due to the unwinding of long-standing local arrangements and concessions sensitive to local conditions, which were forgotten as the emperors stayed away from Gaul. After the civil war, this drift continued. The emperors kept their gaze on the Rhine frontier, while Gaul itself – lightly garrisoned and not apparently unsafe – was for the most part left to its own devices.

When the going was good, Gaul was able to weather this neglect, benign or otherwise. However, when the other pillars of stability were undermined, the entire edifice began to totter. One problem of governance that was never truly solved was the process of planning for the imperial succession. In the third century, following the assassination of the emperor Alexander Severus in 235 on the Rhine frontier after discontent among his troops over his handling of the barbarian peoples, the reasonably orderly successions of the Severan dynasty gave way to bloody struggles for the throne. On top of this, conflict with the Sasanian dynasty of Persia drew attention away from the Rhine and the Danube. Management of the frontiers beyond Gaul broke down, and barbarian warbands from beyond the Rhine made frequent incursions into Gaul, attacking and plundering Romano-Gallic cities and settlements. The long neglect of Gaul's affairs by the centre began to tell. In 260, a breakaway polity – the Imperium Galliarum ('Empire of the Gauls') – was founded by a local Roman army commander named Postumus. It lasted for fourteen years before being crushed, but at its height it claimed the allegiance of all the Gallic provinces, as well as the Germanic frontier and Britain also.

The Imperium Galliarum has been interpreted by some writers as an early manifestation of Gallic nationalism, but despite its institutions of government being closely modelled on Rome's, with an emperor, senate and consuls, it is unlikely that nationalism was the impulse behind it. Rather, it was the need for the proximity of high power, the desire once again, as in the earlier imperial period, for Gaul to be close to an emperor as its patron and protector – an emperor able to solve problems, look to the frontier and dispense patronage and largesse. A new emperor, keeping his courts in Lugdunum and Trier and focusing his concern on the immediate surrounding provinces, was able to fulfil this deep-seated need.

The Imperium Galliarum was suppressed in 274 and the period of instability known as the 'Third Century Crisis' came to an end. It was probably the instability of this age that led to the construction of the walls of Le Mans, and many other such fortifications throughout Gaul. Although the unity of the empire was saved and the empire was, in the propaganda of the age, 'restored', the measures taken to ensure this appear to have stored up problems for the decades to come. Diocletian, who came to the throne in 283, changed the settlement of imperial government, sharing power with a college of four emperors, the so-called Tetrarchy, each of whom would be allotted a portion of the empire. This was, if anything, an acknowledgement that those who had supported the Imperium Galliarum had had a point. One of the members of the imperial college would always be present in the Gallic provinces or their vicinity to provide the leadership, close management of the frontiers and imperial functions that were so desired. Although the Tetrarchy did not survive in its original form into the fourth century, the division of the government of the empire into a de facto western and eastern half followed; and in the fourth century Trier was developed as a new imperial capital, recreating the close connection between Gaul and the heart of imperial power that had been lost since the century after the conquest. This presence seems in some ways to have injected new life into Gaul, giving opportunities to talented people such as Ausonius and his cultural circle to play a part in the imperial service, and again bind Gaul more closely to the institutions of empire. The sheer volume of Ausonius's work – and indeed its very survival from this era – may in itself be a reflection of the sense of invigoration which Gaul felt at its new proximity to the imperial nimbus. The unity of the empire was maintained, but at the cost of institutionalizing disunity, and recognizing that the regions could not be ignored.

In order to make it difficult for regional governors to build up power bases to challenge for the throne, Diocletian reformed the entire organization of imperial government. Originally, the civil service, such as it was, had been lightly staffed with a small number of people responsible for large geographical areas. Many powers were concentrated in a few hands, and there was little exercise of oversight. Diocletian changed this early imperial arrangement. Provinces were broken up into smaller areas. Military and civil areas of authority were divided so that officials in general should only hold authority in one particular sphere. The mechanisms of oversight were developed, and stricter hierarchies were instituted for the formal regulation of the provinces by the centre. To achieve this, the civil service had to take on many more recruits. This was a boon for those, such as Ausonius, who came from the educated classes. On top of this, the army was also increased in size and restructured. However, all these reforms called for an increase in tax revenue. In the long run, this was difficult for the empire to sustain.

The old long-distance trading routes that had flourished from the start of the early imperial period were interrupted during the Third Century Crisis, and they did not return with their previous vigour even once the stability of the empire had been restored in the early fourth century. Trade and prosperity were also damaged over the course of the third century by debilitating inflation, as the coinage of the empire was debased to near worthlessness: rival claimants to the imperial throne had to pay their armies, and the only way to do so was by 'printing' money: reducing the silver content of the coin to almost nothing but keeping the face value of the coin the same. The collapse of the currency in this period encouraged greater local production and local self-sufficiency rather than long-distance trade. In some ways, the economy was demonetized: barter and payment in kind began to return, and the stimulus to excess production – the usual symptom of a money economy – was removed. On top of this, some scholars argue that manufacturing technologies that were originally the preserve of the Mediterranean littoral were dispersed towards the periphery of empire. Thus it was not just the capacity for long-distance trade that declined, but also the imperative to conduct it in the first place.

The demands for tax and the new configurations of the government and army created social pressures. Gaul became polarized. The old civic and mercantile classes were hollowed out. Fewer members of the aristocratic classes wished to undertake the old civic roles, which demanded the underwriting of tax shortfalls. The poor placed themselves in virtual servitude to local magnates in exchange for protection from military service and taxes. Wealth was increasingly concentrated in fewer hands. In earlier times, the practice by the well-to-do of displaying their wealth through benefactions for the construction of public buildings was seen as a social virtue. But this habit now went into decline. A good part of this impulse was absorbed by the growth of the Christian church, which provided an outlet for rich Gauls to display their wealth by financing new ecclesiastical buildings; but more and more wealth was displayed in a private context. As had happened in Rome itself at the start of the crisis that brought about the end of the Republic centuries before, greater numbers of estates fell into the ownership of smaller numbers of people. Some villas were abandoned as not needed or not viable. Over the course of the fourth and fifth centuries, others became larger and more opulent than ever, and some – like the cities – were fortified. The traces of early medieval society and what later historians would refer to as the feudal system began to appear. This might even have owed something to earlier patterns of Gallic society, which re-emerged as the traditional Roman order declined. The word 'vassal', for example, is one of the few survivals from the Celtic tongues to enter medieval and modern usage.

All of these trends are reflected in the walls that encircle Le Mans and other late Gallo-Roman settlements. Civic life seems to have been less viable, and was perhaps of less importance than in earlier centuries. Those public markers of prestige that mattered so much at the beginning of the imperial period were now considered less important – little surprise therefore if great public works were cleared, and old memorials of grand Gallo-Roman aristocrats were broken up and built as rubble into the bastions of Le Mans and elsewhere. Likewise, after the third century, the habit of leaving proud inscriptions detailing one's glorious career as a priest or magistrate seems to have come to a halt. For those lucky enough to possess prestige from wealth or imperial office, its display became a more restricted and private affair. It took place among a closed circle of high-class families, the means of display the grandeur of their villas or their literary endeavour. This may explain why so much Gallo-Roman literature survives from this period: the upper classes were busy writing to prove their class credentials. With Gallo-Roman society in such a highly-strung state, it should have been little surprise that any attack on its essential foundations, as described above, would ultimately have even graver repercussions for imperial unity than the Third Century Crisis.

In 376, the decision to allow a large group of Goths into the empire to settle as soldiers and farmers backfired horribly when a revolt by the newcomers – provoked by Roman mismanagement – culminated in the Battle of Adrianople (fought near modern Edirne, in eastern Thrace). Some 20,000 men, nearly two-thirds of the Roman force present on the battlefield, were lost as a result of incompetent generalship. The eastern Roman emperor, Valens, was also killed. Although the immediate situation was recovered, the heavy losses had serious implications for the western frontiers on the Rhine. Ultimate power over the empire at the time lay in the east, which was then wealthier and more populous than the west. To restore their forces after the calamity of Adrianople, the eastern emperors ran down the frontier establishments in the Germanic provinces. As a force, the western armies essentially evaporated. Trier lost its status as an imperial capital by the end of the fourth century, with Arles taking up the role for a while.

Rather than using its own military establishment to ensure the security of the western frontier, the empire began to rely on federate barbarian warbands (*foederati*), who rather than being integrated into the Roman army acted as discrete forces under their own commanders. This cost-cutting measure of convenience is unlikely to have seemed especially radical or dangerous to the late imperial government; groups of barbarians had frequently been settled in Gaul and relied upon for military service. Indeed, for some time the army had been 'barbarized', assuming types of clothing from beyond the frontier, and even naming various units after barbarian tribal groups renowned among the Romans for their ferocity. The importance of high Roman military officers, in particular the master of the soldiers, who could maintain good relations between the imperial court and the barbarian *foederati*, became ever greater. However, this step meant that the traditional Roman imperial method of controlling the frontier peoples effectively came to an end.

On top of this, conflicts over the succession once more began to damage the western empire by the end of the fourth century. The death of Gratian at the hands of Maximus in 383 has already been recorded. The eventual victory of Theodosius, the eastern emperor (the last to rule both halves of the Roman empire before the rule was again divided) in 388 led to the sudden disenfranchisement of those Gauls, such as Ausonius, who were by then playing their full part at the centre of the imperial system. The period of civil war following the death of Gratian further weakened the military strength of the western empire. In 383 Maximus had removed Roman troops from

Britain in large numbers to support his bid for the imperial throne.*
Furthermore, the various imperial claimants used barbarian federate
troops in their armies, thereby enhancing their autonomous importance in the Gallic provinces.

In the popular imagination, the incursion of a large force of barbarians across the Rhine in 406 – another traditionally resonant date
– is seen as a cataclysmic moment, heralding the end of the empire
in the west. The image of a vast horde of vicious outsiders, breaking
down the fortress walls of the empire to plunder and destroy a precious and sophisticated civilization, built up over centuries, haunts the
European imagination to this day. However, the decline of the western
empire did not take the form of an immediate and brutal collapse,
but a haphazard unravelling of long-standing ties. As Italy looked ever
more to its own defence and welfare, cutting its connections with the
Gallo-Roman aristocracy, it made more sense for the Gallo-Romans to
deal directly with the leaders of the barbarian warbands, which were
now acting as much in the defence of Gallo-Roman society as pos-
ing a threat to it. Thus, the regions north of the Loire appear to have
detached themselves from central Roman control by the first quarter
of the fifth century. The Visigothic branch of the barbarian force that
invaded in 406 – and which was probably not very big – was settled
in Aquitaine by 418 and given autonomous status in return for promising to act in defence of the empire's interests. It appears that they
were given either shares of land following a received procedure for the
settling of federate forces, or even a right to take the tax revenues that
were due from estates. Various other groupings were settled throughout Gaul in this fashion. In the middle of the century, when the Roman
general Flavius Aetius defended Gaul from the inroads of Attila's Huns
and their allies, he relied on a confederation consisting primarily of
'barbarian' forces. At the Battle of Châlons (451), Aetius fought alongside the Visigothic king Theodoric. Aetius's success in driving away

---

* Some early commentators declared Maximus's departure from Britain in 383 to be the
  effective end of Roman rule there, rather than the traditional date of 410.

a genuinely threatening and unified enemy paradoxically led to the weakening of the ties within this confederation. With no enemy to unite against, the pressure for cohesion declined and, despite his successful defence of the empire, Aetius himself was assassinated by the emperor Valentinian III, who was still smarting over Aetius's support for his rival Joannes at the beginning of his reign; he also feared that Aetius wanted to make his own son the heir to the throne. As the office of western emperor became more detached from Gaul, more hotly disputed among rival claimants, and of ever less practical importance, the leaders of the barbarian groupings in Gaul and the indigenous aristocracy were less disposed to look towards Rome for legitimacy or support. Rule in their own name rather than in that of Rome became viable, and the barbarian polities such as the Frankish and Visigothic kingdoms began to develop out of the body of Roman Gaul.

It was a transition that was certainly tainted with violence. However, the arrival of a barbarian kingdom could also be seen as a liberation from the violence and pressures that had become endemic in late Roman Gaul. One churchman, Salvian of Marseilles, preaching around the middle of the fifth century, gives a vivid picture of a fractured society, in which the Roman aristocracy used their position to extort money mercilessly from the poor: 'Widows groan, orphans are trodden down, so that many, even people of good birth and liberal education, seek refuge with the enemy to escape death under the trials of the general persecution. They seek among the barbarians the Roman mercy, since they cannot endure the barbarous mercilessness they find among the Romans.' Some Roman citizens of Gaul who suffered on account of absent government or at the hands of creditors banded together in self-defence. Although they were simply trying to uphold Roman ways, they found themselves branded *bagaudae* (a Celtic word for bandits) or even stigmatized as 'barbarians' by the Roman establishment – a piece of spin that Salvian decried bitterly.

Much of the violence that erupted during the fifth and sixth centuries took the form of fighting between different barbarian parties jockeying for position and control of territory, rather than a wanton assault on Gallo-Romans and Roman culture. Indeed, the incoming peoples *wanted* Roman and Latin culture, and their governing classes needed access to it in order to control the levers of local government, which had been conducted in Latin for hundreds of years. The barbarian leaders issued law codes in Latin that drew heavily on previous Roman bodies of jurisprudence. They respected the hierarchies, rights and traditions of the Catholic Church with its Roman ways, although many of them had previously converted to the Arian form of Christianity, which was regarded as heretical by the Catholics and vice versa. Moreover, the new barbarian rulers of Gaul wished to portray themselves as rulers in the Roman imperial mode.

Sidonius portrays this desire most vividly of all. In 475 the central Roman authorities surrendered Clermont, the city of which he was then bishop, to the Visigothic King Euric in return for a guarantee that the Visigoths would not attempt to extend their control in the southernmost portions of Gaul, closest to Italy. Sidonius, devoted to the Roman cause, was bitter and disgusted at what he saw as this betrayal by Rome, especially given his absolute devotion to the maintenance of Roman rule in the area and to the wider Roman ideal. However, he chose to work with the new regime and, by co-operating, tame it. Around 461, he had written a poem about having to feed a number of Burgundians who had been billeted on him. He complains about their 'German speech', their habit of 'spreading rancid butter on their hair' (presumably in contrast to the more refined Gallo-Roman *sapo*) and their tendency to belch garlic and onion breath over him from their customary ten-course breakfasts. Yet, after 475, he is able to put this ostentatious disgust behind him. When Clermont was ceded he was sent into exile and imprisoned for his original resistance to the Visigoths; but in an effort to win favour he turns his pen to the praise of the Visigothic king. He employs the idioms of those most Roman of poets, Virgil and Horace, to laud in pastoral verse the man who had taken his ancestral city from Roman to barbarian rule: 'You Tityrus, with your land restored to you, range through the groves of myrtles and planes, and so you strike your lyre… it is your warbands, Euric, that are called for, so that the Garonne, strong in its martial settlers, may defend the dwindled Tiber…'

It was Roman praise in this mould that had been heaped on Augustus half a millennium previously; it pleased Euric, and he allowed Sidonius to return to his city. This probably confirmed Sidonius in his belief that although the material elements of Rome had collapsed around them and the vacuum filled by the barbarian 'other', something of value remained that preserved their unity not just as aristocrats, but as Romans: the literature and the culture of Rome. The institutions of imperial government were being run down, there was no money and no inclination to build in the old Roman fashion of the early empire, but the inherited culture of Rome was in itself a blessing that could maintain the evaporating sense of unity. 'The second bond of our spirits', writes Sidonius to a cousin, 'comes from the similarity of our studies.' It was for this that, as the power of Rome receded, Sidonius clung ever more closely to literature. 'Because the imperial ranks and offices have now been swept away, through which it was possible to distinguish each best man from the worst, from now on literature will be the only indication of nobility.' The rule of Rome over Gaul had passed away, but the ideal survived in its culture. It was now open to anyone to be a noble Roman and to share in the ideal of a Europe-wide confraternity whose reality had passed away. The price of admission was the love of its letters, and the pursuit of its Latin poetry and culture.

It is always a foolhardy venture to look to the ancient world for guidance in the modern. In many ways, ancient and modern societies were different in such fundamental ways – security and abundance of food supply, access to education and information, ease of movement, to name but a few – that in seeking or even observing grand comparisons it is easy to be led astray. However, at a point in time when the European Union is struggling to cement the political unity of Europe – a Roman project if ever there was one – in the face of a prolonged economic crisis and fears over migration, it is impossible to restrain oneself from considering how Rome succeeded in its project for unity for such a prolonged era (around 500 years), and how, in the light of this, contemporary Europe may be falling short.

Two aspects of the Roman conquest of Gaul and its absorption into the Roman empire are deeply distasteful to modern sensibilities. First, it arose out of extreme violence and suffering; second, it was a product not of some grand vision, but a result of political expediency, brought about by the manipulation of Roman fears concerning the 'barbarian' outsiders. Rhetoric that emphasized the danger, violence and degeneracy of the barbarians was a constant note in the Roman justification for its presence in Gaul, even before the time of Caesar and up until the evaporation of the empire in the fifth century AD. Indeed, to an extent, it was the notion of the 'barbarian other' that developed and maintained the Romans' sense of their own – civilized – identity. However, Roman practice was always more pragmatic and reasonable than Roman rhetoric. The frontier was not a solid fence but a permeable zone. The maintenance of the empire was dependent not on keeping barbarians out, but on constant engagement with them, understanding their situation, trading with them, subsidizing them, admitting them as migrants to the empire and making them part of the army and institutions of government. There was a recognition that, as a general rule, barbarians did not want to overthrow Rome or wreck its culture. Given the chance to play a part in Roman society, they would become loyal, and would even help Rome to protect itself from other, more sinister, peoples beyond the frontier zone. It was only when engagement with the barbarians was mismanaged, or settlers were used as political tools or cannon fodder in civil wars, that existential danger to the empire arose.

Although Caesar brought the empire to Gaul in a wave of bloodshed and personal ambition, justifications were later found for the Roman presence to which the Gauls, particularly their upper classes, were happy to acquiesce. The Roman presence undoubtedly contributed to a fast and widespread increase in standards of living, social stability and freedom of movement enjoyed by all classes of Gauls. It propagated a government that was effective, but also reasonably cheap to administer and which stimulated the economy. There were opportunities for Gauls at different levels of society to participate in the machinery of government and the wider empire, whether as governors, councillors, administrators, lawyers, merchants or soldiers. In the best periods, the imperial presence felt close to Gaul. It was not distant, but manifested itself in a close association between the emperor and individual Gallic cities. All in all, the empire changed the face of the country, with the development of cities and settlements that remain to this day, roads, the supply of water, and rural villas, some of which may have been the predecessors of present-day towns and villages. Despite the terrible harm inflicted by Caesar on the earlier Gallic culture and way of life, the Roman presence brought benefits for everyone in virtually every area of human activity.

But it was the introduction of Roman culture that was perhaps the greatest triumph on top of all of these material victories. Roman culture, open as it was more to the elite than wider society, had the remarkable effect of making that Gallic elite feel loyal and engaged in the Roman project, while also allowing the Gauls a sense of success within the old indigenous cultural hierarchies. In Roman eyes, it turned them from barbarians to members of the civilized world. In the same way that worship of Roman gods and adherence to the imperial cult could coexist happily with visits to the shrine of Sequana, it was complementary and enhancing, not exclusive: an aid, if anything, to cultural self-realization.

If contemporary Europe could rediscover the sensible Roman pragmatism towards the 'barbarian outsider'; if it could make its high echelons of power feel as close to the people as Claudius was to Lugdunum; if it could rediscover the touch that ensured the flow of trade and prosperity between north and south; if its conduct in the fiscal sphere was not worthy of the sort of rebukes that Salvian threw at the late Roman aristocrats for their financial oppression; if it could foster the sort of shared culture that so entranced and comforted Sidonius and that made him not only a proud Arvernian but also a proud Roman, then, perhaps, contemporary Europe would be have a chance of emulating, without bloodshed, the successes that Caesar and those who came after him wrought in the provinces of Gaul.

Mosaic depicting Orpheus playing his lyre, St-Romain-en-Gal, second century AD.

Bibliographical Notes

For a discussion on the difficulty regarding the use of 'Gauls', 'Celts', etc., see *The Celts*, Collis, pp. 98 ff.

For those wishing to visit the sites of Roman Gaul, the two guidebooks by James Bromwich, *The Roman Remains of Brittany, Normandy and the Loire Valley*, and *The Roman Remains of Southern France* are highly recommended.

CHAPTER 1

An account of the sea-going nature of the Phocaeans is given by Herodotus in 1.163, and their migration in the sixth century BC in Strabo 6.6.1. It is also referred to in Pliny's *Natural History*, 3.5. Trogus's account of the foundation of Massalia is recorded in Justinus's *Epitome*, 53.4ff, and Aristotle's is to be found in Athenaeus, 13.36. More detail is also found in Strabo, Book 4. For an introduction to Celtic society in Gaul before the Roman presence, *The Ancient Celts* by Cunliffe is recommended. For trade and cultural interactions between the Greeks and Gauls before the Roman conquest see King, *Roman Gaul*, Ch. 1, and Rankin, *Celts and the Classical World*, Ch. 2, and also Ebel, *Transalpine Gaul*. For Roman and Greek perceptions of the Gauls see Rankin Chs. 4 and 6, which includes quotations from Posidonius. For the migrations into Italy and the attack on Rome see

Livy, Book 5.34ff and Polybius 2.14ff, as well as Collis, *The Celts*, pp. 107ff, and Cunliffe, *Ancient Celts*, Ch. 4. King's account of the relationship between the Romans and the Gauls from the third to first century BC at the beginning of Ch. 2 is very useful and concise. The Roman movement into Transalpine Gaul on behalf of the Massalians is covered in Livy *Periochae* 60–1, Florus 1.3.17, Strabo 4.1, Diodorus 34.23, Pliny *Natural History* 3.36, Appian *Gallica* 1.5; see also 'Conquest of Eastern Transalpina' in Ebel, King pp. 34–42. The campaign of Marius is covered primarily in Plutarch's *Life of Gaius Marius*, and also touched on in Livy, *Periochae* 66–7. Headlam and Durrell both write evocatively about Marius and the battlefield, but some of the theories Headlam puts forward about the detail of Marius's movements are disputed.

CHAPTER 2

There are many biographies on Caesar and his political life. Goldsworthy, is, in my view, one of the best currently available, both detailed and readable. Also useful as a substantial biography with a focus on politics is Meier. Garland provides a usefully concise work which is a good short introduction. For an introduction to this period of Roman history with a good description of the decay of the republican settlement, see Scullard. Suetonius on the *Life of the Divine Caesar* contains much of the anecdotal information about Caesar's rise to power. For the organization of Gallia Transalpina after the Roman conquest, see the relevant chapters in Ebel, Chapter 6 in Rankin, and also Cicero *Pro Fonteio*.

Caesar narrates his campaign against the Helvetii in his *Commentaries*, 1.2–29. Rice Holmes, in *Caesar's Conquest of Gaul*, gives exhaustive detail of the scholarly debates over the movements of Caesar and the Gauls throughout the period, and is a most useful reference despite its age. Michael Sage, *Roman Conquests: Gaul*, is a useful modern account of the conquest with a focus on its military aspects. The article by E. W. Murray, 'Caesar's Fortifications on the

Rhône', discusses the movement of the Helvetii and the practicalities of securing the south bank of the river. The article by Water Dennison describes a visit to the putative battlefield of the Helvetii at Montmort at the beginning of the twentieth century. Riggsby, *Caesar in Gaul and Rome*, discusses the literary construction and impact of Caesar's *Commentaries*. Osgood's article 'The Pen and the Sword: Writing and Conquest in Caesar's Gaul' is also useful in this regard. Caesar's account of the war against Ariovistus is in his *Commentaries*, 1.30–53.

CHAPTER 3

The actions of Caesar from 57–54 BC are covered in Books 2–5 of the *Commentaries*. The uprising of 53 BC, culminating in the execution of Acco, is described in Book 6. See also King, pp. 42–61. Lewuillon's guide to Gergovia provides a most useful account of the archaeology, the site's broader setting and an introduction to its literary reception in later ages. Graham Robb, in the *Discovery of France*, discusses the naming of Gergovie (p. 304). Luciano Canfora looks at the contemporary criticisms of the destructive nature of Caesar's campaign in Ch. 15 of *Julius Caesar: The Life and Times of the People's Dictator*.

Caesar describes his campaign against Vercingétorix in Book 7 of his *Commentaries*. A full account of the historical texts and archaeological evidence regarding Vercingétorix and an attempt to construct as full a biography of him as possible is given in Goudineau, *Le Dossier Vercingétorix*, pp. 267–445. A history of the site of Alésia and its reception in later French history and literature is given by Büchsenschütz and Schnapp in the monumental *Les Lieux de mémoire*. For the section on the later reception of Vercingétorix I am indebted to André Simon's *Vercingétorix et l'idéologie française*, and the first section of Goudineau's *Le dossier Vercingétorix*. Also useful in this regard are Ch. 9 of Collis, *The Celts*, and also his recent chapter 'The Role of Alésia, Bibracte and Gergovia in the Mythology of the French State', the recent PhD thesis by Laure Boulerie *Le Romantisme français et l'antiquité romaine*, and Annie Jourdan, 'The Image of Gaul during the French Revolution: Between Charlemagne and Ossian'. Maria Wyke also has an excellent chapter focused on the reception of Caesar and the Gallic conquest in later culture, Ch. 3 of *Caesar, a Life in Western Culture*. Mary Beard has an essay on the popularity of Asterix in *Confronting the Classsics*, Ch. 31. Recommended for further reading is Rowell, *Paris: The New Rome of Napoleon I*, regarding the use made of the Caesarian past and the classical world more generally by the French monarchs and emperors.

CHAPTER 4

Caesar's expeditions to Britain are dealt with in his *Commentaries*, Book 4.20–36 for the 55 BC invasion and Book 5.1–23 for the 54 BC invasion. Rice-Holmes's monumental work *Great Britain and the Invasions of Julius Caesar*, although again early like his work on Gaul, is a great compendium of scholarly argument on the locations and practicalities of Caesar's two forays to Britain along with much subsidiary detail. Salway, Ch. 2, contains an account of the two invasions and their political impact as well as Caesar's motivations. For the long-term cultural impact of Caesar's invasions of Britain I am particularly indebted to the two articles by Homer Nearing, 'Local Caesar Traditions in Britain' and 'The Legend of Julius Caesar's British Conquest'. For an overview of some of the German legends of Caesar, see Scales, pp. 309ff. For a discussion of the possible political impact of Caesar's invasion, see Ch. 2 of Webster, *The Roman Invasion of Britain*, and for the impact on the Celtic population of the Roman invasions see Laing, Ch. 2. Cottrell, *Seeing Roman Britain*, touches on the sites associated with Caesar, and Charlotte Higgins, *Under Another Sky*, begins her investigation of Roman Britain at Caesar's landing site of Deal; this is an excellent recent introduction to the broader subject.

CHAPTER 5

Roth's guide to Glanum provides a further description of Les Antiques, as does Headlam, but his identification of them as monuments erected by Caesar in commemoration of Marius is not generally accepted. For Glanum, see also King, pp. 68–70. For the period of Roman control in Gaul after the departure of Caesar in 50 BC to the early imperial period and the development of Roman government see Drinkwater, *Roman Gaul*, Ch. 1–2, and 5. The account in Brogan, Ch. 2, is also useful. The essays by Goudineau in the *Cambridge Ancient History* are especially helpful. Fernand Braudel gives a sweeping account of the impact of Roman government in Vol. 2 of *The Identity of France*, pp. 60–83. For the difficult geographical concept of Gaul, I am grateful to Professor David Kovacs for sight of an unpublished paper and helpful discussions on the subject. For the Druids, see Ellis. For Licinius, see Cassius Dio 54.21ff. For Caligula in Lyons, see Cassius Dio 59.21ff. The article by Christopherson 'The Provincial Assembly of the Three Gauls in the Julio-Claudian Period' discusses the imperial altar at Lyons, as does Drinkwater in *Roman Gaul*, pp. 114–117. Drinkwater's articles, 'A Note on Local Careers in the Three Gauls under the Early Empire' and 'The Rise and Fall of the Gallic Julii' provide further detail on the careers of Gallic aristocrats and the status of the new towns in Gaul in this period. Also useful for the cultural impact of Rome in this period are MacMullen, *Romanisation in the Time of Augustus*, and particularly for the question of cultural identities Woolf's article 'Beyond Romans and Natives' and also his book *Becoming Roman: The Origins of Provincial Civilisation in Gaul*. There are also useful chapters on the concept of Romanization in *The Early Roman Empire in the West*, edited by Blagg and Millett.

CHAPTER 6

An overview of the history of Arles is given in Headlam, along with its literary reputation. The conflict between Arles and Massalia during the Roman civil war is described in Caesar's *Civil War*, 1.34ff. Brogan, in the relevant sections on Roman Gaul, gives a useful summary of the Roman monuments of the city, as well as an account of urbanization in Ch. 4. A recent full history of Arles is Eric Teyssier, *Arles La*

Romaine. Useful information on the amphitheatre is to be found in Bomgardner, *The Story of the Roman Amphitheatre*. The development of material culture is discussed in MacMullen, Ch. 4. Goodman, *The Roman City and its Periphery*, has a discussion of Arles and in particular the development of its suburbs in Roman times. For Vaison, the archaeological guide by Goudineau is an excellent starting point. More generally for the development of urban life, see King, Ch 3, and Drinkwater, *Roman Gaul*, Ch. 7.

CHAPTER 7

An introduction to rural life in Roman Gaul is to be found in Drinkwater, *Roman Gaul*, Ch. 8 King, Ch. 4, and Brogan, Ch. 6. Detailed material on the Orange cadastral maps is found in the following articles: Martine Assénat, 'Le cadastre colonial d'Orange' and André Chastagnol, 'Les cadastres de la colonie romaine d'Orange'. On tracing Roman field boundaries, see the illuminating article by Cheyette. For an account of rural crafts and agricultural produce, see the relevant sections in Coulon, *Les Gallo-Romains*. For the Barbegal Aqueduct, see King, pp. 100–101. The descriptions of villas in Ausonius's *Moselle* are to be found from ln. 298ff. The letter of Sidonius to Domitius is in 1.2 of his collected letters, and his *propempticon* is no. 24 in his collected poems. Pliny writes on Gallic wheat in *Natural History* 18.12. The use of the combine harvester in Gaul is discussed in Palladius 7.2. References to Gallic wines are in Pliny *Natural History* 14.18, 26, 57, 67. The Martial epigram on Munna is in 10.36.

CHAPTER 8

Sabine Baring-Goud writes of the Alyscamps in Ch. 6 of *In Troubador Land*, a witness to the time of its nineteenth-century neglect. Many of the inscriptions quoted are visible in the regional museums, but they are also to be found in compilations of Latin inscriptions, in particular the volumes of the *Corpus Inscriptionum Latinarum* mentioned in the bibliography. A useful reference was also Maureen Carroll,

Spirits of the Dead. For discussions of crafts and trade in Roman Gaul, see King, Ch 5, Drinkwater, *Roman Gaul*, Ch. 9, and also Coulon, *Les Gallo-Romains*, passim. Nicholas Tran's chapter 'The Social Organisation of Commerce and Crafts in Ancient Arles' is also most helpful.

CHAPTER 9

Haarhoff, *Schools of Gaul*, makes an excellent starting point for education in Roman Gaul, and Marrou, *A History of Education in Antiquity*, offers further depth and background for Gaul in the context of education of the ancient world more generally. The quotations on Julius Agricola's use of Roman education in Britain come from Tacitus *Agricola*, 21. For an overview of the Roman development of Autun, see the article by Alain Rebourg, 'L'urbanisme d' Augustodunum (Autun, Saône-et-Loire)' and for some detail of the Greek mosaics see Michèle Blanchard-Lemée and Alain Blanchard, 'Épicure dans une anthologie sur mosaïque à Autun'. The address of Eumenius on the restoration of the schools with an English and Latin text is to be found in *In Praise of Later Roman Emperors: The Panegyrici Latini*, edited by E.V. Nixon and others. For Juvenal on the Gallic orators, see *Satires* 7.148 and 15.111. Martial on the Vienne booksellers is epigram 7.88, and the presence of his works in Narbonne and Toulouse in epigrams 8.72 and 9.99. Pliny the Younger on the availability of his books is in epistle 9.11. A useful introduction to Ausonius can be found in Raby, *Secular Latin Poetry*, Ch. 2; this also includes a wider discussion of Gallic writers during the period. There are also more recent surveys of Ausonius's work, including the essay by Harold Isbell in Binns's *Latin Literature of the Fourth Century*, and also Kay's *Ausonius, Epigrams*, which contains a text with commentary that makes an excellent starting point for those who wish to study Ausonius's work in the original. Ausonius's epigram to his wife (*Uxor, vivamus quod viximus et teneamus...*) is no. 20 in the collection by Kay. There is also a 2017 English translation of the poems with notes by Deborah Warren.

CHAPTER 10

Good introductions to religion in Roman Gaul are to be found in King, Ch. 6, and also in Miranda Green, *The Gods of the Celts, passim*. King also writes a chapter 'The Emergence of Romano-Celtic Religion' in *The Early Roman Empire in the* West, edited by Blagg and Millett. For further detail of the ex-votos at the source of the Seine, see the essay by Anne-Marie Romeuf, 'Les ex-voto en bois de Chamalières (Puy-de-Dome) et des Sources de la Seine (Côte-d'or): essai de comparaison'. Ton Derks, *Gods, Temples, and Ritual Practices*, is a detailed recent work, with an emphasis on the northern regions. For the Cybele shrine in Vienne, see the articles by André Pelletier, 'Les Fouilles Du "Temple De Cybèle" A Vienne' and Charles Picard, 'Le théâtre des mystères de Cybèle-Attis à Vienne'. The inscriptions about Cybele are to be found in *Corpus Cultus Cybelae Attidisque*, Vol. 5, and further information about the Cybele cult in Vermaseren, *Cybele and Attis*, with a particular focus on Gaul in Ch. 6. For the development of Christianity in Gaul, an excellent account is given in the two works by Peter Brown, *The World of Late Antiquity* and *The Rise of Western Christendom*. For the early Christian religious sites of Gaul, see Jean Guyon and Anne Jégouzo, *Les premiers chrétiens en Provence*. The letter reporting the religious persecution in Lyons is in Eusebius, *History of the Church*, 5.1. The dating of the persecution is challenged in the article by Thompson, J. F., 'The Alleged Persecution of the Christians at Lyons in 177'. The reports of the heresies of Marcus are in Irenaeus *Against Heresies*, 1.13ff. For Martin of Tours, see the primary source material by Sulpicius Severus. A modern biography, very much in the hagiographic vein but still useful is Donaldson, *Martin of Tours*. Van Dam, *Leadership and Community in Late Antique Gaul*, contains discussions of the Christianization of Gallic society, with particular attention paid to the aristocracy, Sidonius and relic cults. The letter quoted from Sidonius to Bishop Lupus is epistle 9.11. Mathisen, *Roman Aristocrats*, similarly has an excellent overview of the role played by the Gallo-Roman aristocracy in the hierarchy of the Catholic Church. Klingshirn, *Caesarius of Arles*, contains further detail not only on Caesarius but also this aristocratic background. The impact of Christianity on the built environment of Arles is covered in the chapter by Loseby, 'Arles in Late Antiquity'. For Paulinus, see Trout, *Paulinus of Nola*, and also the accounts by Raby and Waddell, which have a touching account of the famous correspondence between Paulinus and Ausonius.

EPILOGUE

The academic literature on the decline and fall of the Roman empire has grown considerably in volume and complexity over recent years. An excellent way to orient oneself in this literature, not to mention the period, is to read the relevant chapters of Rollaston's *Early Medieval Europe*, which has an excellent overview of the academic arguments currently raging over the fall of the Roman empire. The *Introduction to Early Medieval Europe* is another valuable textbook in this regard. The view that the Roman empire was brought down by its inherent flaws (the view of Gibbon) is represented principally by the work of A. H. M. Jones. Peter Heather counters with the notion that the collapse of the western empire was as a result of overwhelming barbarian attacks that exhausted the capacity of Rome to maintain resistance, though he argues that the empire was in a strong state for most of the fifth century, and that misfortune also played a role in its collapse. He does however admit to some level of cultural continuity, but points to a sudden decline in the order and prosperity of the former Roman territories. Ward-Perkins hammers home this point most stridently of all, seeing the fifth century in the west as a period of cataclysm. Other historians, such as Goffart, maintain that the fifth century was a time of managed retreat and that the settlement of barbarians in the empire was for the most part a managed and intentional process. Guy Halsall argues that the movements of the barbarians into the empire did not cause its collapse, but were rather caused by a decline in its authority. Chris Wickham charts the continuities from the fifth century onwards in his monumental *Framing the Early Middle Ages* and *The Inheritance of Rome*. The continuities are also discussed in Volume 2 of Braudel. Also worth reading are Cameron, *The Later Roman Empire*, Goldsworthy, *The Fall of the West* and Grant, *The Fall of the Roman Empire*. For more specialist discussion of specific aspects of late Roman Gaul, see the compendium of essays edited by Drinkwater and Elton, *Fifth-Century Gaul*. For the Imperium Galliarum, see Drinkwater, *The Gallic Empire*.

Bibliography

PRIMARY SOURCES

Ammianus Marcellinus, *History*, (tr. J. C. Rolfe), Loeb Classical Library, 2005

Appian, *Roman History*, (tr. Horace White), 4 vols, Loeb Classical Library, 1913

Athenaeus, *The Learned Banqueters*, (tr. S. Douglas Olson), 8 vols, Loeb Classical Library, 2012

Ausonius, *Epigrams*, (ed. N. M. Kay), Bloomsbury Academic, 2001

Ausonius, *Works, with Paulinus of Pella's Eucharisticus*, (tr. Hugh G. Evelyn White), 2 vols, Loeb Classical Library, 1961

Ausonius, *Moselle, Epigrams and Other Poems* (Routledge Later Latin Poetry) (tr. Deborah Warren), Routledge, 2017

Cassius Dio, *Roman History*, Vol. 3, (tr. Earnest Cary), Loeb Classical Library, 1914

Chronicle of St Martin of Dover, Cotton MS Vespasian B XI, ff. 72–79, British Library; see also notes in T. D. Hardy, *Descriptive Catalogue of Materials Relating to the History of Great Britain and Ireland* (Rolls Ser.), II, 263.

Cicero, *Letters to Atticus*, (tr. D. R. Shackleton Bailey), Loeb Classical Library, 1999

Cicero, *Pro Fonteio*, (tr. N. H. Watts), Loeb Classical Library, 1953

Corpus Cultus Cybelae Attidisque, Vol. 5 (*Aegyptus, Africa, Hispania, Gallia et Britannia*), (ed. M. J. Vermaseren), Brill, 1986

Corpus Inscriptionum Latinarum, Vol. 12 (*Inscriptiones Galliae Narbonensis Latinae*, (ed O. Hirschfeld), Vol. 13 (*Inscriptiones trium Galliarum et Germaniarum Latinae*, (eds O. Hirschfeld and E. Zangemeister), Berlin-Brandenburg Academy of Sciences and Humanities, 1888–1906

Diodorus of Sicily, *Library of History*, Vols 3, 6, (tr. C. H. Oldfather), Loeb Classical Library, 1935

Eumenius, *Pro Instaurandis Scholis Oratio* ('For the Restoriation of the Schools'), Ch. 9 from *In Praise of Later Roman Emperors: The Panegyrici Latini*, (eds Nixon, E. V. and Rodgers, Barbara Saylor), University of California Press, 2015

Eusebius, *History of the Church*, (tr. G. A. Williamson), Penguin Classics, 1989

Florus, *Epitome of Roman History*, (tr. E. S. Forster), Loeb Classical Library, 1929

Geoffrey of Monmouth, *The History of the Kings of Britain*, (tr. Lewis Thorpe), Folio Society, 1966

Gregory of Tours, *The History of the Franks*, (tr. Lewis Thorpe), Penguin Classics, 1974

Herodotus, *The Persian Wars*, (tr. A. D. Godley), 4 vols, Loeb Classical Library, 1920

Irenaeus, *Adversus Haereses (Against Heresies)*, (ed. A. Roberts), Wm. B. Eerdmans, 1950

Julius Caesar, *The Civil Wars*, (tr. A. G. Peskett), Loeb Classical Library, 1957

Julius Caesar, *The Gallic War (De Bello Gallico)*, (tr. H. J. Edwards) Loeb Classical Library, 1917

Justinus, *Epitome of the Philipic History of Pompeius Trogus*, (tr. John Selby Watson), Henry G. Bohn, 1853

Juvenal, *Satires*, (tr. Susanna Morton Braund), Loeb Classical Library, 2004

Livy, *History of Rome*, (tr. B. O. Foster et al), 13 vols, Loeb Classical Library, 1919

Martial, *Epigrams*, (tr. D. R. Shackleton Bailey), 3 vols, Loeb Classical Library, 2006

Myvyrian Archaiology of Wales, (eds Jones, Owen; Morganwg, Iolo; Pughe, William Owen), Denbigh, T. Gee, 1807

Napoléon III, *Histoire de Jules César*, Paris, Henri Plon, 1866.

Palladius, *The Fourteen Books of Palladius Rutilius Taurus Aemilianus on Agriculture*, (tr. T. Owen), London, 1807

Perceforest, (tr. Nigel Bryant), D. S. Brewer, 2011

Plutarch, *Life of Gaius Marius*, in Vol. 9 of *Lives*, (tr. Bernadotte Perin), Loeb Classical Library, 1920

Polybius, *The Rise of the Roman Empire*, (eds Frank Walbank and Ian Scott-Kilvert), Penguin Classics, 1979

Rutilius Namantianus, *De Reditu Suo* ('On his Return'), (eds C.H. Keene and F. Savage-Armstrong), George Bell & Sons, 1907

Scriptores Historiae Augustae, (tr. D. Magie), 3 vols, Loeb Classical Library, 1922

Sidonius, *Poems and Letters* (tr. W. B. Anderson and E. H. Warmington), 2 vols, Loeb Classical Library, 1964

Strabo, *Geography*, (tr. H. L. Jones), 8 vols, Loeb Classical Library, 1932

Suetonius, *De Vita Caesarum* ('The Lives of the Caesars'), (tr. J. C. Rolfe), 2 vols, Loeb Classical Library, 1970

Sulpicius (Sulpitius) Severus, *On The Life of St Martin*, (tr. A. Roberts), *A Select Library of Nicene and Post-Nicene Fathers of the Christian Church*, Second Series, Volume 11, New York, 1894

Tacitus, *Agricola, Germania and Dialogus*, (tr. M. Hutton and W. Peterson), Loeb Classical Library, 1992

Tacitus, *Histories and Annals*, (tr. C. H. Moore and J. Jackson), 4 vols, Loeb Classical Library, 1937

Wace, *Roman de Brut*, (ed. Judith Weiss), *Wace's Roman de Brut: a History of the British: Text and Translation*, University of Exeter Press, 2002

In addition to the printed versions of the sources, I also found two websites of very great assistance for searching and quick reference of primary sources: Bill Thayer's excellent Lacus Curtius (http://penelope.uchicago.edu/Thayer/E/Roman/home.html) and The Latin Library (http://www.thelatinlibrary.com).

SECONDARY SOURCES

Allen, Walter, 'The British Epics of Quintus and Marcus Cicero' in *Transactions and Proceedings of the American Philological Association*, Vol. 86 (1955), pp. 143–159

Assénat, Martine, 'Le cadastre colonial d'Orange' in *Revue archéologique de Narbonnaise*, tome 27–28 (1994), pp. 43–54

Audouze, Françoise and Büchsenschütz, Olivier, *Towns, Villages and Countryside of Celtic Europe*, J. T. Batsford, 1992

Bachrach, Bernard. 'The Alans in Gaul', in *Traditio*, Vol. 23 (1967), pp. 476–489

Baring-Gould, Sabine, *In Troubador-Land*, W. H. Allen & Co, 1891

Beard, Mary, *Confronting the Classics*, Profile, 2014

Behr, John, 'Gaul' in *The Cambridge History of Christianity* (ed. Mitchell, Margaret), pp. 366–379, Cambridge University Press, 2006

Benbassa, Esther, *The Jews of France: A History from Antiquity to the Present*, Princeton University Press, 1999

Binns, J. W., *Latin Literature of the Fourth Century*, Routledge Revivals, 2015

Blagg, Thomas and Millett, Martin (eds), *The Early Roman Empire in the West*, Oxbow Books, 2002

Blanchard-Lemée, Michèle and Blanchard, Alain, 'Épicure dans une anthologie sur mosaïque à Autun' in *Comptes rendus des séances de l'Académie des Inscriptions et Belles-Lettres*, 137ᵉ année, N. 4 (1993), pp. 969–984

Bomgardner, David, *The Story of the Roman Amphitheatre*, Routledge, 2000

Boulerie, Laure, *Le Romantisme français et l'Antiquité romaine.*

Literature. Université d'Angers, 2013. French. (PhD Thesis)

Braudel, Fernand, *The Identity of France* (tr. Siân Reynolds), 2 vols, Collins, 1988

Bréan, Adolphe, *Vercingétorix*, Orleans, Gatineau, 1864

Brogan, Olwen, *Roman Gaul*, Harvard University Press, 1953

Bromwich, James, *The Roman Remains of Brittany, Normandy and the Loire Valley: A Guidebook*, Lucina Books, 2014

Bromwich, James, *The Roman Remains of Southern France: A Guidebook*, Routledge, 1996

Brown, Peter, *The Rise of Western Christendom: Triumph and Diversity, AD 200–1000*, Wiley-Blackwell, 2013

Brown, Peter, *The World of Late Antiquity*, Thames and Hudson, 1973

Büchsenschütz, Olivier and Schnapp, Alain, 'Alésia' in *Les Lieux de mémoire*, Vol III, pp. 272–315, Gallimard, 1992

Camden, William, *Britannia*, G. Bishop and J. Norton, 1610

Cameron, Averil, *The Later Roman Empire*, Fontana Press, 1992

Canfora, Luciano, *The Life and Times of the People's Dictator*, (tr. Marian Hill and Kevin Windle), University of California Press, 2007

Carroll, Maureen, *Spirits of the Dead: Roman Funerary Commemoration in Western Europe*, Oxford University Press, 2006

Chadwick, Nora, *The Celts*, Penguin, 1991

Chastagnol, André, 'Les cadastres de la colonie romaine d'Orange' [André Piganiol, *Les documents cadastraux de la colonie romaine d'Orange*, XVIe Supplément à Gallia] in *Annales. Économies, Sociétés, Civilisations*, 20ᵉ année, N. 1, (1965), pp. 152–159

Cheyette, F. L., 'The Disappearance of the Ancient Landscape and the Climatic Anomaly of the Early Middle Ages: A Question to be Pursued' in *Early Medieval Europe*, Volume 16, Issue 2 (May 2008), pp. 127–165

Christie, Neil, *The Fall of the Western Roman Empire: An Archaeological & Historical Perspective*, Bloomsbury, 2011

Christopherson, A. J., 'The Provincial Assembly of the Three Gauls in the Julio-Claudian Period' in *Historia: Zeitschrift für Alte Geschichte*, Bd. 17, H. 3 (Jul., 1968), pp. 351–366

Collis, John, *The Celts: Origins, Myths, Inventions*, The History Press, 2010

Collis, John, 'The Role of Alésia, Bibracte and Gergovia in the Mythology of the French State' in *The Harp and The Constitution: Myths of Celtic and Gothic Origin* (ed. Joanne Parker), pp. 209–288, Brill, 2015

Congès, Anne Roth, *Glanum: From Salluvian Oppidum to Roman City*, (tr. Ralph Häussler and Chrisoula Petridis), Éditions du Patrimoine, 2001

Cottrell, Leonard, *Seeing Roman Britain*, Pan Books, 1967

Coulon, Gérard, *Les Gallo-Romains: Vivre, travailler, croire, se distraire*, Éditions Errance, 2006

Cunliffe, Barry, *The Ancient Celts*, Oxford University Press, 1997

Cunliffe, Barry, *The Celtic World*, Constable, 1992

Dennison, Walter, 'A Visit to the Battlefields of Caesar' in *The School Review*, Vol. 13, No. 2 (Feb., 1905), pp. 139–149

Derks, Ton, *Gods, Temples, and Ritual Practices: The Transformation of Religious Ideas in Roman Gaul*, Amsterdam University Press, 1998

Dietler, Michael, '"Our Ancestors the Gauls": Archaeology, Ethnic Nationalism, and the Manipulation of Celtic Identity in Modern Europe' in *American Anthropologist*, New Series, Vol. 96, No. 3 (Sep., 1994), pp. 584–605

Donaldson, Christopher, *Martin of Tours: Parish Priest, Mystic and Exorcist*, Routledge & Kegan Paul, 1980

Drinkwater, J. F., 'A Note on Local Careers in the Three Gauls under the Early Empire' in *Britannia*, Vol. 10 (1979), pp. 89–100

Drinkwater, J. F., *The Gallic Empire: Separatism and Continuity in the North-western Provinces of the Roman empire A.D.260–274*, Steiner, 1987

Drinkwater, J. F., 'The Rise and Fall of the Gallic Iulii: Aspects of the Development of the Aristocracy of the Three Gauls under the Early Empire' in *Latomus*, T. 37, Fasc. 4 (Octobre–Decembre 1978), pp. 817–850

Drinkwater, J. F., *Roman Gaul: The Three Provinces 58 BC–AD 260*, Croom Helm, 1983

Drinkwater, J. F. and Elton, H. (eds), *Fifth-Century Gaul: A Crisis of Identity?*, Cambridge University Press, 1992

Durrell, Lawrence, *Caesar's Vast Ghost: Aspects of Provence*, Faber and Faber, 1990

Ebel, Charles, *Transalpine Gaul: The Emergence of a Roman Province*, Brill, 1976

Ellis, Peter Beresford, *The Druids*, Robinson, 2002

Enikel, Jansen, *Weltchronik*, (ed. P. Strauch), Munich, 1980

Fischer, Herman, 'The Belief in the Continuity of the Roman Empire among the Franks of the Fifth and Sixth Centuries' in *The Catholic Historical Review*, Vol. 10, No. 4 (Jan., 1925), pp. 536–553

Garland, Robert, *Julius Caesar*, Bristol Phoenix Press, 2003

Goffart, Walter, *Barbarian Tides: The Migration Age and the Later Roman Empire*, University of Pennsylvania Press, 2006

Goldsworthy, Adrian, *Caesar*, Phoenix, 2006

Goldsworthy, Adrian, *The Fall of the West: The Death of the Roman Superpower*, Weidenfeld & Nicholson, 2009

Goodman, Penelope, *The Roman City and its Periphery*, Routledge, 2007

Goubert, Pierre, *The Course of French History*, Routledge, 1996

Goudineau, Christian, *Regard sur la Gaule, Recueil d'Articles*, Babel, 2007

Goudineau, Christian, 'Gaul', in *The Cambridge Ancient History* (eds A. K. Bowman, E. Champlin and A. Lintott), pp. 464–502, Cambridge University Press, 1996

Goudineau, Christian, 'Gaul', in *The Cambridge Ancient History* (eds A. K. Bowman, P. Garnsey and D. Rathbone), pp. 462–495, Cambridge University Press, 2000

Goudineau, Christian, *Le Dossier Vercingétorix*, Babel, 2001

Goudineau, Christian and De Kisch, Yves, *Archaeological Guide to Vaison La Romaine* (tr. Chérine Gebara), Guides Archeologiques de la France, 1984

Goudineau, Christian and Lontcho, Frédéric, *En survolant la Gaule*, Éditions Errance, 2007

Grant, Michael, *The Fall of the Roman Empire*, Weidenfeld & Nicholson, 1990

Green, Miranda, *The Gods of the Celts*, The History Press, 2011

Grey, Cam, 'Two Young Lovers: An Abduction Marriage and Its Consequences in Fifth-Century Gaul' in *The Classical Quarterly*, New Series, Vol. 58, No. 1 (May, 2008), pp. 286–302

Grey, Sir Thomas, *Scalacronica; The Reigns of Edward I, Edward II and Edward III as Recorded by Sir Thomas Gray*, (tr. H. Maxwell), James Maclehose & Sons, 1907

Guyon, Jean and Jégouzo, Anne, *Les premiers chrétiens en Provence: guide archéologique*, Éditions Errance, 2001

Haarhoff, Theodore Johannes, *Schools of Gaul: A Study of Pagan and Christian Education in the Last Century of the Western Empire*, Oxford University Press, 1920

Halsall, Guy, *Barbarian Migrations and the Roman West 376–568*, Cambridge University Press, 2009

Harvey, Brian (ed.), *Daily Life in Ancient Rome: A Sourcebook*, Focus, 2016

Headlam, Cecil, *Provence and Laungedoc*, Methuen, 1912

Heather, Peter, *Empires and Barbarians: Migration, Development and the Birth of Europe*, Pan, 2009

Heather, Peter, *The Fall of the Roman Empire: A New History*, Pan, 2005

Heather, Peter, 'The Huns and the End of the Roman Empire in Western Europe' in *The English Historical Review*, Vol. 110, No. 435 (Feb., 1995), pp. 4–41

Higgins, Charlotte, *Under Another Sky: Journeys in Roman Britain*, Vintage, 2013

Highet, Gilbert, *The Classical Tradition*, Oxford University Press, 1951

Huysmans, Joris-Karl, *Against Nature* (tr. Margaret Mauldon), Oxford World's Classics, 1998

Innes, Matthew, *Introduction to Early Medieval Europe, 300–900: The Sword, the Plough and the Book*, Routledge, 2007

John of Fordun, *Chronicle of the Scottish Nation*, (ed. W. F. Skene) in *The Historians of Scotland*, vol. 4, Edmonston and Douglas, 1872

Johnson, Boris, *The Dream of Rome*, Harper Collins, 2006

Jones, A. H. M., *The Decline of the Ancient World*, Longman, 1966

Jones, R. F. J., 'A False Start? The Roman Urbanisation of Western Europe' in *World Archaeology*, Vol. 19, No. 1, *Urbanization* (Jun., 1987), pp. 47–57

Jourdan, Annie, 'The Image of Gaul during the French Revolution: Between Charlemagne and Ossian' in *Celticism* (ed. Terence Brown), Brill, 1996

Kelly, Christopher, *Ruling the Later Roman Empire*, Belknap Press, 2004

King, Anthony, *Roman Gaul and Germany*, British Museum Publications, 1990

Klingshirn, William, *Caesarius of Arles: The Making of a Christian Community in Late Antique Gaul*, Cambridge University Press, 1994

Koch, John. T and Carey, John (eds), *The Celtic Heroic Age: Literary Sources for Ancient Celtic Europe & Early Ireland & Wales*, Celtic Studies Publications, 2003

Kulikowski, Michael, 'Barbarians in Gaul, Usurpers in Britain' in *Britannia*, Vol. 31 (2000), pp. 325–345

Laing, Lloyd and Laing, Jennifer, *Celtic Britain and Ireland: Art and Society*, Herbert Press, 1995

Lambarde, William, *Perambulation of Kent (1570)*, B. W. Burrill, 1826

Leland, John, *Itinerary*, (ed. Lucy Toulmin Smith), 1907

Leslie, John, *History of Scotland* (1578, tr. James Dalrymple, ed. E. G. Cody), Scottish Text Society, 1888

Lewuillon, Serge, *Gergovie et le pays arverne*, Éditions du Patrimoine, 2013

Loseby, S. T., 'Arles in Late Antiquity: Gallula Roma Arelas and Urbs Genesii' in *Towns in Transition: Urban Evolution in Late Antiquity and the Early Middle Ages* (eds N. Christie and S. T. Loseby), pp. 45–70, Scolar Press, 1996

Lucki, Emil, 'The Role of the Large Landholders in the Loss of Roman Gaul: A Case Study in the Decline of the Roman Empire in the West' in *The American Journal of Economics and Sociology*, Vol. 20, No. 1 (Oct., 1960), pp. 89–98

McCormick, Thomas, *A Partial Edition of Les fais des Rommains, with a Study of its Style and Syntax: A Medieval Roman History*. Studies in French literature 20. Lewiston, New York, Mellen, 1998

MacMullen, Ramsay, 'Barbarian Enclaves in the Northern Empire' in *L'Antiquité Classique*, T. 32, Fasc. 2 (1963), pp. 552–561

MacMullen, Ramsay, *Romanization in the Time of Augustus*, Yale University Press, 2000

Marrou, H. I., *A History of Education in Antiquity*, Mentor Books, 1956

Mathisen, Ralph Whitney, *Roman Aristocrats in Barbarian Gaul: Strategies for Survival in an Age of Transition*, University of Texas Press, 1993

Meier, Christian, *Caesar*, Fontana Press, 1996

Moorhead, Sam and Stuttard, David, *AD 410: The Year that Shook Rome*, The British Museum Press, 2010

Murray, E. W., 'Caesar's Fortifications on the Rhône' in *The Classical Journal*, Vol. 4, No. 7 (May 1909), pp. 309–320

Nearing, Homer, 'The Legend of Julius Caesar's British Conquest' in *Proceedings of the Modern Language Association of America*, 64 (1949), pp. 889–929

Nearing, Homer, 'Local Caesar Traditions in Britain' in *Speculum*, Vol. 24, No. 2 (Apr., 1949), pp. 218–227

Osgood, Josiah, 'The Pen and the Sword: Writing and Conquest in Caesar's Gaul' in *Classical Antiquity*, Vol. 28, No. 2 (Oct., 2009), pp. 328–358

Parker, Earle, 'Caesar's Battlefields in 1908' in *The Classical Journal*, Vol. 4, No. 5 (Mar. 1909), pp. 195–204

Pelletier, André, 'Les fouilles du "Temple de Cybèle" à Vienne (Isère), Rapport Provisoire' in *Revue Archéologique*, Nouvelle Série, Fasc. 1 (1966), pp. 113–150

Pelletier, André, *Vienna (Vienne)*, Presses Universitaires de Lyon, 2001

Picard, Charles, 'Le théâtre des mystères de Cybèle-Attis à Vienne (Isère), et les théâtres pour représentations sacrées à travers le monde méditerranéen' in *Comptes rendus des séances de l'Académie des Inscriptions et Belles-Lettres*, 99 année, N. 2, (1955), pp. 229–248

Potter, David, *The Roman Empire at Bay AD 180–395*, Routledge, 2014

Provini, Sandra, 'Les rois de France sur les traces de César en Italie', in *Cahiers de recherches médiévales*, 13 spécial, 2006

Raby, F. J. E., *A History of Secular Latin Poetry in the Middle Ages*, 2 vols, Oxford University Press, 1957

Rankin, David, *Celts and the Classical World*, Routledge, 1996

Rebourg, Alain, 'L'urbanisme d'Augustodunum (Autun, Saône-et-Loire)' in *Gallia*, Volume 55, No. 1 (1998), pp. 141–236

Rice Holmes, Thomas (T. R. E. Holmes), *Caesar's Conquest of Gaul*, Oxford, 1911

Rice Holmes, Thomas (T. R. E. Holmes), *Great Britain and the Invasions of Julius Caesar*, Oxford University Press, 1907

Riggsby, Andrew, *Caesar in Gaul and Rome: War in Words*, University of Texas Press, 2010

Rivet, A. L. F., *Gallia Narbonensis: Southern France in Roman Times*, B. T. Batsford Ltd, 1990

Robb, Graham, *The Discovery of France*, Picador, 2007

Roddaz, Jean-Michel, 'Jules César dans la tradition historique française des XIXe et XXe siècles' in *Cesare: Precursore o visionario. Atti del convegno internazionale Cividale del Friuli, 17–19 settembre 2009 (I convegni della Fondazione Niccolò Canussio. 9)* (ed. G. Urso), pp. 333–352, Fondazione Niccolò Canussio, 2010

Rollason, David, *Early Medieval Europe 300–1050*, Pearson, 2012

Romeuf, Anne-Marie, 'Les ex-voto en bois de Chamalières (Puy-de-Dome) et des Sources de la Seine (Côte-d'or): essai de comparaison' in *Gallia*, T. 44, Fasc. 1 (1986). pp. 65–8

Rowell, Diana, *Paris: The 'New Rome' of Napoleon I*, Bloomsbury, 2012

Sage, Michael, *Roman Conquests: Gaul*, Pen & Sword, 2011

Salway, Peter, *Roman Britain*, Oxford University Press, 1981

Savay-Guerraz, Hugues, *Le Musée Gallo-Romain de Lyon*, Fage Éditions, 2013

Scales, Len, *The Shaping of German Identity: Authority and Crisis, 1245–1414*, Cambridge University Press, 2012

Scève, Maurice, *The Entry of Henri II into Lyon, September 1548*, Medieval & Renaissance Texts & Studies, 1997

Scullard, H. H., *From the Gracchi to Nero: History of Rome from 133 BC to AD 68*, Routledge, 1982

Simon, André, *Vercingétorix et l'idéologie française*, Editions Imago, 1997

Sivan, Hagith, 'Numerian the Intellectual: A Dynastic Survivor in Fourth Century Gaul' in *Rheinisches Museum für Philologie*, Neue Folge, 136. Bd., H. 3/4 (1993), pp. 360–365

Smith, Julia, *Europe after Rome: A New Cultural History 500–1000*, Oxford University Press, 2005

Teyssier, Eric, *Arles la romaine*, Alcide, 2016

Thiollier-Alexandrowicz, Gabriel, *Itinéraires Romains en France d'après la Table de Peutiager et l'Itinéraire d'Antonin*, Editions Faton S. A., 1996

Thompson, J. F., 'The Alleged Persecution of the Christians at Lyons in 177' in *The American Journal of Theology*, Vol. 16, No. 3 (Jul., 1912), pp. 359–384

Tran, Nicholas, 'The Social Organisation of Commerce and Crafts in Ancient Arles: Heterogeneity, Hierarchy, and Patronage' in *Urban Craftsmen and Traders in the Roman World* (eds Andrew Wilson and Miko Flohr), Oxford University Press, 2016

Trivet, Nicholas, *Nicholas Trevet's Chronicle*, (ed W. V. Whitehead), Harvard University Press, 1961

Trout, Dennis, *Paulinus of Nola: Life, Letters, Poems*, University of California Press, 1999

Van Dam, Raymond, *Leadership and Community in Late Antique Gaul*, California University Press, 1992

Vermaseren, Maarten, *Cybele and Attus: The Myth and the Cult*, Thames & Hudson, 1977

Vigier, Arnaud, 'Dévôts et dédicants: Intégration des élites dans la ciuitas des Allobroges sous le Haut-Empire', Thèse de doctorat, Université de Franche-Comté, Besançon, 2011

Wacher, John, *The Coming of Rome*, Book Club Associates, 1979

Waddell, Helen, *The Wandering Scholars*, Constable, 1927

Ward-Perkins, Bryan, *The Fall of Rome and the End of Civilisation*, Oxford University Press, 2005

Webster, Graham, *The Roman Invasion of Britain*, Routledge, 1993

Webster, Jane, 'At the End of the World: Druidic and Other Revitalization Movements in Post-Conquest Gaul and Britain' in *Britannia*, Vol. 30 (1999), pp. 1–20

Weever, John, *Ancient Funeral Monuments, of Great-Britain, Ireland, and the Islands Adjacent*, W. Tooke, 1767

Wells, Peter, *Barbarians to Angels: The Dark Ages Reconsidered*, W. W. Norton & Co, 2008

Wickham, Chris, *Framing the Early Middle Ages: Europe and The Mediterranean, 400–800*, Oxford University Press, 2006

Wickham, Chris, *The Inheritance of Rome: Illuminating the Dark Ages 400–1000*, Penguin, 2009

Wightman, Edith, *Gallica Belgica*, University of California Press, 1985

Woolf, Greg, *Becoming Roman: The Origins of Provincial Civilisation in Gaul*, Cambridge University Press, 2003

Woolf, Greg, 'Beyond Romans and Natives' in *World Archaeology*, Vol. 28, No. 3, *Culture Contact and Colonialism* (Feb., 1997), pp. 339–350

Woolf, Greg, 'Imperialism, Empire and the Integration of the Roman Economy' in *World Archaeology*, Vol. 23, No. 3, *Archaeology of Empires* (Feb., 1992), pp. 283–293

Wyke, Maria, *Caesar: A Life in Western Culture*, Granta, 2007

Picture Credits

page 193 Bijan Omrani

page 195 Bijan Omrani

page 198 Bijan Omrani

page 203 Bijan Omrani

page 210 Bijan Omrani

page 215 Bijan Omrani

page 218 Bijan Omrani

page 221 Bijan Omrani

page 224 akg

page 229 wikimedia commons

page 231 Bijan Omrani

page 236 Bijan Omrani

page 239 Bijan Omrani

page 244 Bijan Omrani

page 253 Bijan Omrani

page 255 wikimedia commons

page 258 wikimedia commons

page 266 wikimedia commons

page 276 Bijan Omrani

page 280 Bijan Omrani

page 286 Bijan Omrani

page 288 wikimedia commons

page 291 Bijan Omrani

page 298 Bijan Omrani

page 309 wikimedia commons

page 320 alamy

page 324 wikimedia commons

page 346 Bijan Omrani

Acknowledgements

I owe much to Yolande Crowe for helping my travels in search of Caesar and the Romans to get off to such a good start. My warmest thanks to her for her Provençal hospitality and her discussions of French history. My thanks also to the many staff at French archaeological sites and museums who have assisted me in the course of my journeys and researches.

Robert Twigger, Jason Webster and Tahir Shah have all been brilliantly supportive of my writing. My thanks are due to them for their encouragement and helping me to bring this work to completion. I am also forever in the debt of Matthew Leeming and Magnus Bartlett.

I would also particularly like to thank for their encouragement and assistance: Gareth Mann, Dr Sebastien Blache, Professor David Kovacs, Nick Lane, Jules Stewart, Sian and Philip Bell, Sha Crawford, Rebecca S. Davis, Justin Rushbrooke, Nell Butler, Caroline Barron, John Davie, Owen Matthews, Paddy, Di, Ella and Tara Magrane, the late William Smethurst and his wife Carolynne, Allegra Mostyn-Owen and Tom Edlin. I should also like to thank Professor John Paul Russo for the opportunity to lecture on Caesar at the University of Miami.

Many of my colleagues and students at Eton, Westminster and the other schools at which I have taught have been hugely inspirational, and I have learned much from them. My obligation to my own teachers at school and university never lessens, and their influence never wanes. They are too many to name in their entirety, but I shall always be especially grateful to James Breen, the late Dr Robert Buttimore, Mike Fox, Raine Walker, Dr David Howlett and Dr Tony Hunt.

I could have not wished for a better agent than Andrew Lownie, or a better editor than Richard Milbank. My thanks also to the team at Head of Zeus who have worked together with me on this project: Blake Brooks, Jessie Price, Suzanne Sangster, Gill Harvey and Clémence Jacquinet.

I would never have been able to write this book without the amazing support and practical help of my immediate family: Jane, Jason, Michael, Judy, Danesh. My wife Sam has also been extraordinarily patient, loving and supportive whilst I have been immersed in this project. She is a constant inspiration to me, and the book is dedicated to her, as well as our own two Visigoths, Cassian and Beatrix, whom I hope will in time embrace some of our antique Roman ways.

Index

Images are denoted by the use of *italic* page numbers.

Acco 87
Aconii (tribe) 211
actors 237
Adrianople, Battle of 336–7
Adriatic Sea 47
Aduatuci (tribe) 83, 84, 158
Adversus Haereses (Irenaeus) 297, 299
Aedui (tribe)
  allied to Rome 33, 66, 89, 254
  capital 94, 169
  at Dijon 61
  oral tradition 67
  and other tribes 76–7, 158, 252
Aeneas 31, 137, 186
aerial photography 100, 206
Aetius, Flavius 338–9
Afarwy 141
Against Nature (Huysmans) 247–8
Agamemnon 31
Agricola, Julius 251

agriculture *see* farming
Agrippa 154, 155, 164, 284, 287
Ahenobarbus, Gnaeus Domitius 59
Aix-en-Provence 35–6, 39, 40–2
Albinus, Junius Brutus 152–3
Alésia 89, 109, 111, 114–16, 196
Alésia, Battle of 99–102, *100*, 110, *112–13*
Alexander, Julius 234, 235
Alexander the Great 47
Alfred, King 135
Alise-Sainte-Reine 103
Allia, River 27
Allobroges (tribe) 33, 34–5, 61, 63, 287, 301
Alpilles, the 188
Alps, the 23, 24, 31, 33, 39
altars 164–5, *166*, 169, 171, 185–6
Alyscamps, Les (Arles) 227–31, *229, 231*, 237
Ambiorix 87
Ambrones (tribe) 40
Ambrussum *156*
Androgeus, duke of

Trinovantum 138, 139–40
Antonine dynasty 325
Antonine Wall, Scotland 131
Apollinaris 212
Apollo 15, 186, 254, 283
Appian 34
Appian Way 53
Aquae Sextiae, Battle of 40–1
Aquae Sextius *see* Aix-en-Provence
aqueducts 188, 214–15
Aquileia 72
Aquitaine Gaul 155, 157, 158, 194, 221, 222, 328, 338
Arausio *see* Orange
Arausio, Battle of 38, 40
Arborius 265, 268
Arborius, Magnus 261
Arc, River 40
Archelaus, Herod 289
Arelate 178–9
  see also Arles
Ariovistus 77, 83
aristocracies 49, 313–18, 335, 339
Aristotle 13, 14, 20, 25
Aristoxena *see* Gyptis

Arles 177–90
  altars 185–6
  Alyscamps, Les 227–31, *229*, *231*, 237
  amphitheatre *174*, 177, 178, *183*, 188–90
  baths 186–8
  Cathedral of St Trophimus 177
  Chapelle de la Genouillade *231*
  Church of Saint Honorat *229*
  Cryptoporticus 182
  deities 293
  imperial capital 337
  layout of 179–81
  Place du Forum 181, 182
  rue de l'Hôtel de Ville 179, 181
  sculptures 180
  theatre 182–4
  Tour de Roland 183
Arminium *see* Rimini
Artemis 15
Arthur, King 131, 140–1
Arthur's-Hoven 131, *134*
Arverni (tribe) 33, 76, 87, 158, 328
Arviragus 130
Asclepiodotus, Pisonius 234
Asia Minor 12, 20, 56
Astérix (Goscinny and Uderzo) 115–16
Athena 20
Attila the Hun 338
Attis 290, 291, 292, 307
Attusia (wife of Ausonius) 261, 267
Aude, River 36

Augusta Raurica, Switzerland 154, 156
Augusteum (precinct in Nîmes) 288
Augustine, St 127
Augustodunum *see* Autun
Augustonemetum *see* Clermont-Ferrand
Augustus
  and Cleopatra 165
  and Druids 161
  as emperor 149, 171, 180
  in Gaul 164, 168, 331
  memorials 186, 285, 289
  as Octavian 154, 164
Aurelian Way 227
Ausonius 260–75
  consulship 328
  imperial service 334, 337
  journey along the Moselle 207–8, 217, 249
  and Paulinus of Nola 308–11
  poet 179
  sculpture of *266*
  Ephemeris 263–5
  Parentalia 265, 267–9
Ausonius, Julius 261, 262
Austria 36
Autun (Augustodunum)
  cardo maximus 244
  comparison with Le Mans 323–4
  deities 284
  education in 169, 253–9, 254–6
  layout of 252

  mosaics 257–8
  name 168
  Porte d'Arroux *244*
  Porte Saint-André *255*
  Temple of Janus *258*
  theatre 253
  walls 253, *253*
Auvergne 33, 76, 88, 89, 208
Avaricum *see* Bourges
Avitus, Lucius Duvius 194, 312

Baiae, Italy 208
bakeries 241–2
barbarians 328–30, 337, 339–40, 342
Barbegal aqueduct and mill 214–17, *215*
barges 240
bas-reliefs *241*
Bastide-l'Évêque, Aveyron 236
Bath 130
baths, Roman 186–8, 207–8, 209
Beaucaire 39, 59
Belgic Gauls 83, 94, 157, 208
Bellicus *224*, 236
Bellovaci (tribe) 84, 151, 153
Benignus, Quintus Candidus 232
Bernard, Henri 107
Berthelier, Philibert 62
Beryllus 237
Besançon (Vesontio) 77
Bibracte (*oppidum*) 94, 105, 114, 252, *253*
Bibracte, Battle of 73–4, *75*
Bibulus 57–8

bishops 300, 302–3, 311–18
Bismarck, Otto von 110
Bissula (slave girl of Ausonius) 269
blacksmiths 236
Blandina 296
Boii (tribe) 21, 31, 76
Bologna 22, 30
Bononia *see* Bologna
Bordeaux 272, 308
Boulogne 85, 123, 155
Bourbon monarchy 105, 108
Bourg-Saint-Andéol 292
Bourges 89, 94
Bréan, Adolphe 108
Brenne, River 99
Brenner Pass 42
Brennus 28, 104, 105, 137
bribery 55, 160–1
Bridge (Kent) 136
bridges 63, 121, 192
Britain 86, 121, 129–30, 139–40, 142
  Caesar's invasion of 86, 121–4
Britannia *see* Britain
Brittahel of Demetia 138
Brittany 94, 208
bronze 15, 16, 168, 190, 282
Brutus 52, 106, 137
builders 232–3
Burdeau, Auguste-Laurent 294
Burgundians (tribe) 325, 340
Burgundy 76, 279, 325
burial grounds 227–31
Burrus, Afranius 193–4

cadastral maps 201–2, 204, 205
Caesar, Gaius Julius
  and Alésia, siege of 99–102
  assassination of 154
  and Bibracte, defeat of Helvetii at 73
  biographies of 108–9
  and Britain 121–4
  and Cato 86
  description of Helvetii 66–71
  family 42, 49, 50, 52–3, 148
  and Gallic wars 62–116
  number of Gallic deaths caused by 95
  journey to Geneva 62–5
  and Gergovia, siege of 89–94
  legacy of 130
  and Marseille 179
  politician 170, 180, 325, 328
  and provinces 85, 167, 331
  rise of 47–58
  and tribal leaders 77, 106–16, 134–42
  and tribes 65–7, 70–4, 76, 85, 94–5, 151–2
  and Vercingétorix 116
  see also Commentaries on the Gallic War
Caesarius of Arles, Saint 188, 314–16, 318
'Caesar's Camp' 130
Caesar's Vast Ghost (Durrell) 178, 214, 287

calendars 238, 291
Caligula 160, 168, 170, 331
Calvin, John 300
Calvinus, Sextius 36
Camden, William 127, 129, 135
canals 38, 59, 228
Canterbury 126–7
  Bigbury Hill Fort *128*
  Church of St Martin *126*, 127
  Pilgrims' Way 128, *128*
Canterbury Castle 130
Capitol, Rome 27, 54
Carbo, Papirius 36
Carcassonne Gap 36
cardo (road) 179, 202, 227, 244
Carnutes (tribe) 151
Carnutum (*oppidum*) 105
Carron, River 131
Carthage 19–20, 29, 234, 290–1
Cassian, St John 314–15
Cassis 15
Cassivellaunus *118*, 129, 134–7, 138–42
Casticus 70
Catiline conspiracy 55, 62
Cato the Younger 52, 55, 56, 86
Cato, Valerius 258
Catullus 31
Catulus, Quintus Lutatius 55
Catumandus, prince 20
Catuvellauni (tribe) 136
Celtic culture 95, 98, 104
Celtic Gauls, origins of 22–3

Celtillus 88
Cenabum see Orléans
Certinus, Titus Carsius 237
Châlons, Battle of 338–9
Champagne 24
Chapelle de la Genouil-lade, La (Arles) 229, 230, 231

Chares, Oppius 259
chariot racing 156, 195, 289, 300
chariots 15
Charles IX, King 228
Chichester 130
Chilham, Canterbury 129
Chirac, Jacques 115
Chiragan 211
Chlorus, Constantius 254
Christianity 293–300
   bishops 300, 302–3, 311–18
   in Britain 127
   early presence in Gaul 299
   heresy 297–9
   legend 227–8, 230
   first martyrdoms in Gaul 294
   persecution of 294–7, 304
   rise of 260, 335
   Roman Catholicism 103, 107, 314, 340
   and Vercingétorix 107
   see also Martin, St, bishop of Tours
Chronicle of Dover Mon-astery 136
Chronicle of St Martin of Dover 130

Cicero 18, 55, 61, 62, 66, 87, 248, 249, 258, 271
Cicero, Quintus 87
Cilician pirates 51
Cimbri (tribe) 37, 39, 41–2, 83–4
Cinna 50
cippi (inscribed stones) 101, 234
Cisalpine Gaul 21, 31, 33, 47, 58
Civilis, Julius 173
civitates (city-states) 158, 164–6, 167, 169, 192
Claudian 213
Claudius 127, 161, 168–9, 330, 331
Cleopatra 165, 287
Clermont-Ferrand 94, 110, 115, 168, 208, 340
Clovis, King 103, 114
Clusium 26
coinage see currency
Collonges 63
Cologne 156, 168
Colonia Claudia Ara Agrippinensium see Cologne
Colonia Iulia Paterna Arelatensium Sextano-rum see Arles
Cominius, Caius 234
Commentaries on the Gallic War
   background 66–7
   completion by Aulus Hirtius 152
   on Geneva 62–3
   and Gods 283
   on grain 213
   purpose of 67

   on soldiers 125
   as a source 137
   as teaching material 3–4
   Three Gauls 157
   on tribes 70–1, 83, 85–6, 152
   on Vercingétorix's surrender 107
Como, Lake 30
Condate 162, 163
Condrusi (tribe) 158
Constantine 187, 261, 300, 304
coppersmiths 224
Cornelia (wife of Cae-sar) 50, 52
corruption see bribery
coups 108
Coway Stakes, Walton-on-Thames 135–6
craftsmen 238
Crassus 49, 57, 85
Crau, the 38, 228
Cremona 30
Cridous of Albany 138
Critognatus 101, 102
Cryptoporticus (sub-terranean chamber in Arles) 182
cult complexes 291–3
culture and identity, Roman 327–8, 342
currency 17, 149–50, 165, 166, 335
cursus honorum (se-quence of public offices) 53, 172
curule aediles (office) 54
Cybele 290–3, 291, 307
Cybele sanctuary, Vienne 291

Cyrus, king of Persia 12

Danube, River 47, 65, 332
Daphnus of Vaison 299
de Gaulle, Charles 111, 114
Deal 124, 125, 127
Deal Castle 125
decumanus (road) 179, 202
deities 283–5, 293, 299
Delphi 20
Delphidius 271–2
Devil's Dyke, Wheathampstead *118*, 136
Dijon 61
Dio, Cassius 159–60
Diocletian 333, 334
diplomacy 329
Divico 71
Divitiacus 62
doctors 235
dolium (storage jar) *320*
Domitian 221
Domitius 209, 211
Domitius, Gnaeus 34–5
d'Orléans, Henri, duc d'Aumale 107–8
Dorobellum 138
Dover 123, 124
Dover Castle 129–30
Druids 62, 95, 107, 161, 271, 283
Drusus 164
Dumas, Alexandre 177
Dumnorix 70
Durocortorum 105
Durrell, Lawrence 178, 214, 287

Eburones (tribe) 158
Edirne 336–7
education 250–2, 253–9
Egypt 165, 185, 207, 287
Elysian Fields 227
English Channel 86, 122–3
Entremont (*oppidum*) 22, *23*, 34, 35, *35*
Epicurus 257
epigrams 223, 259, 263, 274
Étang de Thau 59
Etruscans 13, 18, 19, 22, 25
Eumenius 254–6, 257
Euric, King 340, 341
European Union 342
Eusebius 287, 289, 294–5
Euthymenes 250
Euxenus *see* Protis
Exe, River 130
Exeter 130

Fabius, Laurent 115
Fabius, Lucius 115
farming
    animals 217, 219
    and cadastral maps 202, 204–5
    calendar 238
    crops 213–14, 217
    tradesmen and 237–8
Felix, Vitalinus 235
Festus, Maximius 293
First World War 236
flamen dialis (priest of Jupiter) 50
Flanders 85
Flavian dynasty 325
Florus 32, 33, 160
flower-sellers 235

Fonteius, Marcus 61
Fort de L'Écluse 64
fortifications (*oppida*) 34, 88, 128
forums 181, 182, 324
Fos (port near Arles) 38
France 103–5, 106–8, 142, 147
Franco-Prussian War 106, 110
François I, King 104
Franks, the 103, 104–5, 106, 339
French Revolution 104

Gaius 180
Galba 173
Gallia Belgica *see* Belgic Gauls
Gallia Cisalpina *see* Cisalpine Gaul
Gallia Comata 83, 86, 152, 154, 251–2
    see also Three Gauls
Gallia Lugdunensis *see* Lyonese Gaul
Gallia Narbonensis *see* Narbonese Gaul
Gallica Aquitania *see* Aquitaine Gaul
Gambetta, Léon 110
Garlaban (mountain) 12
Garonne, River 36, 157
Gauguin, Paul 229
Genava *see* Geneva
Genesius, St 227
Geneva 36, 62–3, 65, 71
    St Pierre's Cathedral 300–3
Geneva, Lake 62, 65
Geoffrey of Monmouth 137, 138–9, 140–1

Gergovia (*oppidum*)
89–90, 92–4, 99, 105,
110, 111, 115
Gergovia, Battle of 87–9,
91, 93, *96–7*, 99
Gergovie (modern vil-
lage) 92, *92*, *98*, 111
Germania 328
Germany 110–11, 142
Getae (Thracian tribe) 65
Gibbon, Edward 243, 325
gladiatorial games 54,
170, 177, 196, 237
Glanum
Arch of Glanum
147–50, *148*, *150*,
161, 170–1
finds from 21
Glanic mothers 284
Mausoleum of the
Julii *144*
glassmakers 234, 235
Gnipho, Antonius 258
gold 21, 25, 27–8, 33,
124, 180
gorgons 16
Goths *see* Visigoths
Grand-Rue, Marseille 15
Gratian 262, 270, 308,
337
Great St Bernard Pass 24
Greeks 31, 72, 179, 217,
220
colony of Massalia 11,
12–15, 20, 153, 250
impact on Gauls 17,
18, 22
language 17–18, 170,
250–1, 257, 274
philosophy 299
see also migration;
Phocaea; Vix Krater

Greek fire 136
Gregory of Tours 317
Grey, Sir Thomas 131
grottoes 280–2
Gueithaet of Venedotia
138
guilds 233–4
Gyptis 13–14

Hades 37
Hadrian 211
Hallstatt culture 15
Hannibal 28, 30
Harpocrates 293
Hasdrubal 29
Haussmann, Georges-
Eugène 109
Haute-Garonne 211
Headlam, Cecil 178
heads, display of human
21–2, 34, 301
Helvetii (tribe) 70–4
census 76
migration *64*, 65–7,
68–9, *75*
rise of 36
territory of 63, 156
see also Caesar, Gaius
Julius
Hercules 12–13, 284
Herodotus 12
Hesperia 31, 32
Hesperius 268
Hirtius, Aulus 67, 152,
153
Hispania 35
*Historia Regum Bri-
tanniae* (Geoffrey
of Monmouth) 137,
138–9, 140–1
Homer 250
Horace 171, 270, 271

Huysmans, Joris-Karl
247

Illyricum 47, 58, 65, 85
Imperium Galliarum
(Empire of the Gauls)
332–3
imports, luxury 15–16
Inferno (Dante) 228
inscriptions
altars 164
decline in use 336
Gallo-Roman Muse-
um 166, 169, 170
Greek art 18
memorials 136, 232–8
monuments 180,
189–90
Vercingétorix memo-
rial 94, 103, 115
Irenaeus, bishop of
Lyons 297, 299
Isis 293
Italy 22, 25, 37–8, 88, 338
Iucundus 238

Jean, duc des Esseintes
(character in *Against
Nature*) 247–8
Jewish settlers, France
147
John of Fordun 131
Judaism 147
Julia (wife of Marius)
42, 52
Julianus, Septimus
233–4
Julius Caesar *see* Caesar,
Julius
Julius, Titus 180–1
Juno 27
Jupiter 283

Jura Mountains 63
Jurgurtha, King 38
Jutland 37
Juvenal 259

Knights Templar 177, 289
kraters (wine cauldrons)
  16–17, *18*, *44*

La Graufesenque (Avey-
  ron) 240
La Pêne 216
La Roche Blanche 90
La Turbie
  Tropaeum Alpium 164
Labienus, Titus 71, 138
Lac d'Aydat 208
Lambarde, William 126,
  130
Latin 32, 63, 67, 94, 141,
  168, 170, 206, 249,
  281, 282, 306, 308, 340
  doggerel 258
  epigrams 274
  the Gauls and 169,
    190, 251, 341
  Late Latin 248
  literature from Gaul
    260, 270, 271
  metre 263
  names of villa estates
    207
  'Silver Latin' 248
  teaching of 3, 5
  Latium 25, 31
Lavant, River 130
Le Mans (Vindunum)
  Cathedral of St Julien
    324
  comparison with
    Autun 323–4
  forum 324

walls 323–5, *324*, 333,
  336, 338
Le Pen, Jean-Marie 115
Légion Française des
  Combattants 111
Leland, John 125, 130
Lemière, Pascal-Louis
  107
Lenus 284
Leprosum *see* Levroux
Les Baux-de-Provence
  147, 300
Leslie, John 131
Levant, the 13, 56
Levroux 306
Li Fet des Romains
  (anon.) 135–6
Licinius 159–60
Ligugé 305
Ligurian tribes 13
L'Île (Geneva) 62
literature
  authors 177–8,
    247–50, 336
  French 106–8, 142,
    247–8
  German 142
  Latin 248–9, 271, 275
  Welsh 141–2
Livy 21, 23–6, 28, 31,
  32, 37
Locociacum *see* Ligugé
London 137, 138, 139
Louis XII, King 147
Louis XVIII, King 105
Lucan 95
Lucca, Italy 85
Lucius 180
Lugdunum *see* Lyons
Lugdunum Conue-
  narum *see* Saint-Ber-
  trand-de-Comminges

Lugus *see* Mercury
Lupus of Troyes, Bishop
  312–13
Lutetia *see* Paris
Lyonese Gaul 157
Lyons 155, 156, 161, 162,
  196, 265, 287, 293,
  294, 295, 297
  Altar of Peace (*Ara
    Pacis*), Rome 171
  Altar of the Three
    Gauls 164–5, *166*,
    169
  amphitheatre 293–4,
    296
  Christian martyrdom
    in 294–7
  colonies in 154, 155
  Fourvière Hill 162, *163*
  Gallo-Roman Muse-
    um 166, 170–1
  layout of 162–3, 164–5
  Rue Burdeau 168, 293

Macpherson, James 104
Majorian 312
Mandubii (tribe)
  99–102, 158
Marcellinus, Ammianus
  250
Marcellus 272
Marcia, Queen 137
Marcus 297–8
Marignano, Battle of 104
maritime trades 233
Marius, Gaius
  and the Ambrones 40
  Battle of Aquae Sexti-
    ae 41, 42
  and Caesar 54
  consulship 38–42, 49
  monument to 148–9

and the Teutones 38,
    39, 41, 60, 70–1, 74
Mark Antony 154
Marmoutier (near
    Tours) 305
Marne, River 24
Mars 283
Marseille 11–22
    archaeological re-
        mains in *14*
    education in 250–2
    and Rome 12, 32–3,
        35, 153
    siege of 179
    see also Massalia
Martial 223, 259, 274
Martin, Henri 106
Martin, St, bishop of
    Tours 303–7, 311,
    317–18
martyrdom, Christian 294
Mas des Tourelles, Beau-
    caire *218*, 220–2, *221*
Massalia (Greek colony)
    14–20, 21, 22, 24, 25,
    32, 33, 34, 35, 39, 59,
    72, 122, 153, 179, 223,
    250, 251, 258, 300
    see also Marseilles
Massif de l'Étoile
    (mountain) 12
Matres Nemausicae 285
Maximus 262–3, 272,
    337–8
Maximus, Valerius 251
Mediterranean Sea
    12–13
megara (Greek halls) 17
Mela, Pomponius 193
memorials 164–5, 232–5
Menapii (tribe) 85, 94
Mercury 283, 284

Merdogne *see* Gergovie
Merovingians, the 103,
    114
metalwork 15
Metrodorus 257
migration
    of the Helvetii 64–5,
        66
    Gallic 23, 24–5, 29, 37
    Germanic 76–7, 85–6
    of the Phocaeans 12,
        13–14, 24, 32
    tradesmen and 234–5
milestones 59, *60*
Millet, Aimé *80*
mills, flour 216–17
miners 236
Minerva 283
Minervius, Victor 271
Mirabeau, Marquis de 42
Mistral, Frédéric 177, 299
Mithraism 292, 293
Mithridates, king of
    Pontus 51
Mitterrand, François
    114–15
Modena 30
Molmutius, Dunvallo
    137
Mont Auxois 99–100,
    103
Mont Lassois 16, 17, 18
Montagne de Bussy 99
Montagne de Flavigny
    99
Montagne Sainte-Vic-
    toire 40–2, *41*
Montmort 73
Morini (tribe) 85
Moselle, River 207, 217,
    269
Mulhouse 77–8

Mutina *see* Modena
Mystères du peuple, Les
    (Sue) 106
Myvyrian Archaiology
    142

Nannus, King 13–14
Napoleon III 90, 92, *92*,
    103, 108–10, 123, 280
Napoleonic Wars 104,
    105, 106
Narbo Martius *see* Nar-
    bonne
Narbonese Gaul 36, 156,
    157
Narbonne 36, 156
Nemausus 285
    see also Nîmes
Nennius 138
Nero 172, 193–4, 331
Nervii (tribe) 84, 94
nettle, Roman 127
Nicomedes, king of
    Bithynia 51
Nîmes
    amphitheatre *vi–vii*
    Augusteum 285, 286
    'Latin Rights' 153
    symbol of 287
    'Temple of Diana'
        285–6, *288*
    theatre 285–6
    tombstones *239*
    Tour Magne 285, *286*
Noricum 36, 39
Norma (Bellini) 107
Normandy 208
Noviodunum (*oppidum*)
    88

Octavian 154, 164, 180
    see also Augustus

Odysseus 37
offerings (ex-votos) 282, 285
olives 17, 214, 217, 238
olive oil 22, 34, 234
Olympus, Marcus Julius 237
Oppidum Ubiorum *see* Cologne
Orange, Vaucluse
cadastral maps 201–2, 204, 205
theatre 184–5, *184, 203*
tombs *195*
oratory 51, 259, 271
Orcet, Great Camp at 89–90, *91*
order, social 28, 242
Orgetorix 70, 73
Orlando Furioso (Ariosto) 228
Orléans (Cenabum) 87, 88
Orosius 135
Ouvèze, River 191, 194

paganism 227, 249, 307, 315–17
Palladius 213–14
Paris (Lutetia) 89, 109
Parkinson, John 127
Parma 30
Pas de L'Écluse 63–4, *64*, 65–6, 72
Patera, Attius 271
Paulinus, Lollius 164
Paulinus of Nola, St 249, 308–11, *309*
Paulinus of Pella 249
Paulus, Axius 272, 273
Pax Romana 192, 234
Perceforest (anon.) 142

perfume-sellers 234
Pérignat-lès-Sarlière 89
Pétain, Marshal Philippe 111, 114
Petta *see* Gyptis
Phocaea, Greece 12
Phocaeans 12–13, 19, 24, 32
Phoenicians 13
Piacenza 30
pilgrims 281–2
Pilgrims' Way 128
Piso, Lucius Calpurnius 73
Placentia *see* Piacenza
Plancus, Lucius Munatius 153, 154
Plato 271
Plautus 185
Pliny the Elder
background 22–3
on bread 213, 241
on Caesar 95
on religion 161
on shampoo 234
on wine 193
Pliny the Younger 259
Plutarch 28, 39, 40, 47
Po, River 25
Po Valley 30, 39
Polybius 23, 25, 29–30
Pompey 56–7, 60, 85, 151, 153, 194
Pont du Gard (aqueduct) 1, 214
Ponticus 296
pontifex maximus (chief priest) 54–5
Pontius Pilate 287, 289
populism 49
Portus Itius *see* Boulogne

Posidonius 21, 37
Postumus, Lucius 21–2, 332
Pothnius, bishop of Lyons 295–6
pottery 220, 240
Pourrières (valley) 40, *41*, 42
priesthood 50, 165–7, 180–1, 234, 290
Priscillian 307–8
Priscus, Gaius Munius 189–90
Protis 13–14
Pulcher, Publius Clodius 87
Punic Wars 30, 290–1
Puy d'Issolud (Uxellodunum) 151, 188
Puyloubier 40, 41
Pyrenees, the 157
Pyrrhus, King 28
Pytheas 122

Raeti (tribal federation) 153, 154
Red Book of Hergest 141–2
Reformation, the 300
Regulianus, Gaius Sentius 234
reliefs *224*, 240, *241*, 284, 290, 292, 300
religion 287, 289, 292–3, 299
see also priesthood
Remi (tribe) 84
Renaissance 104
Republic, Roman 48–9
Rhine, River 86, 121–2, 153, 332
Rhône, River

conflict along 36
crossing the 63, *64*, 65–6
head of 62
map of *68–9*
mouth of 179
settlements along 153, 155
trade route 15, 38
Richard II (Shakespeare) 130
Richborough, Kent 140, *141*
Richborough Castle 126
Rimini 30
rituals 42
roads, Greek 15
roads, Roman 15, 59, 61, 155–6
  see also Via Aemilia; Via Aquitania; Via Domitia
Rochefort, Henri 110
Rochester Castle 130
Romani, Felice 107
Romanitas 173, 185, 190
Romney 127
Roquepertuse, Acropolis 22
Rosmerta 284
Rufus, Gaius Julius 190
Rutilius 249

Sacrovir 160, 254
St Albans, Hertfordshire 136
Saint Béat, Haute-Ga-ronne 235
Saint-Bertrand-de-Comminges (Lugdu-num Conuenarum) 60
Saint Honorat, Church of, Arles 228, 229

Saint-Martin-de-Crau 13
St Mary in Castro, Dover Castle 130
St Pierre's Cathedral 300–3
Saint-Rémy-de-Provence 38, 147
  Asylum of St Paul 21
  Roman baths 21
St-Romain-en-Gal
  mosaics *198, 210, 236,* 238, *346*
  Orpheus ensemble *210, 346*
Saint-Seine-l'Abbaye 318–19
Saintes 155, 190
Saintes-Maries-de-la-Mer 300
Saluvii (tribe) 33, 34
Salvian of Marseilles 339
Sambre, Battle of the 84
Samian ware (pottery) 240
Samnites (tribe) 25, 29
Saône, Battle of the 72
Saône, River 15, 72, 162
sarcophagi 229, 232
Sarkozy, Nicolas 115
Sarthe, River 323
Sasanian dynasty, Persia 333
Saturninus, Publius Brittius 237
Scheldt, River 157
Scotland 131
Second World War 110, 147, 294
Segobrigii (tribe) 13, 19
Segusiavi (tribe) 169
Seine, River 157, *275,* 280–2, *280,* 318–19

Seine, St 318
Sena Gallica *see* Senigallia
Senate, Roman 48–9, 55–8, 84, 172, 180, 330–1
Seneca 193
Senigallia 30
Senones (tribe) 28, 30, 94
Sequana (goddess) *275,* 281–2, *283,* 284, 343
Sequani (tribe) 66, 67, 76–7, 158, 169
Servilia 52, 55
Severia, Severa 234
Severinus, Julius 169
Severus, Alexander 332
Severus, Sulpicius 304
shrines 93–4, 196, 280–2, 306–7, 318
Sidonius 208–10, 211–12, 249, 312–13, 340–1
sieges
  Alésia *100,* 112–13
  Gergovia *91, 96–7,* 99–101
  Rome 27
Sieyès, Abbé 104
silver 17, 33, 54, 140, 190, 335
'Silver Latin' 248
Simon, André 110
Simos 13
slaves 128–9, 236, 264–5
Socrates 271
soldiers 48–9, 235, 236–7, 285, 316, 330
Solemnis, Titus Sennius 170
Soumet, Alexandre 107

Spanish Civil War 147
Sportisse, Lucien 294
steles, wooden 22, *275*
Stoffel, Colonel Eugène 90, *91*
Stoffel maps *68–9, 75, 96–7, 112–13, 132–3*
Stour, River 128
Strabo
  on Cimbri (tribe) 37
  on farming 212–13, 217
  on Lyons 155, 162, 164–5
  on Marseille 32, 250
Sue, Eugène 106
Suebi (tribal confederation) 77
Suessiones (tribe) 84
Suetonius 51, 52, 121, 259
Sulla 49–51
Sulpicius 306
symbolism 17, 111, 115, *280*, 287, 290
Syracuse, Sicily 25, 28

Tacitus
  background 260
  and culture 253, 254
  on Marseille 251
  on oratory 259
  on uprisings 160, 173
Tarascon 39
taxation 56–7, 159, 164, 329, 332, 334
temples
  Apollo 254
  Athena 20
  Lenus 284
  at the Source of the River Seine 281

Temple of Diana 285–6, *288*
Temple of Janus *258*
Venus Victrix 42
Vienne 289
Tencteri (tribe) 85–6, 94
Tenvantius, duke of Cornwall 138
Terence 185
Terentius, Marcus 238
Tetrarchy 333
Teutones (tribe)
  and Caesar 83–4
  and Marius 38, 41–2, 70–1, 74, 101
  migration 37, 39, 60
Thames, River 129, 134–6
Theline 178
Theodoric, king 338
Theodosius I 262, 273, 337
Theon 273
Therasia (wife of Paulinus) 310
Thierry, Amédée 104, 105–6
Thierry, Augustin 104–5
Third Century Crisis 333, 334–5
Three Gauls 156–9, 330–1
Tiber, River 31, 341
Tiberius 161, 180, 217, 331
Tigurini (Helvetii tribe) 72–3
Togirix 167
Tolosa *see* Toulouse
tombs *144, 195, 241,* 317
  see also burial grounds
tombstones *239, 298*

torture 295–6
Toulouse (Tolosa) 36, 211, 259
Tours, France 305, 306, 318
towers 62, *286,* 287
traders, Greek 15
trades 233–42
trading routes 240, 329, 335
Transalpine Gaul 33, 58, 60, 65, 153, 156
Tres Galliae *see* Three Gauls
Trets 41
Treveri (tribe) 284
tribes
  barbarian 330
  conflicts 36
  depictions of 149–50
  Gallic 61, 158, 167, 169–70, 172–3
  Germanic 86, 121–2, 164
  memorials to 164–5
  upheaval of 205
  vanishing 158
  see also individual names
Tricastini (tribe) 205
Trier 260, 284, 333, 337
Trinovantum (London) 137
Trivet, Nicholas 130
Trogus, Pompeius 12, 13, 18–19, 20, 32–3, 194
Troia Nova (London) 137
Trojans 31–2
Trophimus, St 227–8, 299
Troy 31, 137
tumuli 15
Tungri (tribe) 158

Ubii (tribe) 86, 156
Ucuetis 196
Urbicus, Quintus Lollius 131
Usipetes (tribe) 85–6, 94
Uxellodunum *see* Puy d'Issolud

Vaison-la-Romaine 190–6
  Castle Hill 191
  House of the Dolphin *193*
  House of the Silver Bust *191*
  houses 195
  mosaics and frescoes 195–6
  Puymin site *320*
Valens 336
Valentinian III 339
Valerius 265–6
Valetudo 284
Vallée des Baux 216
Vallonus 237, *239*
vallus (reaping machine) 213–14
van Gogh, Vincent 21, 177, 229–30
Varro 32
Veii 25
Vellaunodunum (*oppidum*) 88
Venarey-les-Laumes 98–9
Venerable Bede, the 135, 137
Veneti (tribe) 85, 94–5

Venus 53, 186
Venus Victrix 42
Vercellae, Battle of 42
Vercingétorix 103–16
  and Caesar 87–9, 101, 102–3
  legacy of 111–12, 114–16
  memorial *80*, 93–4, 99, 103, 109–10
Vercingétorix (Martin) 106
Verecundus, Marcus Licinius 285
Vesontio *see* Besançon
vessels, drinking 17, 21–2, 234, 238
Via Aemilia 30
Via Aquitania 36
Via Domitia
  first Roman road 35, 59–60, 155, *156*
  milestones on *60*
  slip road from 147, 148, 149
Vienne 287–90
  Cybele sanctuary *291*
  'Latin Rights' 153
  odeon 289
  settlement 36, 265
  temple 289
  theatre 289, 290
  tower 287
  walls 161
villas 206–8, 209–12, 220, 242
Vindex, Gaius Julius 172, 331, 332

Vindunum *see* Le Mans
vines 71, 219, 220, 221, 222
vine-dressers 237, *239*
vineyards 17, 219–2
Virgil 31, 130, 171, 205, 273
Visigoths (tribe) 325, 336, 338, 339, 340
Vix Krater *8*, 16–17, *18*
Voconti (tribe) 192
Vorocingus (near Nîmes) 212
Vosges, Battle of 77–8

Wace 130, 141
Walmer 125, 127
Weever, John 136
wells 284, 302
Welsh literature 141, 142
Weltchronik (Enikel) 142
Wheathampstead *118*, 136
Wheeler, Sir Mortimer 136
William of Malmesbury 130
winemaking *218*, 220–3, 222
workshops, craft 220, 238, 240
wrestling 139

'Year of the Four Emperors' 172–3

Zeus 13

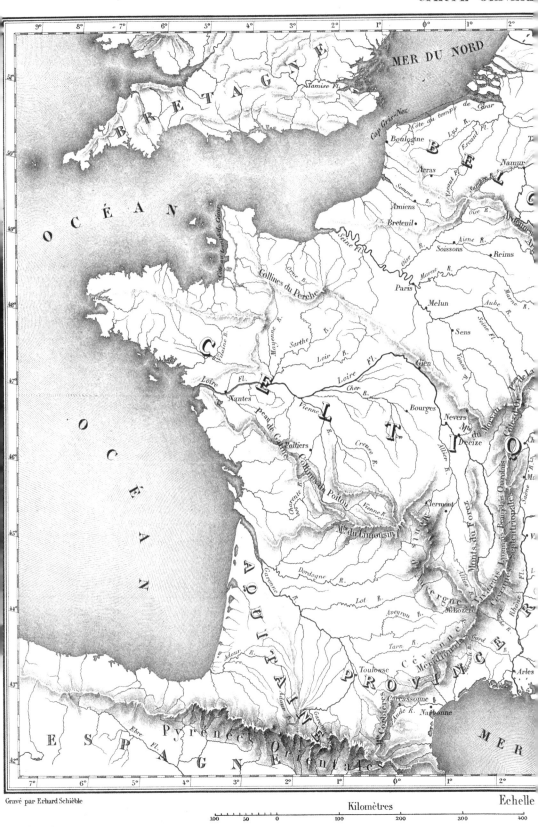

Gravé par Erhard Schièble

Henri Plon. Ed.

Kilomètres   Echelle

100   50   0   100   200   300   400